CAMBRIDGE GEOGRAPHICAL
TEXT BOOKS

General Editor: G. F. BOSWORTH, F.R.G.S.

INTERMEDIATE

CAMBRIDGE GEOGRAPHICAL TEXT BOOKS

INTERMEDIATE

BY

A. J. DICKS, B.A., B.Sc.

Cambridge:
at the University Press
1912

CAMBRIDGE
UNIVERSITY PRESS

University Printing House, Cambridge CB2 8BS, United Kingdom

Published in the United States of America by Cambridge University Press, New York

Cambridge University Press is part of the University of Cambridge.

It furthers the University's mission by disseminating knowledge in the pursuit of education, learning and research at the highest international levels of excellence.

www.cambridge.org
Information on this title: www.cambridge.org/9781107639287

© Cambridge University Press 1920

First published 1920
First paperback edition 2013

A catalogue record for this publication is available from the British Library

ISBN 978-1-107-63928-7 Paperback

PREFACE

THIS text book of Geography aims at presenting the main features of the subject in a manner suitable for pupils in the middle forms of secondary schools, the ground covered being approximately that required for the University Junior Local Examinations.

The earlier chapters deal with Mathematical Geography and the various forms of land and water, so as to provide data for the elucidation of the chief factors determining climate. The importance of climatic conditions in deciding the flora and fauna of a particular region is recognised throughout the book, whilst the distribution of population is considered not only from these conditions, but also from the location of minerals, and from the geographical position of the country in relation to the other land areas. Brief histories of the peoples from the geographical standpoint are included, and their industrial development is associated with the underlying geographical advantages of the country. The results of the recent Census and Trade Returns are introduced, but, as a rule, statistics are sparingly used.

The maps deal with climate and emphasise special features relating to rainfall, winds, etc., which would not be shown in an ordinary topographical atlas. The views illustrate physical features, important industries, and the fauna and flora of certain areas.

It is hoped that the questions and exercises will often suggest new lines of thought to the young student.

A. J. D.

January 1912

CONTENTS

LIST OF ILLUSTRATIONS, MAPS
AND DIAGRAMS

MAPS AND DIAGRAMS

CHAPTER I

INTRODUCTION

GEOGRAPHY is the study of the earth's surface with a view to a knowledge of natural phenomena, and of the conditions of life in different parts of the world. We shall first consider the earth's position and its motion through space, and how these produce alternate day and night and the different seasons (*Mathematical Geography*); next we must examine in some detail the earth's surface and the air above it, deriving from these some important principles underlying climate (*Physical Geography*); we shall then learn that climatic conditions largely determine the nature and distribution of both plant and animal life (*Biological Geography*), whilst all our studies will be directed towards a proper appreciation of man's position on the globe (*Political and Commercial Geography*).

Mathematical Geography.

Shape and Size of the Earth.

The gradual disappearance of ships below the horizon as they travel away from land, the circular shadow of the earth cast upon the moon during an eclipse, and the circumnavigation of the world by sailors lead us to believe that our earth is a globe, and not a flat disc as was thought by the ancients.

It is hard for us to grasp the immensity of this huge body, its radius being about 4000 miles, whilst its circumference measures more than six times that distance. We can, however, gain some idea of the earth's size by imagining that land covered the whole of its surface and that a man set himself the task of walking completely round the globe. If he walked eight hours daily at a rate of four miles an hour, the journey would occupy more than two years ; on the other hand, an express train travelling continuously day and night at a speed of sixty miles per hour would require about eighteen days to encircle the earth.

One further point deserves attention: although we have spoken of the earth as a globe, it is not a perfect sphere. It is very slightly flattened in its most northerly and southerly regions (the poles), the radius here being some thirteen miles shorter than the equatorial radius. As a matter of fact, this departure from the true spherical form is so slight, when compared with the great size of the earth, that any attempt to represent it in a diagram would be an exaggeration. Similarly, the highest mountain masses are negligible in considering the earth as a sphere.

The Solar System.

In olden times men thought that the earth occupied a fixed position in space, and that all the heavenly bodies described immense circles around it; in fact the earth was regarded as the centre of the universe, but nowadays we hold a far different view. Let us consider for a moment what is meant by 'the heavenly bodies.' By day we see the sun and by night the moon and stars, but all the stars are not of the same kind. By far the greater number shine with a twinkling light and are situated immense distances away from us ; they are known as the true or fixed stars, because although they all appear to describe circular paths in the sky, they remain in the same positions relatively to one another. Some few others glow with a steadier light and are much nearer to us than the fixed stars. They are called the planets (or wanderers), because the paths they describe in the sky differ from those traversed by the true stars. The reason for this difference is that they travel around the sun, and in this they resemble the earth, which is also one of the planets.

The sun is one of the fixed stars, and it seems so large because it is nearer to us than the others. It is the centre of the solar system, by which term we include :

(a) the sun,
(b) the planets revolving around it,
(c) the moons (or satellites) revolving around some of the planets.

In geography we are mainly concerned with the sun and the moon, in so far as they affect our own planet.

We had some difficulty in conceiving the earth's size, but this difficulty is as nothing compared with that of appreciating the sizes of the heavenly bodies and their distances from us. For instance, the sun, apparently a small ball in the sky, is really more than a million times the size of the earth, and it would take an express train more than 175 years to reach it, for it is more than 90 million miles away. The moon, on the contrary, apparently as large as the sun, is really smaller than the earth ; it looks large because it is so much nearer to us.

The Motions of the Earth.

The earth has two motions : one, a rotatory movement similar to that of a spinning top ; the other a translatory movement, sweeping out an elliptical orbit or path around the sun.

(a) The Rotatory Movement.

The rotatory movement of the earth can be imitated by spinning a ball (or coin) upon any smooth horizontal surface. There are apparently two stationary spots upon the ball, one at its uppermost, one at its lowest point, and the ball spins about a line joining these two points. This line is the ball's axis of rotation. Applying this to the earth, the *axis* is an imaginary line running through its centre and reaching the surface at the North and South Poles.

Again, that part of the ball's surface lying midway between the two stationary points has the fastest motion; thus places lying upon the earth's Equator have most rapid movement due to rotation. Further, the rate of movement diminishes as we approach the Poles from the Equator. This fact will be found to be of great importance when we come to deal with sea and air movements.

Each rotatory movement of the earth is completed in 24 hours. This is the earth's daily motion, and to it we owe our alternate day and night. If the earth were stationary, one half of its surface would always be receiving the sun's rays and so would enjoy perpetual day, whilst the other half would be in lasting darkness, being always turned away from the sun. The alternation of day and night can only be explained on the supposition that those parts at one time receiving light from the sun are turned away from it later by reason of the earth's rotatory movement.

It is improbable that the earth's axis is always at right angles to the sun's rays, because if this were so every place on the earth's surface would have days and nights of equal length throughout the year. This is contrary to our experience, for in our own country there is a marked variation in the relative lengths of day and night at different seasons, whilst in Arctic and Antarctic regions we know that the summer 'day' lasts for several months and the winter 'night' is equally long.

If we regard the earth's axis as *inclined* to the direction of the sun's rays we can easily explain the latter phenomenon (fig. 1), for although the earth is rotating upon its axis *ab* and consequently one half the world is in darkness, all places lying north of the circle *cd* will have light for many days and nights; yet during this time there will be continuous darkness at all places situated south of the circle *ef*, even during our daytime.

Let us consider more in detail how the position of a place upon the earth's surface will determine the relative lengths of its day and night when the earth and sun are in the positions shown in fig. 1:

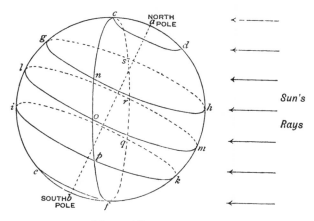

Fig. 1. Day and Night

(*a*) The circle *cd* is wholly illuminated; all places upon it (or north of it) have continuous day.

(*b*) The circles *gh, lm, ik,* are partially illuminated; all places lying between the limits *cd, ef,* have one day and one night in 24 hours.

(*c*) The circle *ef* is not illuminated; all places upon it (or south of it) have continuous night.

(*d*) The circle *gh* has an illuminated portion *nhs* of greater length than the unilluminated *ngs*; places upon it have a longer day than night.

(*e*) The circle *ik* has an illuminated portion *pkq*
       less than the unilluminated portion *piq* ;
       places upon it have longer night than day.

(*f*) The Equator *lm* has equal illuminated and
       unilluminated portions ; places on it have
       day and night of equal length.

To sum up : The length of a day (12 hours at the
Equator) increases as we proceed towards the North
Pole and decreases towards the South Pole ; but the
student should note that this only applies to the
summer positions of earth and sun and as shown in
fig. 1.

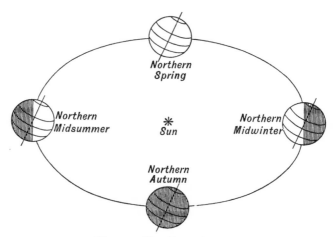

Fig. 2.   The Four Seasons

(*b*) **The Earth's Revolution.**

To the earth's yearly motion round the sun are due
the four seasons.   The path described by the earth is
elliptical, but the ellipse is nearly a circle, with the sun
lying almost at the centre (fig. 2).   The plane of the
earth's orbit is called the plane of the ecliptic and in

this plane lie the centres of both sun and earth. It is essential to note, that although the earth changes its position throughout the year with respect to the sun, the direction of its axis is always the same, or in other words the earth's axis is always inclined in one direction at a constant angle of $66\frac{1}{2}°$ to the plane of the ecliptic.

This inclination is of the utmost importance in causing differences in the seasons. Near Midsummer we have long days and short nights, whilst in the southern hemisphere there are short days and long nights (midwinter). The reason for this is that the northern hemisphere is turned towards the sun at this time, the north polar region having continuous day and the south polar region continuous night. The conditions are reversed at our midwinter : we have short days and long nights, the north polar region is in darkness, and the south has continuous day.

An intermediate condition exists at the *equinoxes* of spring and autumn (Mar. 21 and Sept. 23), when all places upon the earth have day and night of equal length, since at these dates the earth's axis is at right angles to the sun's rays, and consequently all places see the sun for 12 hours out of the 24.

Zones of the Earth.

The whole surface of the earth is divided into five zones or belts according to the visibility of the sun at different times of the year. These zones have well-defined differences in climate, for the temperature of a place depends largely upon the altitude attained by the sun in the sky and the time during which it is visible. Fig. 3 shows the various zones and their bounding circles.

All places in the Torrid Zone have the sun vertically overhead at noon at some time in the year, the sun apparently travelling northwards and southwards over this zone each year. This is in consequence of the planes of the equator and ecliptic being at an angle of $23\frac{1}{2}°$ to each other.

At noon on March 21 the sun is vertically overhead at places situated on the Equator.

At noon on June 21st the sun is vertically overhead at places situated on the Tropic of Cancer.

At noon on Sept. 23 the sun is vertically overhead at places situated on the Equator.

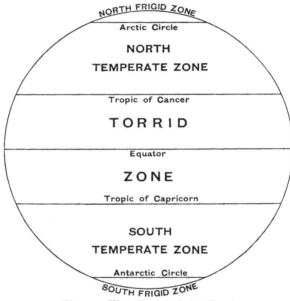

Fig. 3.   The Zones of the Earth

At noon on Dec. 21 the sun is vertically overhead at places situated on the Tropic of Capricorn.

June 21 and Dec. 21 are often spoken of as the *solstices*, because the sun on these dates appears to stand still before beginning its return journey towards the Equator.

All places lying in the Frigid Zones have the sun invisible for some days in the year.

Latitude and Longitude.

It is very necessary that we should be able to fix with accuracy the positions of places upon the earth's surface, and to do this we make use of two series of circles.   One is a series of 180 almost equidistant circles drawn parallel to the Equator (fig. 4), and these serve to mark how far a place lies to the north or south of that line : this distance being the north or south latitude as the case may be.   The circles are called *Parallels of Latitude,* and the distance from one parallel to the next

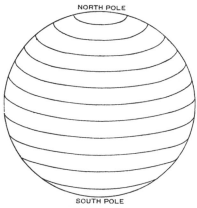

NORTH POLE

SOUTH POLE

Fig. 4.   Parallels of Latitude

is called a *degree* of latitude.   There are 90 degrees (°) of latitude in each hemisphere.   Each degree is divided into 60 *minutes* ('), and each minute is further subdivided into 60 *seconds* (").   London's latitude is 51° 30′ N. lat. The latitudes of the Equator, the Tropics of Cancer and Capricorn, and the Arctic and Antarctic Circles are 0°, 23° 30′ N. lat., 23° 30′ S. lat., 66° 30′ N. lat. and 66° 30′ S. lat. respectively.   Owing to the earth not being a perfect sphere the length of a degree of latitude varies slightly, it being about $68\frac{3}{5}$ miles at the Equator and $69\frac{2}{5}$ miles near the Poles.

Such circles would not suffice in themselves to mark the exact position of a place, because many places lie upon the same parallel of latitude. We must therefore specify how far the place is east or west of some particular line. Greenwich is chosen as a starting point in our maps, and a circle drawn through it and the two Poles divides the globe into hemispheres with east and west longitude respectively. *Longitude* is the distance east or west of the circle passing due north and south through Greenwich. It is measured by a series of 180

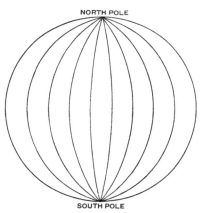

Fig. 5.   Meridians of Longitude

circles running due north and south upon the earth (fig. 5). These circles all cut one another at the North and South Poles; thus forming 360 semicircles which cut the Equator at 360 points about 69 miles from each other.

These semicircles are called *Meridians* of Longitude, because all places situated upon any particular meridian have noon at precisely the same instant. The distance east or west from one meridian to the next is called a degree of longitude, and each degree contains 60 minutes or 3600 seconds, as does the degree of latitude.

The meridian passing through Greenwich is numbered 0°, the successive meridians east and west of it being numbered in rotation from 1° to 180° East and West longitude respectively. The student will note that 180° E. long. and 180° W. long. fall upon the same meridian, and also that each meridional circle forms two meridians, *e.g.* 1° W. long. and 179° E. long. are the two halves of one great circle, similarly 15° W. and 165° E., 84° W. and 96° E.

From our definition of a degree of longitude as the distance east or west from one meridian to the next, it naturally follows that, since the meridians all cut the poles, the number of *miles* in a degree of longitude will vary according to the latitude. At the Equator the degree contains a little over 69 miles, at London about 44 miles, and at 80° N. or S. lat. the longitude degree only contains about 12 miles.

Effect of Longitude on Time.

The sun's apparent motion through the sky from east to west is known to be the result of the earth's rotation upon its axis in an easterly direction. Thus in one day all the 360 meridians have successively faced the sun ; *i.e.* noon has occurred throughout the world. It is strange at first to think that at any moment it is noon at some place on the earth, but this is true nevertheless, for each meridian faces the sun 4 minutes after its predecessor. In other words, the time as shown by local clocks would be 4 minutes slow if compared with clocks at places situated on the meridian lying next to the east, assuming of course that the clocks were set by the sun.

If clocks all over Britain were regulated by the sun as it crossed the particular meridians at noon, there would be great confusion. This is remedied by the use of 'Greenwich time,' the exact moment of noon being wired from Greenwich to different parts of the kingdom.

Maps.

Since the earth is spherical, we can only represent its surface accurately upon a globe ; it is impossible to do so upon a plane sheet, yet, since globes are unwieldy, many attempts have been made to construct flat maps of fair accuracy.   Where the area to be mapped is of small size a very accurate plane map can be made, but

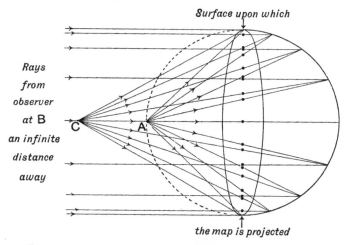

Fig. 6.   Orthographic, Stereographic, and Equidistant Globular Projections

if, for example, a hemisphere is to be mapped upon a plane surface, distortion must necessarily result.

A plane map of a hemisphere may be made by considering it hollow and closed at its base by a transparent plane, through which the observer looks at the concave surface lying beyond.   The points at which the rays of light strike this plane are points on the plane map. By such means we *project* the spherical upon a plane surface, and three kinds of projection arise according as the observer is at *A*, a point on the sphere, *B*, an infinite distance away, or *C*, a point intermediate between *A* and *B* (fig. 6).

When he is considered to be at *B*, the countries, etc. situated near the rim of the hemisphere appear much too small, whereas, viewed from *A*, they are unduly magnified. By taking an intermediate position *C* these two distortions will tend to neutralise one another, but even then we do not get an accurate representation of the whole surface of the hemisphere.

The view obtained from *B* is termed the *ortho-*

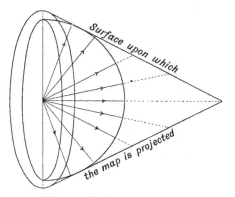

Fig. 7.   Conical Projection

graphic projection, that from *A* the *stereographic*, and that from *C* the *equidistant globular* projection.

In other methods of projection (figs. 7 and 8) the observer is supposed to be at the centre of the hemisphere and the rays to be projected through the spherical surface to meet that of an investing cone or cylinder (*conical* and *cylindrical* projections). The surfaces of these are then unrolled and laid flat to form the plane map. The conical projection will be approximately true only in the region where it touches the hemisphere, whilst the cylindrical projection greatly exaggerates the sizes of regions situated far from the rim of the hemisphere. Mercator's projection is a modification of the cylindrical method.

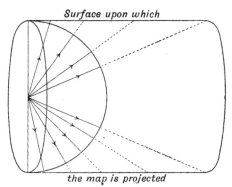

Fig. 8. Cylindrical Projection

From what has been said above, the student will see the importance and necessity of correcting, by a constant reference to a globe, the impressions he has received from plane maps.

CHAPTER II

LAND AND WATER

Land Forms.

The earth was once a molten mass, but cooling has resulted in the formation of a solid rocky crust and the condensation of water vapour upon it. When the cooling began, the earth's surface presented no great variations in elevation. The mountainous regions of to-day, and also the great depressions in which water has collected and which now constitute the oceans and seas, are the direct result of the contraction or shrinkage of the earth whilst cooling. But the original solidified rock has been subjected for countless ages to the influence of the sun's rays, water, air, ice, and frost, with the result that its outer portions have been broken down and powdered to form other rocks of different type, and this process has been repeated again and again.

Kinds of Rocks.

The earth's solid crust thus consists of (*a*) very ancient rocks, which are more or less crystalline in structure, according to their slow or rapid rate of cooling ; these contain many metals, and are the most deeply seated rocks, being found underneath all others ; and (*b*) rocks produced from these by various agents. These are termed the derived or sedimentary rocks. They are found in bands or strata overlying the oldest rocks, and are called *primary, secondary, tertiary,* and *quaternary* according to their ages, the primary being the first formed, whilst the quaternary are the most recent.

Earth Movements.

The shrinkage during the cooling process has in some places caused mutual pressures between the rocks, and this pressure has been relieved by an upheaval of

Chalk cliff, showing strata

huge masses above the surrounding parts. Thus we find that mountains are composed of ancient rocks, flanked by more recent strata. Sometimes the disturbance has been less violent and has resulted in a more gentle folding of the strata into alternating hill and valley, or again into slight uplands standing above an almost level plain. Rolling country is typically that of secondary rocks, whilst more recent strata give a flat land-surface with monotonous scenery.

Crust Blocks and Faults.

In other places the earth's shrinkage has caused whole regions to remain elevated, whilst the surrounding parts have fallen bodily away and been greatly depressed. Such a fracture as this has relieved the strain between the rocks, and a plateau is the result. *Crust block* mountains are of this type, and valleys may be produced in a similar way.

Rifts in the strata are known as *faults*, and since the crust has been weakened in their neighbourhood, outpourings of volcanic material are probable. In some places large areas have been covered by igneous rock in this way, and these rocks, weathering more slowly than the others, have given rise to an elevated region.

Alteration in appearance.

The great alterations produced in the appearance of a region when a widespread elevation or depression has occurred should be carefully noted. In the first case the floors of shallow seas become coastal plains, islands increase in area, rivers become longer, and mountains and hills higher. On the other hand when depression takes place submergence of low-lying coastal districts occurs, valleys may become gulfs, islands of low elevation disappear or at least decrease in area, new islands may be formed by the isolation of coastal districts of fair elevation, whilst the encroaching sea may shorten the lengths of rivers and diminish the heights of mountains.

Destructive Action.

In addition to the changes brought about by earth movements, the land is subjected to destructive action from above. The sun, by heating the rocks, causes their expansion, and if this be unequal, they split apart. The same thing happens if the various portions of the rock-mass cool at different rates. Water assists in this splitting of rocks to form boulders and carries the

work of disintegration still further.   It sinks into
the crevices, and aided by the slightly acid character
it has acquired in its absorption of atmospheric gases,
it dissolves away certain rock constituents, thus deepen-
ing and widening the cracks.   When it freezes it forms
a most powerful expansive, since ice is more bulky than
the water from which it has been produced, and this
action going on year after year results in the separation

Norwegian Glacier

of huge rocks from the parent mass.   On mountain-tops
the snow solidifies into ice, and the glaciers so formed
carry away boulders as well as the small rocky particles
which they have scraped from the underlying rock.

Constructive Action of Rivers.

The action of water as a transporting agent is equally
important.   Rivers are continuously carrying to lower

levels the materials they have swept away from higher
districts.   As they traverse more low-lying lands their
slower rate of flow allows the coarser suspended matters
to settle upon the river bed.   Where the rate of flow
is very slow, sediment may accumulate to such an extent
that sandy shoals and islands are formed in the river.
This deposition is greatest where the current is slowest;
thus long stretches of river-formed land may be produced at the sides of the stream, with the result that
the water is flanked by embankments. This is well seen
in very flat countries.

Floods.

Such banked-up rivers are liable to burst their banks
and take a new course, thus giving rise to disastrous
floods.   Any river-flood on its subsidence leaves the
land covered with a layer of soil (or mud) of great
fertility. The student will remember that the Egyptians
could not exist were it not for the regular Nile floods.

No river deposits *all* its suspended matter whilst on
its course.   A large amount reaches the mouth, where
strong tides may carry it away to sea, or where it may
be deposited under other conditions as a *delta*, sand-
bar, or hidden shoal.   Finally it should be noted that
both river and sea break the rock fragments to smaller
size, although, of course, the sea is by far the more
important in this respect.

The action of the wind as a transporting agent is
best seen in sandy coastal and desert districts where
ever-shifting sand dunes are produced by its aid.

The student must not assume from the above that
the ancient rocks are always covered by those of sedimentary character.   In some places they lie quite at the
surface and contribute in no small degree to the rugged
grandeur of the scenery.

Distribution of Land and Water.

We usually speak of five continents : Europe, Asia
Africa, America, and Australia, but a glance at a globe

or a map of the world shows that there are but three main land-masses upon its surface. Europe, Asia and Africa all form parts of one huge land-mass, whilst the continents of America and Australia form the other two land-masses.

Similarly the five oceans (Arctic, Antarctic, Atlantic, Pacific, and Indian) all form parts of one great water area which surrounds the three land-masses. This can be seen more easily by reference to a globe than to a plane map, for the continuity of the oceans cannot be shown so well upon the latter.

The oceans cover three-fourths of the earth's surface, but what is specially evident from the globe is the uneven distribution of land and water. The hemisphere having Great Britain at the centre of its surface will be found to include the bulk of the land, whilst the opposite hemisphere (with New Zealand as centre) is covered mainly by water.

The Continents.

In the largest land-mass we note that Europe is relatively small, and that it forms but the north-westerly portion. There is no well-marked dividing line between it and Asia, whereas Africa is connected with Asia by the narrow isthmus of Suez only. Just as we may look upon the whole land-mass as an island, so we may regard Africa as an immense peninsula. Africa is very regular in outline, but both Europe and Asia have more indented coasts. A feature of both is their smaller peninsulas which stretch in an approximately southward direction. In Europe we find Scandinavia, Spain, Italy, and the Balkan Peninsula ; in Asia there are Arabia, India, the Malay Peninsula, Kamchatka, and Korea.

The American land-mass includes the two great peninsulas of North and South America, connected by the narrow isthmus of Panama. The island continent of Australia lies to the south-east of Asia, towards which runs a connecting chain of islands.

Their Islands.

Islands are usually found fringing the continents, to which they were formerly attached, as is proved by the similarity of animal and vegetable forms, and rock structure in the two regions.

Europe has Iceland, the British Islands, the Balearics, Corsica, Sardinia, Sicily, Crete, and Cyprus ; Africa has Madagascar ; America has the West Indies, Newfoundland, Greenland and numerous Arctic islands ; with Asia are associated Ceylon, the Japanese islands, Formosa, the Philippines, the Dutch East Indies, Borneo, and New Guinea ; and Australia has Tasmania.

The Oceans and their Seas.

As we have noted above, these are all connected. The Atlantic Ocean merges into the Arctic on the north and the Antarctic on the south.   Also a ship would pass from the South Atlantic into the Indian Ocean by rounding the Cape of Good Hope to the east, or into the Pacific by rounding South America to the west.

Those parts of the oceans, which by reason of their nearness to the land-masses are partially enclosed by the mainland or its adjacent islands, have received special names as seas.   The Atlantic has upon the east the North Sea and the almost land-locked Baltic, Mediterranean, and Black Seas, and upon the west Baffin Bay, Hudson Bay, the Gulf of Mexico, and the Caribbean Sea. The Indian Ocean has the Red, Arabian, and Timor Seas and the Bay of Bengal, whilst in the Pacific Ocean are the seas of China and Japan, and the Yellow Sea.

The Depth of the Oceans.

The oceans are far from being of uniform depth. Around the continents there is a shallow area, the floor of which is known as the *Continental Shelf,* where the depth does not exceed 100 fathoms (1 fathom = 6 feet). In places this shelf is of great width, for instance off

Western Europe it embraces the Baltic, North and Irish
Seas, its southerly boundary being a line drawn from
Cape Clear in Ireland to Bordeaux.   On the eastern
shores of North and South America it is of greater
width than on the western shore.   It is comparatively
narrow round the whole of the African continent.   It
is well developed off east and south-east Asia, joining
Formosa and Borneo to the mainland and also linking
up New Guinea and Tasmania with the Australian
land-mass.

Deep Soundings.

Beyond the continental shelf the sea-floor dips
much more rapidly to a very great depth.   The deepest
soundings obtained as yet in the three most important
oceans are six miles in the Pacific to the east of the
Ladrone Isles, over five miles in the Atlantic to the north
of the West Indies, and less than four miles in the Indian
Ocean to the north-west of Australia.   These figures
show us that the land and water upon the globe attain
about equal limits of height and depth.

Ridges.

The student must not assume any uniformity in the
depth of water in any particular ocean.   The Atlantic
and Indian Oceans, for example, possess a well-pro-
nounced "divide" or ridge, where the depth is about
$2\frac{1}{4}$ miles, passing almost due north and south, and
separating them into eastern and western basins or
troughs.   Both oceans have areas of great depth, both
east and west of this dividing line, but the Atlantic
reaches its greatest depth in the western, the Indian
Ocean in its eastern portion.

The Pacific, on the other hand, is very unequally
divided by a ridge running due south from Central
America.   Its greatest depth is attained in its western
and greater basin.   A knowledge of the ocean's depths
is useful in several ways : it enables navigators to know
when they are near shore in foggy weather or at

night-time; it serves to indicate the best routes for laying submarine cables; finally, it is of great service in explaining differences or similarities between the animals and plants of countries washed by any one ocean.

Sea Water.

Since rivers bring to the sea the mineral matters they have dissolved from the earth, we can understand the salinity or saltness of sea water: a property possessed also by the waters of 'salt lakes' for a similar reason.

The saltness of the ocean in any particular region will vary in accordance with the amount of evaporation going on, as also with the amount of fresh water being received from rivers, rain, or from melting icebergs. The amount of dissolved matters present partly decides the temperature at which the water freezes. Fresh water freezes at 32° F. under ordinary conditions, but sea water has a freezing point of 28° F. This is one of the reasons why the sea is frozen less frequently than freshwater lakes.

Its Temperature.

We shall find the oceans having great effect upon the climate of neighbouring lands. This is largely because water increases and decreases in temperature at a different rate from land. It becomes heated more slowly, but gives off its heat more slowly also. Thus the oceans are cooler than the land-masses in summer and warmer in winter, and consequently exert an equalising effect upon the temperatures of the adjoining lands.

Water at a depth greater than 100 fathoms varies very little in temperature; the surface waters only need be considered as regards variations of temperature, and these do not vary more than 1° from one day to the next.

We find of course the hottest surface waters in the Tropics, for here the sun's rays strike the earth almost vertically, and so exert their greatest heating effect. Such surface waters have a temperature greater than

80° F., the opposite extreme being found in Polar waters
where the surface temperature is always less than 50° F.
The depth of warm water varies at different parts of the
oceans ; speaking generally it is deeper in the north-
western than in the south-eastern parts.   This is due to
the great ocean movements which we are about to
consider.

The Movements of the Ocean.

The ocean's constant motion is another factor which
prevents its freezing.   We may distinguish waves, tides,
drifts, and currents.

Waves.

Waves are surface disturbances due to the combined
action of wind and gravity ; the wind tends to heap up
the water and drive it along in front, whilst the earth's
force of gravity tends to pull the water down again
to its original level.   In the open sea long lines of
rollers are the result, and these 'break' on reaching the
coast.   A large part of the sea's action in wearing down
the coast is due to the tremendous force of the breakers.
It should be carefully noted that the water does not
travel at the same rate as the wave.   The water-
particles have mainly an up-and-down motion ; it is the
condition of elevation or depression which travels
onwards.   The truth of this can be seen by watching
a piece of paper floating in the sea.

Tides.

The tides are familiar to us by the sea's advancing
and receding twice daily, but these phenomena are
really caused by the whole level of the sea in that part
being raised or lowered at these times.   There is an in-
terval of about $12\frac{1}{2}$ hours between one high tide and the
next.   The tides are due to attractive influences exerted
by the sun and moon.   They will be more fully discussed
in a later volume of this series.   It will suffice here to
notice that the highest or 'Spring' tides occur at new

and full moon, *i.e.* at a time when the sun reinforces the
moon's attractive power, whilst the lowest or 'Neap'
tides occur when the sun's influence is antagonistic to
that of the moon : the latter being in its first or third
quarter.

The height of the tidal rise is greatly modified by
the contour of the coast : in funnel-shaped bays and
estuaries it becomes greatly increased, the Bay of Fundy
and the estuary of the Severn being familiar examples.

The Severn Bore at Bridgwater

The tide deepens coastal waters, especially the mouths
of rivers, and helps commerce, since large ships can
penetrate much further inland, as well as receive help
onwards from the tidal movement.

Drifts.

Drifts are irregular or spasmodic surface movements
caused by, and in the same direction as, the wind.
They disappear as the wind dies down, and are only of
importance when produced by constant winds.   One of

the best examples is the Gulf Stream Drift promoted by
the south-westerly winds blowing over the North Atlantic.
The ameliorating influence of the Gulf Stream is thus
enabled to reach Western Europe ; without the aid of
the wind the current would lose itself in mid-ocean,
although off the American coast it is fifty miles wide
and one mile deep.

The Circulation of the Oceans.

This is brought about by *ocean currents*—movements
more forcible and persistent than the drifts mentioned
above.   They are due to several causes :

(*a*) The warm light surface waters of the Torrid
Zone tend to flow north and south to colder regions.

(*b*) The colder polar waters tend to replace these
by creeping towards the Equator along the ocean floor.

(*c*) This deep flow also replaces the great loss of
water due to evaporation in the Tropics.

(*d*) The earth's rotatory motion from west to east
tends to cause the water to lag behind and to form a
westerly drift.   This will naturally be most pronounced
in the Torrid Zone where rotation is most rapid.

(*e*) This westerly drift becomes a distinct current
under the influence of the Trade Winds.

CHAPTER III

CLIMATE AND THE DISTRIBUTION OF LIFE

The Atmosphere and Climate.

By the climate of a place we mean the average condition of its atmosphere, with particular reference to temperature, pressure, and moisture.

The temperature of the air varies according to

- (*a*) the latitude (cf. polar and tropical climates);
- (*b*) the altitude (cf. the temperature of a mountain top and the valley at its foot);
- (*c*) the direction and character of prevailing winds (*e.g.* the warm south-westerly winds reaching Britain from the Atlantic);
- (*d*) the distance from the sea (*e.g.* the extreme temperatures of continental interiors);
- (*e*) the character of ocean currents (cf. the effect of the warm drift from the south-west upon Britain with that of the 'cold wall' current from the north upon Labrador);
- (*f*) the amount of rainfall (*e.g.* the great ranges of temperature in rainless districts);
- (*g*) the character of the soil; and
- (*h*) presence or absence of vegetation.

Isotherms.

These are lines drawn upon the map to connect places having equal temperatures. These temperatures may be the mean or average daily, monthly, or yearly temperatures as the case may be. Perhaps the most instructive of temperature maps are the two which show January and July isotherms respectively.

We notice first of all that the isotherms do not coincide with the latitude parallels ; that they do not do so is the result of the other factors mentioned above ; yet the change from high to low temperatures is seen to proceed from torrid and temperate to polar regions, thus showing the effect of latitude upon temperature.

The effect of altitude cannot be traced upon these temperature maps, for all temperatures have been reduced to sea level ; it being usual to add 1° F. for every 300 feet elevation, because a mountain top is colder than its base.

A comparison of the two maps shows the seasonal effect, the whole system of isotherms moving northwards during our summer and southwards during our winter, thus following the sun in its apparent journey north and south over the Torrid Zone.

The winter and summer isotherms really show the relative temperatures of the *air* above the land and water areas during these seasons. Where no great landmasses interrupt the oceans there is no abrupt change in the course of the isotherm (*e.g.* isotherm 48° in the southern hemisphere approximates very closely to the 50th parallel in January and the 40th in July), but in the northern hemisphere the isotherms depart very considerably from the lines of latitude. Take for example the isotherm 32° in January : it arches northwards and reaches much higher latitudes over the oceans than over the continents, where it bends southwards. This shows us that in winter oceanic places have a higher temperature than we should expect from their latitude, and that continental ones have a colder temperature.

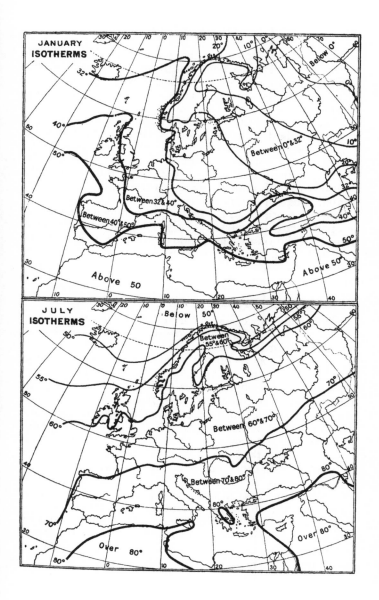

Similarly we note that the summer isotherms in the northern hemisphere bend southwards over the oceans and take a course in higher latitudes over the continents; from this we see that the sea is cooler than the land in summer.

The January isotherms show the genial effect of wind and ocean drift from the south-west upon West Europe, where the whole coast southwards from the Arctic Circle comes within its influence.

By placing a tracing of the July isotherms over the map of those of January we get interesting examples of annual range of temperature.   By the *annual range of temperature* we mean the *difference* between the average temperature of January and July—the coldest and hottest months of the year. The coasts of California, N.E. Brazil and S.W. Cape Colony will be found to possess very equable climates ; S.W. Norway has a range of about 30°, whilst Central Asia has 50°—100° range.

Atmospheric Pressure.

The atmosphere, like all gases, possesses weight and exerts pressure.   In order to measure its pressure we use the barometer, where the air pressure is usually made to support a column of mercury in a glass tube. The amount of pressure is expressed by the height of the supported column, measured in inches.   But the air's pressure is found to vary from day to day, and the chief causes of this are the varying temperature and the amount of moisture present.   *Warm* air expands and exerts less pressure than cold air, and *moist* air also exerts less than dry.   The variation in temperature is, however, the more important of the two causes.

Isobars are lines drawn upon the map to connect places having equal atmospheric pressures at the same time.   Such lines are important, for from them we can deduce the directions of the wind.   A wind is merely a passage of air from a region of high pressure to one of lower pressure ; by winds the air pressure in different places tends to become equal.

A weather chart is a familiar example of a map showing isobars, the barometric readings being taken at many places and telegraphed to the Meteorological Office, where the pressure chart is constructed. These readings are all taken at the same time of the day, usually at 7 o'clock in the morning, but before being inserted upon the chart they are reduced to sea level ; *i.e.* the reading is increased by 1 inch for each 900 ft. elevation of the station, this being necessary because air pressure diminishes with increased altitude.

Pressure Systems.

Monthly or yearly isobars are also constructed to show the average barometric conditions for any month or year. We also note from pressure maps that the isobars are not straight lines ; one of their most frequent forms is that of a series of lines running roughly parallel to some central oval line. The central area is either one of high or of low pressure, and if we examine the numbers (*i.e.* heights of the barometer) placed upon the successive isobars, we shall find that the pressure decreases or increases as we proceed from the central region. A system with a low-pressure area at its centre is called a *cyclone*, one with high pressure at its centre an *anticyclone*.

Directions of Winds.

A cyclone draws in air from surrounding regions, but the winds do not pass directly to its centre by crossing the isobars at right angles ; they pass inwards in a spiral course, travelling in the *northern* hemisphere in an *anti-clockwise* direction, and in a *clockwise* direction in the *southern* hemisphere. Air passes out spirally from a high-pressure system clockwise in the northern, and anti-clockwise in the southern hemisphere. The earth's rotation is responsible for these spiral movements.

In Britain we usually have rainy weather at the eastern part of a cyclone, but anticyclones give us a spell of fine weather.

Not only can we gauge the direction of the wind from a pressure map but we can also estimate its *speed*, since it travels more quickly over regions which have the isobars close together. (The rapid flow of water down a steep slope is a useful parallel to consider here.)

Cyclones and anticyclones are but *local* disturbances of the atmosphere. In this they resemble land and sea breezes which are so frequent at places on the coast during night and day respectively. During a summer day the land becomes hotter than the sea and consequently the air above it becomes heated, expands, and forms a low pressure area, to relieve which the air passes in from the sea. At night rapid radiation of heat from the land cools it so that the air above is at high pressure, and then a breeze rises from the land to equalise the lower pressure over the sea.

Regular Winds and their Causes.

(i)   The Effect of the Earth's Rotation.

The Earth's daily motion not only tends to produce an accumulation of air, and so a high-pressure region, over the Tropics, but also causes winds to be deflected from their course. The high-pressure belt which we should expect to find in equatorial regions is relieved, however, by expansion of the air due to the sun's intense heat, so that we actually find a low-pressure belt flanked about latitudes 30° north and south by two belts of high pressure. Winds should pass due north and south from these belts towards the Equator and the Poles, but if a wind be blowing from the north towards the Equator it is passing over a more rapidly moving part and this gives it an apparent motion *from* the east, so that it becomes a north-east wind. Similarly a wind blowing from the south towards the Equator becomes a south-east wind. This is well seen in the *trade winds* which blow in these two directions towards the Equator, where they meet and are lost in the strong up-draught which produces the *doldrums* or equatorial belt of *calms*.

Likewise, the winds passing from the same high-pressure belts (lat. 30° N. and S.) towards the Poles are apparently deflected *towards* the east, because they have come to a more slowly rotating part of the earth. Thus the British Isles receive *south-westerly* winds from the Atlantic all the year round and the climate greatly benefits thereby.   Part of the west coast of North America is influenced in a similar way by south-westerly winds from the Pacific Ocean.

(ii)   **The Effect of the Seasons and of the Distribution of Land and Water.**

A belt of low pressure or rarefaction follows the sun in its yearly journey over the Torrid Zone; the student will consequently understand the *migration* of the Trade Wind system, northwards during our summer and southwards during our winter.   The greatest seasonal effect however is due to the unequal rates of heating and cooling of the great land and water areas.   We will consider first the northern hemisphere in January. Low-pressure areas exist over the relatively *warm* North Atlantic and Pacific Oceans, high-pressure areas over the *cool* continental masses of America and Asia. Cold air tends to pass out from these continents.   The north-east monsoon blowing over India is a direct result of the high pressure area over Central Asia.

The July isobars reveal an opposite condition : low-pressure areas exist over the heated continents, whilst the cooler oceans have high-pressure areas developed above them.   Winds thus blow from ocean to continent, and in the Indian Ocean they are strong enough to counteract the North-East Trades completely.   In the southern hemisphere there is less variation owing to the lack of great land-masses.   The high-pressure belt exists throughout the year in the neighbourhood of 30° S. lat. ; but during the southern summer low-pressure areas exist over South America, Africa, and Australasia about latitude 10° S.

Character of Winds.

The character of the wind depends upon that of the region it has previously traversed. Winds from the oceans are moist, those from continental regions are dry. During the summer months winds from the oceans are cool, but they bring warmth during the winter ; the opposite holds good for winds blowing from a continent. The temperature of a wind depends upon its direction : speaking generally winds blowing from high to low latitudes are cool, those blowing towards higher latitudes are warm.

The great value of winds rests upon the fact that they distribute heat and moisture, and thus modify the climate. They do this also by promoting ocean currents. The student has only to compare a map showing prevalent winds with one of ocean currents to see the truth of this.

Moisture in the Atmosphere.

The air receives water-vapour by evaporation from the exposed water areas upon the earth's surface, but its capacity for water-vapour depends upon its temperature, as the following figures will show :

1 cubic foot of air at 30° F. can hold about 2 grains of water-vapour.

1 cubic foot of air at 60° F. can hold about 6 grains of water-vapour.

1 cubic foot of air at 90° F. can hold about 15 grains of water-vapour.

When air contains as much water-vapour as possible it is said to be *saturated*. If it then be cooled, its capacity for moisture is decreased and the excess is condensed in the form of dew, mist, rain, or snow.

Air naturally tends to become saturated when lying over or traversing the oceans ; whether it deposits any of this moisture on reaching a land surface depends upon the temperature and elevation of the latter. Northern Europe, Asia, and America would receive little or no rain from a wind passing in from the Arctic ocean, for although the air might be saturated with moisture, it would have its temperature raised in passing over the land and little condensation would result.

The *elevation* of the land has a great effect upon the amount of rainfall, for when a moisture-laden wind passes over mountain slopes it is deflected upwards to mix with the higher, cooler layers of the atmosphere. Condensation then takes place and rainfall results. The depth of rainfall at Llyn llydaw (Snowdon), 237 inches during 1908, shows well the effect of warm, moist winds striking an elevated district.

The wind may be deprived of its moisture to such an extent in passing over a mountain range that no condensation takes place as it traverses the low-lying region beyond, notable examples being the districts to the east of the Rockies and the Andes. As the wind passes a further distance over a land-mass, it becomes poorer and poorer in contained moisture, and consequently little condensation takes place even when it is deflected upwards by mountain slopes.

Dry continental regions sometimes owe their climate to the fact that the prevailing winds blow *from* the land. This is well seen just beyond the Trade Wind Zone, where extreme dryness characterises the western districts of N. and S. America, N. and S. Africa, and W. Australia. The deserts of the Sahara, Arabia, and Central Asia, on the other hand, are traversed by winds which have already crossed wide land areas ; these are passing to lower latitudes and consequently are becoming relatively drier as their temperature increases.

Rainy Districts.

Excluding the western Canadian coast, where constant south-westerly winds blow from the Pacific, and the Himalayan and Burmese slopes, where altitude wrings the moisture from the south-west monsoon, the rainiest districts in the world are found within the tropics. Great evaporation takes place in this zone, and much condensation is caused by the heated air rising to cooler layers of the atmosphere. Equatorial South America and Malaysia have exceedingly heavy rainfalls, as also have the African Guinea coast, the western Indian coast, and Ceylon. In the last-named place rain is brought by both monsoons, the north-east having traversed the Bay of Bengal, and the south-west the Indian Ocean.

It is important to note that rainfall lessens the range of temperature, for during the summer the lower layers of the air are cooled by the evaporation of falling rain, whereas in winter condensation takes place nearer to the earth's surface and this process gives heat to the atmosphere.

Distribution of Life on the Globe.

Plants as well as animals can only live in certain regions of the globe if they are fitted by their structure for life in those places. Even if they are so fitted, there may be other agents (*e.g.* enemies) to prevent them from establishing themselves firmly, and their race may dwindle and die out in a particular district.

(*a*) Plants.

Green plants require a soil of a certain degree of fertility from which to draw *water* and *mineral matters*, and they also require *warmth* and *sunlight* in order for them to make food and grow. In the North Polar regions the alternately frozen and waterlogged soil paralyses the absorptive action of plants' roots and lessens their powers of breathing and absorption. If we add to this that the food-making process is at a standstill during the long 'night' and proceeds but slowly during the short summer, that the ground is long snow-covered and spring consequently delayed, that bleak winds sweep the plains, we can easily understand the few and insignificant plants of the Frigid Zone. Lowly lichens and mosses, together with dwarfed

Harvesting, Ontario

willows and stunted conifers, practically complete the
vegetation.

Further south a vast coniferous forest belt is found,
such trees being fitted for life in cold regions by reason
of their root structure and their evergreen needle-like
leaves.   This forest belt gradually changes its character
in its southerly part: the broader-leafed deciduous
trees—oak, beech, maple, etc.—are found in increasing
numbers. They are less fitted for extreme climates, yet
can better utilise the greater warmth of the sun.   Broad
grass plains appear in drier regions, and under cultivation the larger grain-bearing grasses have gained the
upper hand over the wild kinds.

The cereals differ amongst each other in the temperature requisite for their ready growth and proper
ripening ; thus oats, rye, and barley give place to wheat
farther south, and this in its turn to maize and rice.
Along with these cereals we find the many temperate
crops—potatoes, flax, turnips, beet, hemp, tobacco,
grapes and so on.

In the Torrid Zone the great heat, heavy rainfall,
and brilliant sunshine are so favourable to rapid growth
that tangled forests extend for many miles.   So rapidly
does natural vegetation spread, that constant labour is
required to keep the cultivated plantations clear.
Ornamental woods, rubber, spices, and oils are obtained
from the virgin forests ; sugar, coffee, tea and cocoa
plantations occupy the cleared areas.

The southern hemisphere, with its cereals and grass
lands, its fruits and forests, offers in general a repetition
of the vegetation of the northern hemisphere.

Whilst we have been mainly tracing the effect of
latitude upon vegetation, we must not forget the
existence of practically rainless districts—east of the
Rockies and the Andes, the Kalahari, Sahara, and
Arabian deserts, Turkestan, Central Australia—where
no plant can live unless it can hoard up any water it
may have absorbed, and resist the destructive action
of burning sun and tearing wind.

A Rubber Estate

Finally, we note that *altitude* exerts the same effect
as latitude upon temperature, and therefore upon vegetation.   Thus, in passing from a valley to the summit of a
mountain in the tropics, we leave behind us in succession
tropical, subtropical, temperate, subarctic, and arctic
zones of vegetation, until finally we come to broad snow
and ice-fields where nothing will grow.

(b) Animals.

Since man, by virtue of his activity and intelligence,
is found practically all over the globe, going as he does

Hippopotamus on the Zambesi river

to almost uninhabitable regions in search of natural
products, it will be well to consider first the distribution
of the lower animals.

In the North are the reindeer, polar bear, arctic fox
and fur-bearing animals generally, these alone being
capable of withstanding the great cold.   Passing to
more temperate regions we find the brown bear, boar
and wolf in more sparsely peopled parts, whilst accompanying mankind in the moister or drier districts
are vast herds of cattle or flocks of sheep.   Pigs are

largely bred throughout the North Temperate Zone, particularly in the United States, where vegetable food is plentiful. Open grass lands are suitable for horse-breeding. Camels and goats are widely found in south-west Asia, whilst herds of yak form the basis of weaving and kindred industries in Tibet.

Tropical wild animals are both large and numerous. They include the tiger, elephant, rhinoceros, hippo-potamus, lion, leopard, panther, crocodile, giraffe, zebra, monkey, and jaguar.

In the South Temperate Zone horses, cattle and sheep have been introduced upon the grassy plains, thus displacing native deer and other animals. The animals peculiar to Australia are the kangaroo, opossum, platypus, and emu. Her mammals are of the marsupial or pouch-bearing kind.

Birds are equally varied, ranging in size from the tiny humming-bird to the ostrich, and in plumage from the snow-white birds of the Arctic winter and the sober-garbed songsters of the temperate zones, to tropical kinds which possess most brilliant colouring.

Fish, varying in kind according to their habitat, thrive in the rivers and shallow seas. The deep ocean is of little value in this respect.

(c) Distribution of Population.

Latitude, altitude, rainfall, temperature, proximity to the sea, fertility of the soil, and the character of minerals found under it are all factors determining the distribution of man upon the earth.

In the far North man makes a bare living by a continuous struggle against adverse conditions of life. The sea and particularly the rivers provide him with much of his food, which is mainly animal since the frozen land is incapable of cultivation. His herds of deer supply most other necessaries. The scattered population is thus mostly found along the shores and is migratory, going north in summer and south in winter as the herds pass from one feeding ground to another.

In sub-arctic regions hunting is the staple occupation and this of necessity can support but few persons per square mile. A little further south lumbermen work in the vast forests, but such men are few in proportion to the area of the land.

In the temperate zones the wide grass lands support cattle and sheep, but again their guardians are few in number. Comparatively more persons are engaged when the plains are devoted to agriculture, and the number varies according to the crop raised and the fertility of the soil. The dense populations of India and China are good examples of how fertile plains can support a great population. Another important point is that the number of persons engaged in agriculture has decreased owing to the use of modern machinery.

Men engaged in the above pursuits are essentially food-producers. But man requires more than food; hence the necessity for the industrial workers—men engaged in spinning, weaving, tanning, mining, metal-working, ship-building and countless other labours. Many of these industries are dependent on the pastoral and agricultural ones : *e.g.* weaving depends upon sheep-rearing, cotton and flax culture ; tanning upon cattle-breeding and horse-raising ; and commerce upon the dependence of one set of workers upon the others.

The close connection between density of population and distribution of minerals (especially coal and iron) will be seen when we consider the countries in detail, for we shall find whole groups of large towns lying upon the coal fields, with inhabitants engaged in manufacturing processes requiring steam power. In the tropics, the population is thinnest in desert and forest areas, the first offering no food, the second being almost impenetrable.

CHAPTER IV

EUROPE

Position and Size.

The continent of Europe is the north-westerly part of the largest land-mass. It is continuous with Asia on the east, whilst the land-locked Mediterranean Sea separates it from Africa on the south. It is but one-third the size of Africa and one-fourth that of Asia, yet size is no index to its importance, for it is situated almost entirely in the temperate zone and to this its peoples owe their vigour and hardihood. Its boundaries are roughly the 35th and 70th parallels of north latitude and, omitting Iceland, the 10th and 60th meridians of west and east longitude. Its extent thus gives it great variety of climate and natural productions, but these are greatly modified by various causes.

General Features: the Seas of Europe.

Europe is much more deeply indented by the sea than are Asia and Africa. Its irregular coast-line and numerous good harbours are of great commercial importance. The seas readily divide into two groups, the northern and southern; the former group including the Irish, North, and Baltic Seas. These seas, being a sub-merged portion of the great Central Plain of Europe, are remarkably shallow, the depth seldom exceeding 600 ft. Well-marked tides enhance the value of the outer seas, but the Baltic is practically tideless, and its flat sandy shores contrast strongly with the rugged fjord scenery of West Scandinavia and Scotland. Its flat shores and lack of tides, combined with the slow

rate at which rivers flow into it, combine to form
deltas and lagoons. Its high latitude causes little
evaporation and consequently its waters are fresher
than those of the ocean. Two results follow :

    (i)   There is an outflow from it through the Katte-
           gat and Skager Rak to the North Sea.

    (ii) Its waters freeze more readily than those of
           the outer seas. It is useless commercially
           for one-third of the year, being ice-bound
           during this time.

The southern seas include the Mediterranean, Black
Sea, and Caspian Sea. These land-locked, practically
tideless seas resemble the Baltic in that deltas and marsh
formation are frequent, but all three are *deep* seas, both
the Mediterranean Sea and the Black Sea reaching a
depth of 6000 ft. The high temperature of the Mediterranean due to its lower latitude causes a greater loss of
water by evaporation than is supplied by its rivers.
Thus there is an inflow of water from the Atlantic and
also a high degree of salinity, with the result that this
sea is never frozen.

The Black Sea on the other hand does freeze. It has
a more northerly situation than the Mediterranean, and
further, it shares the continental climate of S.E. Russia.
The slower rate of evaporation from its surface, the large
volume of water it receives, and its comparatively small
size all help to weaken its saltness and so promote
freezing. This sea is characterised by sudden storms
and thick fogs.

The Caspian Sea is entirely inland. So much evaporation goes on from its surface that it is 85 ft. below
'sea level,' and its waters are very salt.

The Build of Europe.

A relief map of the continent shows it to consist of
a central plain flanked by mountainous regions on the
north-west, east and south.

The north-west highland district includes the axes
of Scandinavia and the Scottish highlands. Both are

composed of very ancient rocks, weathered during countless centuries, and providing grand fjord scenery. The Scandinavian system reaches an altitude of 8000 ft. —a height double that of our Scottish mountains. In both cases the 'divide' is situated nearer the western than the eastern coast, so that the rivers flowing westwards are the shorter and more rapid.

The Alps, showing the Weisshorn.

The southern highland system is both more extensive and of greater elevation than the north-western. It embraces practically the whole of southern Europe and its elevation varies from 8000 ft. in the Karpathians to 18,000 ft. in the Caucasus. It consists of a southern series of folded ranges—Pyrenees, Alps, Apennines,

Karpathians, Balkan sand Caucasus,—flanked on the north-west by crust-block formations in Spain, S.E. France, and High Germany. The fertile plains of the Danube and the Po are enclosed by the folded ranges of this southern system.

Watershed and Rivers.

The main European watershed or divide lies upon a line drawn from the centre of the Pyrenees to Perm, and from it rivers flow in approximately opposite directions. The following rivers have a northerly element in their direction : Garonne, Loire, Seine, Meuse, Rhine, Weser, Elbe, Oder, Vistula, N. and S. Dvina, and Petchora. Of these the North Russian rivers are practically useless since they flow into the Arctic Ocean. Being of great length, of low elevation at their source, and flowing through high latitudes, they are icebound for many months.

The three or four months' ice of the Baltic lessens the commercial value of its rivers, but in the case of those flowing northwards through low latitudes we must note their value as lines of communication between Central Europe and the sea.

The rivers flowing into the unfrozen North Sea, the English Channel, and the Bay of Biscay, are of much greater importance commercially, owing to their accessibility at all times of the year. The Rhine and Elbe are exceedingly valuable as inland waterways, for they lead into the heart of the continent, and the ports of Hamburg and Rotterdam are ideally situated for supplying the needs, and exporting the surplus produce, of the inhabitants of Central Europe.

The Rhone, Danube, Dniester, Dnieper, Don, and Volga flow from the southerly slope of the great 'divide,' and vary in speed (and also in commercial value) according to the height of their sources and their distance from the sea. The Rhone and the Volga are interesting contrasts in this respect.

The Rhine at Bingen

Lakes.

Associated with both Scandinavian and Alpine mountain systems will be found a series of long, narrow 'ribbon' lakes, occupying the lowest parts of some of the valleys. These are most frequently found along the courses of the rivers; indeed we may regard them as local expansions of the rivers, on the waters of which they exercise a filtering effect—the deposition of much suspended matter being due to the slower rate of flow

A chalk pit overlain by glacial gravel

through them. This is particularly well seen in lakes Constance and Geneva.

Other lakes of larger size and broader shape are found in the north-west of the great plain. Their formation dates from the Glacial Epoch when the great ice sheet descended from the Scandinavian axis over Northern Europe, much of which is now covered with clay, boulders, etc. brought down by its agency. The bulk of the great plain, as also the valleys and smaller plains lying between the mountains, is covered by rocks of comparatively recent age, and these form soils of high fertility.

Temperature.

We should naturally expect to find temperature varying with *latitude.* We may take as examples the three towns, Archangel, Riga, and Athens, and compare their average January and July temperatures :

Town	Latitude	Jan. temp.	July temp.
Archangel	65° N.	10° F.	55° F.
Riga	57° N.	20° F.	65° F.
Athens	38° N.	50° F.	80° F.

The student should note from the above how temperature decreases as latitude increases, but if latitude were the only determining factor the isotherms would coincide with the latitude parallels. European isotherms however run roughly from N.W. to S.E. in winter and from S.W. to N.E. in summer. In other words, if we proceed eastwards along a parallel of latitude in winter we come successively to places of colder and colder temperature ; whereas if we do so in summer, higher and higher temperature will be experienced.

Effect of the Sea.

One great cause of this is the ameliorating *effect of the sea* upon temperature. This influence is exceptionally marked in Europe where we have a *peninsula of peninsulas* in the western half. The average January temperatures of Riga, Nijni Novgorod, and the Central Urals are 20°, 10°, and 0° F. respectively, and not only do the winters become more severe as we recede from the sea but the summers become hotter (or a more extreme climate is the result), and climatic conditions resemble those of W. Asia. The North Sea, and the Baltic and Mediterranean, which lie deep in the land, prevent their littorals having very great ranges of temperature. The 20° range of Wales should be contrasted with the 60° range of central Russia lying in the same latitude.

Effect of Winds.

The sea's moderating influence is reinforced by that of the *winds* blowing from it. We have already seen these to be due to the different rates of heating and cooling of land and water, and to the regions of high and low pressure so caused.

In winter the relatively warm North Atlantic produces a low-pressure area over Iceland, whilst a high-pressure zone exists over S.E. Europe and extends over the cold Asiatic land-mass. The winter isobars run approximately in a north-easterly direction over Europe and the winds, blowing from the south-west, swerve to the north in their passage over the continent.

In summer a high-pressure area exists over that part of the Atlantic west of Spain, and from this area the westerly winds pass with a more or less southerly sweep over Europe, to equalize the low pressures existing over Asia and Africa.

Dry winds blow across the Mediterranean in summer towards the heated Sahara, but at times the Mediterranean coast is subject to the *Sirocco*, a hot sand-laden wind blowing from the same district.

Effect of Elevation.

The *elevation of the land* has also a marked influence both upon the general temperature of the continent and upon the local temperature in different districts. Since Europe has a lower elevation than Asia, we find that its temperature, speaking generally, is the higher of the two. Again, the effect is well seen in comparing the temperatures at the summit and foot of a mountain : Mont Blanc, for instance, has a snow-capped summit with 10 to 20 degrees of frost, at a time when the valley at its base is enjoying a temperature of 70° F.

Rainfall.

From what has already been said, we see that North-West Europe receives winds from the south-west practically all the year round, and these both lessen the temperature range and increase the rainfall. These winds are deflected upwards on meeting the highlands of Britain, Norway and N.W. Spain, and consequently the rainfall of W. Europe greatly exceeds that of the eastern plain.

Other mountains besides those mentioned above are instrumental in causing rain ; thus the Pyrenees, Alps, Karpathians and Caucasus all have heavy rainfalls, whilst plains lying beyond or partially surrounded by mountains are relatively dry ; examples of this are found in N. Italy, Hungary and Bohemia. The dryness of the Spanish tableland and of that part of Sweden lying immediately to the east of the Scandinavian mountains is explained by similar conditions.

Rainfall decreases as we pass from the west to the east of the Iberian peninsula—Madrid has an annual rainfall of only 16″ as contrasted with Lisbon's 29″ ; and the same phenomenon is found in Ireland, Great Britain, Scandinavia, the Balkan peninsula, and in Caucasia.

If we compare Europe with North America we find that our own continent has no great mountain range running due north and south. This circumstance, aided by the great inland seas, results in a much more gradual diminution of rainfall from west to east. Ireland has more than 200 rainy days in the year, whilst in the Volga basin there are less than 100. North and south-east Russia are among Europe's driest districts.

Bordeaux has 33″ of rainfall annually, Berlin has 23″, and Moscow only 21″.

Rainy Seasons.

Striking differences also exist in the seasonal variations of rainfall. The western fringe of Europe has rain at all seasons of the year, although more in winter as a

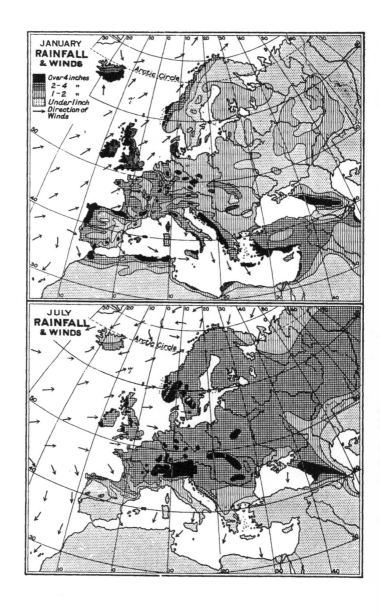

consequence of the air over the land being cooler at that season ; but the bulk of the Central Plain has most rain during the summer months. This is explained by the south-easterly deflection of the winds and by the greater amount of evaporation from rivers and lakes during that period. The Mediterranean region however receives its greatest rainfall during the winter months. Its summers are dry, for it is subject to dry north-easterly winds, which have blown over Asia to replace air withdrawn from the Mediterranean by the low-pressure area existing over the heated Sahara. These same north-easterly winds are largely the cause of the hot, dry summer of the Russian steppes.

We may say that in summer the Mediterranean district comes within the sphere of influence of the North-East Trade Winds. The dry summers of Spain, Italy and the Balkan peninsula have a great effect upon the vegetation of these countries.

Vegetation.

(a) The Frozen North.

The *tundra* region of N. Russia and Finland bears only cotton-grass, mosses, lichens, and dwarf shrubs, the latter giving place to the coniferous forest further south.

(b) The Trees of Europe.

Spruce firs, pines, and larches comprise this forest and clothe Russia and Scandinavia down to latitude 60° N. Heathy moors and bogs occupy the Scandinavian plateau, whilst on the west of the peninsula heavy rains have washed away much of the surface soil and rendered extensive forest growth impossible. Conifers clothe also the slopes of the German uplands and much timber is floated down to the North Sea and Baltic in the form of rafts. Such trees are found generally upon the higher, colder parts of the mountains in central Europe.

Black Forest Pines

About latitude 60° the broader-leafed deciduous trees begin to supplant the conifers. They are better fitted for warmer conditions of life, and they stretch through central Europe to South France and to the western shore of the Black Sea, being found also on the lower slopes of the mountains. Typical deciduous forest trees are the alder, beech, birch, chestnut, elm, lime, oak, sycamore and plane.

A vast deciduous forest once stretched to the Mediterranean, but in past years much of the southern portion has been cleared ; the result has been disastrous, for the soil, no longer bound by the roots of the trees, has been washed away by the winter rains, and the water now runs straight to the rivers, which are alternately swollen or shrunken in consequence. The land, too, having lost its power of retaining the moisture, is parched and dry during the hot summer, and vegetation suffers. The only trees which can withstand such adverse conditions are those of the evergreen type with thick leathery leaves. Thickets, rather than continuous forests, of these trees are characteristic of the Mediterranean region (Spain, Italy, and the Balkan peninsula). The laurel, holly, myrtle, mulberry, olive, evergreen oak, and pine are most frequently found in this district, and with them are sub-tropical drought-resisting plants.

The fruit trees of southern Europe—orange, lemon, fig, and pomegranate—contrast strongly with the apple, pear, plum, and cherry of our own islands and of that part of the continent lying in latitudes a little further south of us.

(c) The Cereals of Europe.

Much forest land has been cleared for cultivation of corn and other crops. Cereals on the whole prefer a rather dry soil, although they vary among themselves in the amount of moisture and heat required for growth and ripening. Barley, oats and rye will thrive in regions which are too damp and cold for other grain. They are therefore found cultivated in the more northerly as well as in the more elevated parts of the continent. In Bohemia and Bavaria hop culture is carried on together with that of barley, the two crops being used in the beer industry.

Wheat requires a drier and warmer summer to ripen its grain. It is widely grown between latitudes 45° and 52°, although its northerly limit of culture may be taken as the line drawn through Aberdeen and St Petersburg. It comes to greatest perfection in France, Hungary, Italy, and the Russian Black Lands.

Maize requires a higher temperature than wheat and consequently is cultivated farther south. Much of it is grown in South France and the Danube basin. A line through Orleans and Astrakhan would approximately mark its northerly limit. Rice, demanding abundant moisture and heat, is grown in the Po valley, but not to the same extent as other cereals.

(d) Other Cultivated Plants.

Flax and hemp, both valuable fibre-producing plants, are cultivated on the central plain. Flax has the more northerly habitat. It thrives in moist, cool districts and is found in Ireland, N. France, Belgium, Holland and the south-east Baltic region ; hemp is produced in Central Russia.

Vegetables require a moister soil than cereals. Potatoes and beet are perhaps the two most important root-crops. The poorer soils of Ireland, S. Scandinavia and N. Germany are largely given up to potato culture, whilst beet is a staple crop in N. France, Germany and S. Russia, and its increased production has gone hand in hand with the growing and zealously fostered sugar manufacture. The European production of beet has increased to such proportions that many of the West Indian sugar planters are faced with ruin.

The cultivation of the vine is one of Europe's greatest industries. This plant grows best on well-drained slopes exposed to genial summer heat ; thus one naturally looks to southern Europe as its area of cultivation. France,

Italy, Spain and Hungary are the four countries producing most wine. Latitude 50° may be regarded as
the northern limit of vine culture. In Europe the
southern slopes of the hills are used for vineyards, but
in Australia the *northern* slopes are preferred ; the
student will easily see the reason for this difference.

(*e*) **Grass Lands.**

These fall into two main groups :

  (i) Rich, lush, meadow-lands where the soil and
      general climate are too damp for cereal
      culture (*e.g.* Denmark, Holland).

  (ii) Wide, open, dry plains, subject to extremes of
      heat and cold, where forest growth is
      impossible by reason of lack of rain,
      shortness of summer, and friability of the
      soil, and yet where quick-growing grasses
      can recover from the drought, and ripen
      their grain during the few hot months
      (*e.g.* the steppes of Russia).

The Russian steppes lie to the south-east of a line
joining Perm to the N. Karpathians and passing eastwards to Odessa. Their western portion, the Black
Earth region, is now being transformed into a great
wheat-growing area. The eastern steppes are practically
a desert ; they lie to the north of the Caspian, and
although scorched in summer, they are snow-covered
for half the year.

The moister meadow lands support cattle, and give
rise to dairy occupations, whilst the drier plains are of
necessity devoted to sheep.

Animals of Europe.

As man proceeds to clear the forest with a view to
agriculture, so he exterminates the wild animals living
therein, and these are fast decreasing. There remain
the reindeer, elk, and Polar bear in the north, and the
bear, boar, wolf and various kinds of deer in central and
southern Europe.

Man exterminates wild animals; but he protects, and fosters the increase of those which he has domesticated for purposes of supplying food, clothing, or means of transport. The grass lands are suitable for horses, cattle, and sheep. The latter—as also goats— feed on the higher, drier, and poorer pastures, cattle occupying the moister lands. The horse, mule, ox, camel, and reindeer are used as beasts of burden in different parts of the continent.

Lowestoft Trawlers

Both seas and rivers are rich in fish, but the most valuable fisheries are those of the shallow North Sea, from which cod, herring, mackerel and many other kinds of fish are obtained. The tunny and sardine fishery of the Mediterranean is much less important. Indeed the Roman Catholic nations of southern Europe receive tons of fish in the dried state every year from Britain and Scandinavia. The rivers of the north-west are fished for salmon, those of the south-east for sturgeon.

The Minerals of Europe.

Coal and Iron. The European coalfields are widely scattered. Their importance in promoting the development of the different nations cannot be over-estimated, especially when, as frequently happens, iron is found in their vicinity. In the following list of coalfields the regions with accompanying iron are italicised : *Great Britain, N. Spain, S.E. France, Meuse Valley, N.W. Germany,* S. Germany, *S. Sweden,* S. and Central Russia, *Poland.* The Mediterranean and Baltic regions are practically without coal ; so also are the very high mountainous districts. Iron is also found in Sweden and the S. Urals.

Copper exists in the Harz Mountains, S.W. Spain, the Urals and Sweden. Swansea receives much copper from Spain. *Clay* for pottery purposes is found in England, Holland, and Bohemia. *Gold* is comparatively scarce, the Urals being the chief district where it is mined. *Graphite* or black lead has given rise to the lead pencil industry of Bohemia.

Mercury is obtained from Spanish ores, and *marble* is found in Italy, whilst *petroleum* wells are numerous in S.E. Russia, on the shore of the Caspian Sea. *Salt* is obtained either by evaporation of sea water or from mines of rock salt. The latter are found among the secondary rocks in Britain, Central Germany and Austria. Many chemical industries have arisen in their neighbourhood.

Silver is found in the Harz Mountains, the Urals, S. Germany and Bohemia, and *lead* is frequently found in conjunction with it. *Sulphur* occurs in districts which are, or have been, volcanic ; Sweden and Italy, particularly Sicily and Stromboli, are the most important sources. Spain, Belgium and Germany have supplies of *zinc,* and England produces *tin.*

Distribution of Population.

If pastoral, agricultural, and fishing pursuits were the only ones, we should find the population distributed along the shores near the richer fishing grounds, and over the interior of the land in proportion to its quality, pastoral land being more sparsely peopled than agricultural. But two other factors have much to do in modifying this distribution. These are (i) the presence of minerals, and (ii) the necessity for commercial relations between various countries.

The presence of minerals, and in particular coal and iron, gives rise to densely peopled manufacturing areas ; e.g. the districts around Glasgow, Manchester, Liège, Düsseldorf, Chemnitz, and St Etienne. On the other hand, commercial relations between peoples tend to gather the population at spots conveniently facing their neighbours oversea. This is well seen in London, Rotterdam, Hamburg, Liverpool, Havre and Stockholm.

The most sparsely populated regions in Europe are N. Scandinavia and Russia lying to the north of lat. 60°, the Scottish highlands, and the south-eastern Russian steppes. In all these districts there are less than 16 persons per square mile. By way of contrast we may note that there are more than 2000 people per square mile in some of the busy manufacturing districts referred to in the preceding paragraph.

The Peoples of Europe and their Religions.

With the exception of the Finns and Lapps of the extreme north, the Magyars of Hungary, the Turks, and the Tartars of the Russian steppes, the peoples of Europe belong to the great Indo-European or Aryan race. They are distinguished among themselves as

Celts in the extreme north-west—Ireland, Scottish highlands, Brittany, Wales.

Teutons—the great German group—inhabiting Norway, Sweden, Holland, Germany, Belgium, Denmark, Britain, Northern Austria.

Graeco-Latins—occupying France and South Europe.

Slavs in Russia, E. and S. Austria, and the northern part of the Balkan peninsula.

The Turks are the only Mohammedan nation. Their capture of Constantinople and the Balkan peninsula took place about 1450 A.D.

The other European nations profess Christianity, either in the Protestant or Roman Catholic form, according as they did or did not separate from the parent church at the time of the Reformation. Speaking generally, it was the Teutonic nations who participated in this movement. At the present day the Slavs belong to the Greek Church, whilst southern Europe generally professes Roman Catholicism. The separation of the Roman Church into eastern and western churches goes right back to Roman times, and was consequent upon the splitting of the Roman realm into eastern and western empires.

The British Isles.

Position and Size.

The British Isles, consisting of Great Britain, Ireland, and numerous smaller islands, are situated off the north-west coast of continental Europe, from which they are separated by the North Sea and the English Channel. They lie between the 50th and 59th parallels of north latitude, and the 2nd east and 10th west meridians of longitude. Their size is relatively small, the extreme length being but 600 miles, and the area of the whole group of islands about 120,000 sq. miles. This area should be carefully remembered, because we shall use it as our unit of area in later parts of the book. We must not, however, regard size as a standard of importance, for many other factors have combined to make our own country the foremost in the world.

Surface and General Features.

Of the three countries, Scotland is the most mountainous, Ireland the least so, whilst England is intermediate between the two.

In Scotland the highest elevation is that of Ben Nevis (over 4000 ft.). As regards build it may be conveniently divided into

> (i)   A mountainous region lying to the north of the Firths of Tay and Clyde,

Snowdon

> (ii)   A central and lower region lying to the south of these firths, and separating the highlands from
>
> (iii)   A southern upland region.

The mountainous district includes the North-West Highlands and the Grampians, the highest peaks being Ben Wyvis, Ben Macdhui and Ben Nevis. The Ochil and Sidlaw Hills lie in the central district, and in the southern uplands are the Lead, Pentland, and Cheviot Hills. Whilst these uplands stretch in a north-easterly direction right across the country from Stranraer to the Firth of Forth, and give place to the rolling country of Kirkcudbright and Dumfries on the south, the Grampians lie on the whole nearer to the west, so that the eastern counties have a lower elevation.

In England and Wales there are two great elevated regions : the Cambrian with Snowdon (about 3500 ft.), and the Pennine-Cumbrian with Crossfell and Scafell (about 3000 ft.), as their highest peaks. These are the only parts of the country that deserve to be called mountainous. With the exception of the moors of North Yorkshire and Devon all the remainder of the country is a great plain crossed by low hills. These hills may be regarded as three series :

(i) The Cotswolds, Edge Hill, and Lincoln Heights, ending in the North York Moors.

(ii) The Chilterns, East Anglian Heights, and Lincoln Wolds, ending in the York Wolds.

(iii) The Western Downs, with their continuations the North and South Downs, running through S.E. England.

In Ireland the mountains fringe the coast, the most important being those of Donegal, Antrim, Mourne, Wicklow, Kerry, and Connemara. Both in Wicklow and Kerry peaks reach an elevation of 3000 ft. The centre of Ireland is a great plain.

The Watersheds of Great Britain and Ireland.

In Great Britain the main divide runs north and south in an irregular line, lying nearer to the west coast than the east, as far south as Marlborough. At this point it branches and crosses the country from east to west, so that we may regard its shape as ⟂. From this we should expect to find two sets of rivers, one flowing generally in an easterly or a westerly direction, and the other in southern England flowing with a northerly or

southerly course. The student should recognise the
approximate truth of this from his atlas. He will find
many deviations from these principles, and he should
explain all these deviations by reference to a relief
map. The following points are especially noteworthy :

    (i)   The greater length of the rivers flowing east.

    (ii) The action of the Cambrian mountains in
           causing rivers to flow N., E., W. and S.

    (iii) The directions taken successively in their
           courses by the Trent, Thames, and Severn.

    (iv) The parallel courses of the various tributaries
           of the Yorkshire Ouse ; of the Welland,
           Nen, and Great Ouse ; and of the Severn,
           Wye, and Usk.

The situation of the Irish mountains near the coast
gives rise to the phenomenon of rivers rising from their
inland slopes quite near the sea, yet reaching it at a far
distant spot after traversing the interior. The Bann,
Liffey, Blackwater, Lee, and Shannon all flow in this
way. The central ridge of Slieve Bloom determines the
south-westerly direction of the Shannon in its lower
reaches and also sends the Barrow and Suir southwards.
A comparatively slight elevation lying to the north of
this range gives rise to the Erne and Boyne.

Lakes.

The lakes of Great Britain differ from those of the
Irish plain in that they are of the ribbon type, occupying
long valleys in the northern highlands, Grampians and
Cumbrian group. In Ireland many of the lakes are
shallow, with a much greater expanse of surface. The
flat character of the country accounts for this. On
the other hand, the mountain lakes of Killarney recall
both in situation and beauty the lakes of Great Britain.
The majority of the lakes in the British Isles are expansions of the rivers ; this is seen very well in the
Irish rivers Erne and Shannon, which connect long
strings of lakes.

The Coast of Britain.

(a) The West Coast.

The elevation and geological formation of the land does much to decide the character of the coast and its scenery. The huge mountainous masses lying near the sea give a rugged grandeur to the north and west Scottish coasts. Numerous lochs run far into the land and recall the fjord scenery of Norway. The Hebrides add to the beauty, and, interposed between the main-land and the Atlantic, form a natural breakwater which calms the sea considerably. Thousands of tourists visit Scotland every year, one of the greatest attractions being the basaltic caves of Staffa, an island which was covered with lava in Tertiary times. The Firth of Clyde is protected by the southerly peninsula of Kintyre. It stretches far into the Grampian district, and the scenery of the Kyles of Bute and Lochs Fyne and Long is widely renowned. As we proceed southwards the west coast loses its grandeur, until along the southern coast of Scotland there are the flat sandy shores of the plain which lies to the south of the southern uplands.

The Solway Firth is low and sandy along both its shores. The projecting St Bees Head is the point where the Cumbrian mountains lie nearest the sea. From Walney Island to North Wales level stretches of sandy coast are the rule. When the sea recedes from the land, great expanses of sand are left bare. The Isle of Man has a coast scenery of a different type : beaches are few, the coast being usually occupied by high cliffs of volcanic rock. It is a favourite holiday resort by reason of its mild climate and the beauty of its glens.

The coast from North Wales to Land's End is of a more rugged nature than that lying further north, the nearness of the mountains and the wearing force of the Atlantic accounting for this. Great Orme's Head in North Wales is a projecting limestone mass. The tides flow with very rapid current through the Menai Strait which separates Anglesey from the mainland. The sweeping curve of the Welsh mountains determines that of Cardigan Bay, ending at St David's Head. The strong tides of the Bristol Channel and the funnel-shaped estuary of the Severn produce the tidal wave called the *Bore*. The coast scenery of West Cornwall is majestic. Cliffs of granite and other ancient rocks rise sheer from the sea for several hundred feet. Land's End is a granitic mass.

The Needles

(*b*) The South Coast.

The south coast of England ranges from the rugged Cornish cliffs to the more gentle type at the east. Safe anchorage is afforded at Falmouth and Plymouth, at the latter place by an immense artificial breakwater. From Start Point to Portland Bill a great bay has been

formed by the softer rocks being worn away. Chalky
rocks prevail from Portland Bill to the Forelands. The
main capes (the Needles, Beachy Head, Dungeness, N. and
S. Foreland) occur where the hill-ranges reach the sea.
Opposing tides meet off Dungeness and deposit much
transported matter. The roadsteads, the Solent and
the Downs, are sheltered by the Isle of Wight and
the Goodwins.

(c) **The East Coast.**

The estuary of the Thames and the eastern coast as far
as the chalky mass of Flamborough Head have low, uninteresting shores. Mud flats occur at the mouth of the
Thames, much material having been deposited by this
river. A sandbank lying off Yarmouth produces the
calm water of the Yarmouth Roads. The shores around
the Wash are flat, and fringed with low sand hills, bound
together by coarse grass and prickly sea-thorn.

The eastern Scottish coast is rocky from the Tweed
to St Abb's Head, where the southern uplands reach
the sea. A lower coast is found round the Firth of
Forth, this being a part of the central lowland area
of Scotland. A rocky but somewhat low coast with
interspersed sandy stretches occupies the eastern coast
as far north as Tarbat Ness. From this cape high rocks
prevail until the majestic Dunnet Head is reached.

The Coasts of Ireland.

These are much more rugged and lofty on the
western and south-western shores, where they are exposed to the full force of the Atlantic. Since the Irish
mountains lie mostly near the sea, they are responsible
for much of the grandeur of the cliff scenery. The
numerous islands and the greatly scarred western coast-
line with its narrow fjord-like indentations remind us
of the west coast of Scotland. The south-eastern and
eastern coasts are more regular and less rocky, bold
headlands being found only where the Wicklow and
Mourne mountains abut upon the sea. The basaltic

plateau of Antrim is the chief feature of the north-east. The Giant's Causeway is a part of this volcanic region. The north-west corner of the island has a high rocky coast due to the mountains of Donegal.

Giant's Causeway

The Climate of the British Isles.   Temperature.

The average annual temperature of the British Isles is 48° F., but places situated in the extreme north or south have an average temperature some three or four degrees lower or higher than this, a result due, among

other causes, to difference in latitude and the consequent difference in the angle at which the sun's rays
strike the land.

(a) **Winter Temperature.**

The distribution of temperature varies very much
according to the season. Thus, in winter, the isotherms
run approximately north and south, whilst in summer
they traverse the land in curves arching towards the
north. The N.–S. direction of the January isotherms is
the result of the warming influence of the ocean drift
from the south-west and the prevalent south-westerly
winds blowing from the Atlantic. The presence of the
colder continental mass upon the east also favours this
distribution of temperature in winter. The country may
thus be divided into successive belts from west to east,
each with a higher January temperature than the next.
The warmest parts of the country during this month are
west and south-west Ireland, the Cornish peninsula, and
the westerly regions of Anglesey and Wales. In all
these districts the temperature is above 42° F.

The coldest parts are east Scotland and the eastern
Midlands in England, where the temperature is below
38° F. The heating effect of sea and wind referred to
above cannot be too strongly emphasised. There is
only a difference of 1° F. in the average January temperatures of London and the Shetland Isles. The 40°
isotherm passes due south through western Scotland
and mid-Wales. It then curves to the south-east
through the Isle of Wight, next southwards to the
Pyrenees, and then eastwards through north Italy and
Turkey. Thus in winter the Shetlands (lat. 60° N.) have
an average temperature equal to that of Milan (lat.
45° N.) and Constantinople (lat. 40° N.).

(b) **Summer Temperature.**

The summer isotherms follow the latitude parallels
more closely. The cooling effect of the Atlantic is
greater than that of the shallow North Sea, which
becomes heated the more quickly of the two, and

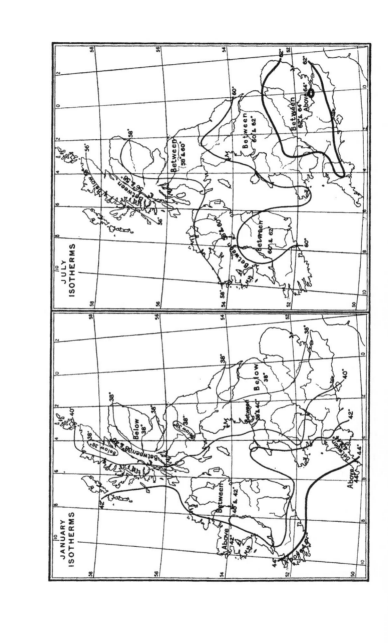

furthermore is largely enclosed by heated land-masses. The isotherms consequently form curves arching towards the north and striking the east coast at a higher latitude than the west. In other words, the summer is warmer on the east coast than at places on the west coast in the same latitudes. South-west Ireland has a July temperature of 59°, Cardiff has 62°, and London 64°.

Latitude exerts considerable effect on temperature in summer. London's summer temperature of 64° is 10° above that of the Shetlands. The path of the 60° July isotherm is very instructive. In its passage across Europe it traverses Finland and N. Russia, yet in the British Isles we find upon it Youghal, Limerick, St David's Head, Carlisle, and York. Such British places have a July temperature 10° cooler than those situated in the same latitudes in the eastern part of the Russian plain.

(c) **Winds.**

The continuous low-pressure area over the Atlantic in high latitudes ensures that south-westerly winds shall be the most prevalent over the British Isles. These winds blow twice as frequently as those from any other single direction. They do not however blow continuously, for they are subject to interruption by other winds, particularly the cold north-east winds blowing towards us from Europe. We all know by experience the changeable nature of our own climate. Much of this is due to alterations in position of the areas of high and low pressure over the continent lying to the east of us. Our country is especially liable to the visits of cyclones, or local low-pressure systems, which have reached our islands from the Atlantic, and we associate rainy weather with them.

(d) **Rain and Rainfall.**

The prevalent south-westerly winds do more than moderate the cold of winter and heat of summer, for they are moisture-laden and deposit much of their moisture **when** cooled by blowing up the mountain sides in our islands.

Rainfall is heavy throughout Ireland (the 'Emerald' isle) except in the east of Meath and Dublin counties, where it is less than 30″ annually. The heaviest rains are experienced in the mountainous districts of S.W. Cork and Kerry and W. Galway (60″ or more). This is just such a distribution as we should expect.

The following places in England and Scotland also have an annual rainfall of over 60″: Skye, Mull and the western mainland of Scotland near these islands, Lead Hills, Cumberland, the heights of Wales and those of Cornwall and Devon. A rainfall of 40″ to 60″ is found in the western parts of Ireland, the southern Scottish uplands, the Pennines, Wales, and the Cornish peninsula.

The central plain of England is drier than that of Ireland. Its dryness increases towards the east, for the winds are by this time robbed of the bulk of their moisture, and the level land does not tend to cause rainfall. The driest parts of the English plain are Lincolnshire, Cambridgeshire, Huntingdonshire, and the eastern halves of Sussex and Essex. The importance of this distribution will be evident in our later work.

The amount of rainfall has been previously noted as affecting the range of temperature. We can trace this effect in our own islands : eastern England has an average range of 23° F., whilst the Irish mountains have a range of about 16° F.

In concluding this section we give the annual rainfall in the year 1908 at twelve British stations. The student should account for the remarkable differences between the rainfall at these places.

Kerry	86″	Kingstown (Ireland)	24″
Swansea	135″	Colchester	16″
Llyn llydaw (Snowdon)	237″	Harwich	16″
Seathwaite (Cumberland)	127″	Bourne (Lincs.)	15″
Loch Shiel (W. Inverness)	121″	Dundee	19″
Dublin	22″	Arbroath	19″

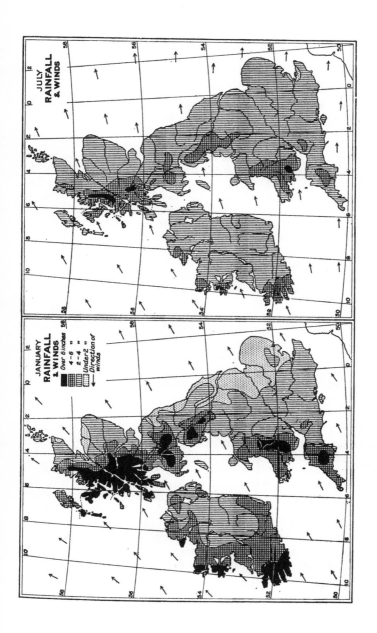

The Plants of the British Isles.

In ancient times the surface of Britain was practically covered by forest and marsh, but with the advance of civilisation these conditions have been greatly altered. The bulk of the forests has been cut down, so that now they occupy but 4 % of the surface of the land, although the geographical names *weald* and *wold* remain as testimony of their ancient extent. Many of the important plants in Britain to-day have been introduced from abroad. Among the trees we may note the oak, beech, birch, alder, poplar, aspen, hornbeam, willow, thorn, ash, rowan, maple, and Scots fir as being truly British.

The area under cultivation has been greatly increased by the drainage and improvement of marsh lands (*e.g.* the Fen district), but in Ireland large expanses of bog still remain. The heavy rainfall of that country, as also its level nature, is largely responsible for these.

Not only the area occupied by, but also the number of, our native plants has been reduced by drainage and deforestation, and we seek them either in lanes and odd corners of cultivated fields, or in upland regions where poorness of soil renders agriculture impossible.

The Native Animals.

The destruction of native animals has accompanied that of the plants. Formerly bears, boars, and wolves were common in the land, but now they have been completely exterminated. The smaller carnivora have escaped somewhat. They include the wild cat, the jealously preserved fox, the badger, polecat, stoat, weasel, and otter. Red, fallow, and roe deer all exist wild. The hare, rabbit, rat, and squirrel, with a number of smaller creatures, complete the list of wild quadrupeds. Snakes number but few species, the viper being the only venomous kind.

Agriculture.

By this term we mean strictly the cultivation of the ground, but since the agricultural and pastoral occupations are so closely connected we will consider them together.

(a) Very Poor Lands.

Some land is productive, some quite unproductive. Examples of the latter will be found in the elevated masses of ancient rocks—the Millstone Grits, granites and slates of our mountainous districts. We have already seen that the mountains receive most rainfall ; consequently surface soil is absent from their upper and steeper slopes. Further down the mountain side a moss and heather zone occurs, the thin soil being sufficient to provide these plants with anchorage and sustenance. These give place at a lower elevation to short wiry grass, which is the beginning of the hill pastures. The soil of these pastures is not rich enough to repay cultivation and so it is left for sheep grazing. Sheep can exist upon much poorer and drier grass lands than can cattle or horses, so we should expect to find them reared extensively in the highlands and uplands of Scotland and Wales, and upon the dry secondary ridges of limestone and chalk in England.

(b) Moist Meadows.

On the other hand, cattle thrive upon moister pastures. They are thus particularly numerous in Ireland and in the low-lying regions in the west of England and Wales. Scotland rears but few cattle by contrast with the other two countries. Eastern England produces on the average less cattle than sheep ; the reasons for this will be made clear by a study of rainfall and geological maps. East Scotland rears in general more cattle than West Scotland, elevation and rainfall being the two great determining factors.

Moderately dry grass lands are suited for horse rearing. This industry consequently becomes important in N.E. Yorkshire, Suffolk, and the Midlands.

(*c*) **Crops.**

Farmers are decided by geological and climatic conditions what crops to raise, although usually they have been taught by experience rather than by theory. The nature of the soil, the temperature of the air and the amount of rainfall exercise the greatest influence in this connection. The warm dry summer of Lincolnshire, Cambridgeshire, Norfolk, Suffolk and Essex makes these great wheat-producing districts. The clayey soil,

Gathering cider apples, Devonshire

especially when properly limed, is particularly suited for wheat, and also for potatoes and other root crops. Wheat requires a higher temperature for ripening than our other cereals. Its northerly limit of cultivation may be taken as Aberdeen, although it is grown but sparsely in Scotland, Ireland, and N. England. A lower temperature suits barley, and so it forms an important Scottish cereal and has given rise to the spirit industry in that country. We also find it grown in England, especially where the soil is a light mixture of chalk

and clay. Most oats are grown in Scotland, for they
demand little warmth and dryness. They form the
staple food of the Scottish peasantry. Certain geological formations are peculiarly suited for particular
crops : a mixture of chalk and upper greensand
forms admirable wheat land; mixed chalky soils, as
those of Hereford, Hants, Kent, Surrey, Sussex and
Worcester, are good for hop culture; whilst the red
sandstones are especially fitted for fruit trees. The
apple and pear orchards of Devon, Hereford, Gloucester
and Somerset are due to this cause.

The moist cold climate of Ireland is fitted for the
growth of the flax plant, and the drained soils of that
country form good potato-growing regions.

Fisheries.

The most important sea-fisheries are situated in the
neighbourhood of the banks and shoals of the North
Sea, where cod, herring, and flatfish abound. Fleets of
trawlers send their catches by steamer to the larger
fishing towns to be forwarded by rail to London. The
herring fishery employs the Scottish as well as English
fisher-folk. This fish is found both on the east and
west coasts of Great Britain. Many thousand barrels
of herring are sent to Europe annually. Mackerel and
pilchard shoals visit our coasts, but the latter fish is
found only on the south coast of Ireland and around
Cornwall. Salmon and trout are the only important
river fish, the Scottish and Irish rivers being the main
sources of supply.

Oysters are cultivated in beds at the mouth of
the Thames, Humber and other rivers, where the beds
of Colchester, Whitstable, and Grimsby are the most
famous.

Minerals of the British Isles.

Coal. We owe our importance as a manufacturing
nation to the plentiful supply of this mineral, yet it is
not found distributed uniformly over our own islands.

Ireland is sadly deficient in coal, and what little she has is of inferior quality. It is found in the south-east in the counties of Carlow, Tipperary, and Kilkenny, and in the north-west in Donegal and Londonderry. Lack of coal has greatly hindered the industrial development of Ireland.

In Scotland, the coalfield is found in the central lowland region (*i.e.* stretching from Fife Ness to Ayr). In this district the majority of Scottish manufacturing towns are situated. These include Glasgow, Paisley, Kilmarnock, Motherwell, Coatbridge, Falkirk, Alloa and Dunfermline.

The English coalfields are both numerous and extensive. They are all associated with ancient rocks, and lie to the west of a line running north-east from Somerset to the mouth of the Tees.

They arrange themselves in two groups: one flanking the Pennines, the other lying to the east and south of the Cambrian system.

The first group includes—

(i) *The Northumberland and Durham Coalfield,* shipping coal to London, and also providing it for smelting purposes in the Cleveland district of Yorkshire. Newcastle, Sunderland, Jarrow, North and South Shields all lie upon this coalfield.

(ii) *The York, Derby, and Nottingham Coalfield,* some 60 miles long, stretching from Leeds to Nottingham, and providing coal for the busy centres of Sheffield and Rotherham as well as for southern England.

(iii) *The Leicester Coalfield,* on which stands Ashby-de-la-Zouch.

(iv) *The Warwick and South Staffordshire Coalfield,* supplying the furnaces of the Black Country.

(v) *The North Staffordshire Coalfield,* providing coal for the pottery towns of Hanley, Stoke and Burslem.

(vi) *The South Lancashire Coalfield,* which supplies motive power for the cotton spindles of Lancashire, and feeds the chemical furnaces of St Helens and similar towns.

A South Wales colliery

(vii) *The Cumberland Coalfield,* with Whitehaven and Maryport as chief centres. Much of this coal is used for smelting the haematite iron ore of the Furness district.

The second group includes the coalfields of Cheshire, Shropshire, Bristol, Somerset, and South Wales. The last-named coalfield is of great extent and its coal (the smokeless anthracite variety) is of great value, much being exported for use by the world's navies. Newport, Merthyr, Swansea, Llanelly, Aberdare, and Cardiff all lie upon this coalfield, and to some of these towns crude tin and copper ores are brought from distant parts of the world in order to be smelted.

Iron. Fortunately for England, much of its iron is found upon the coalfields. This means a smaller cost of production of pig-iron and steel, as also of their manufactured products. Another fortunate circumstance lies in the fact that the flux—limestone—necessary for smelting operations is also found close at hand in the oolitic ridge of secondary rocks crossing England from S.W. to N.E. Iron ores are found in some of these secondary rocks.

In Northamptonshire, Lincolnshire, and the important Cleveland district, iron ores are found in the secondary rocks away from the coal. The smelting of the Yorkshire ores by means of coal brought from the coalfield lying to the north has already been noted, as also has that of the Furness ore by Cumberland coal.

But great bands of iron ore are found directly upon the coalfields. This is especially noteworthy in the case of the Northumberland-Durham, South Staffordshire and South Wales coalfields.

Iron is also found in conjunction with coal in the central lowland area of Scotland. Ireland is poor in iron, as in other metals. Her only important iron district is Antrim.

Copper is mined in Merioneth and Anglesey, and also, together with tin, in Cornwall and Devon. Copper mining does not pay in England, because of the cheapness of foreign ores. The little copper produced is smelted at Swansea and Llanelly in South Wales. Some copper is also found in the Wicklow hills.

Zinc is mined in Cornwall, Cumberland, and Derbyshire.

Lead is associated with mountains, especially in North Wales (Holywell and Mold), the Isle of Man, and the Lowther Hills (Leadhills) in South Scotland. It is also obtained in Durham, Yorkshire, Cumberland, and Derbyshire. The veins of metal are frequently found in limestone mountains.

Tin mining, although one of the most ancient British industries, has much decreased, and some of the Cornish mines have been closed through foreign competition. Tin is brought from Australia and Malaysia for smelting at Swansea, which is the great centre of the tinplate industry. Owing to cheap native labour and the low cost of ocean carriage, this tin is a serious rival to the metal produced from our home mines.

Building Stones, etc. Granite is quarried in Aberdeen, Peterhead, Argyle, Cumberland, Wicklow, Leicestershire and Dartmoor. The Mourne mountains form the Irish supply. Marble occurs in Scotland, Donegal and Kilkenny, Derbyshire and Devonshire, and slate forms many of our mountain masses. It is exported from Bangor, Port Madoc, and Carnarvon in Wales, and is also quarried in Cornwall, Cumberland, and the Isle of Man. Magnesian limestone is obtained from Yorkshire, whilst numerous counties situated on the oolitic ridge have limestone quarries.

Freestone is extensively quarried at Bath and Portland. The chalk hills of south and south-east England provide lime for building purposes and flints for use in the pottery industry. The situation of the latter in North Staffordshire is due to a bed of suitable clay in that district. Dartmoor and Cornwall send to the Potteries and to Worcester their *Kaolin*, which

Granite quarries, Aberdeen

owes its formation to the disintegration of granite rocks in remote ages. The Midlands and the London basin have important brickmaking industries. Stafford tiles have a name in the building trade. The fireclay so largely used in the construction of furnaces and modern fireplaces is obtained from the Sheffield district, where it is found in beds forming part of the coal measures.

People, Race, and Religion.

Although from trade and other reasons we find a large number of foreigners living amongst us, we may say that the United Kingdom is peopled by Teutons, except in the north and west, where the older Celtic race is found.

Celts are found in Scotland, the Isle of Man, Wales, and Ireland. In 1901 only 5% of the Scottish people could speak Gaelic, whilst in the ten years preceding, the number of people speaking Celtic languages in Wales and Ireland had decreased from 70% to 46% and from 18% to 14%. These figures show how the older tongues are dying out, and this is largely due to better communications and improved trade.

More than a quarter of a million British people emigrate each year, and about the same number of foreigners pass out yearly, particularly from our western ports which face America. North America receives three out of every four people who leave the mother country.

All forms of religion are fully tolerated in Britain, the Protestant forms of worship being more prevalent in England and Scotland, and the Roman Catholic in Ireland. Education is in a very forward state : elementary education is free and compulsory ; numerous university colleges, secondary schools, and technical institutions provide intermediate education ; and there are universities in all the countries (viz. at Oxford, Cambridge, London, Durham, Manchester, Leeds, Liverpool, Sheffield, Birmingham, and Bristol, in England ; Aberystwyth, Bangor, and Cardiff in Wales ; St Andrews,

Aberdeen, Glasgow, and Edinburgh, in Scotland ; and
the National University of Ireland at Dublin, Cork, and
Galway, and Queen's University at Belfast, in Ireland).

Population and its Distribution.

In 1911 the population of the United Kingdom was
more than 45 million persons.   England and Wales
had a population of 36 millions; Scotland $4\frac{3}{4}$ millions;
Ireland $4\frac{1}{3}$ millions; the average population being 370
per square mile.

The population is distributed very unevenly.   We
should expect this from the varying altitude and fertility of the land, and from the irregular distribution
of coal.

History explained by Geographical Position and Conditions.

The glory of conquest, and the value of British lead,
tin, iron, grain and fish, led the Romans to invade our
country and to retain their hold for four centuries.
Their long straight roads traversed the flatter parts of
the country in all directions, and their walls and forts
kept back the turbulent Scottish tribes.   Britain's outlying position on the skirts of the Roman Empire led to
the early withdrawal of Roman troops and left her a
prey to the Teutonic hordes which swept westwards
from the Continent.   The natural fertility of Britain
as contrasted with that of N.W. Europe was sufficient
inducement to these Teutonic tribes to make their
permanent home in this country.   The Norman conquest unfortunately connected Britain with France,
an influence from which she was not freed until 1453.
Even since that date she has been repeatedly drawn
into European wars, although we may say that her soil
has been spared desolation at the hands of foreign
armies.   Her insular position is to be thanked for this.

Her industries have varied greatly through the
centuries.   At first she was mainly a pastoral country
exporting wool to the Low Countries for weaving

purposes.   Political disturbances and religious cruelty led to Protestant refugees settling in England and introducing their knowledge of weaving.   The discovery of coal and steam power and the invention of machinery changed Britain in the 18th and 19th centuries into the foremost manufacturing country of the world.   Raw materials and food were required respectively for manufactures and the people engaged in them, and with this went the great development of our mercantile marine.   Increased facilities for both internal and foreign communication became necessary, and the present-day network of canal, railway, and ocean routes has been the result.   The small size of our country and the consequent nearness of all parts to the sea, the pronounced tides in the seas around our shores and the relatively great extent of sea-coast, the humidity of our atmosphere and the character of our fresh-water supply, the moderate range of temperature, the absence of imposts upon raw materials entering the country, the mineral wealth, and the activity of the people both on sea and land have all been factors in making the country what it is to-day.

Industries of the British Isles.

The industries of the British Isles have arisen in almost every case from the natural resources of the country.   At one time agricultural and pastoral pursuits occupied the bulk of the people, but now, owing to the discovery of our minerals, manufacturing processes are more important than either agriculture or stock-raising.   We may say roughly that the two latter pursuits occupy Ireland generally, Scotland with the exception of the central manufacturing district, and England in the south, east, and highland regions.

In agricultural and pastoral regions there have naturally arisen country towns where produce can be disposed of, and necessities obtained.   The fairs held in olden times were means to the same ends, and some of these fairs still continue, although the majority have

disappeared before the all-conquering railway.   Corn
and stock markets are held in most of the country
towns of eastern England.

Industries   dependent   on   Agriculture   and Grazing.

Agriculture directly promotes subsidiary industries.
Modern farming has necessitated the agricultural imple-
ment industry, and Grantham, Ipswich, Bedford and
Lincoln have become important centres, even though
they may have in some cases neither coal nor iron in
the neighbourhood.   In grazing districts the leather
trade comes to the fore ; the boot and shoe industry
of Leicester, Kettering, Northampton and Norwich, and
the glove manufacture of Limerick, Kendal, Yeovil and
Worcester being good examples.   The cheapness of
female labour in agricultural districts also aids in
making these industries semi-rural.

The manufactures of mustard at Norwich and of
biscuits at Reading owe their origin respectively to the
low-lying Fen lands favouring the growth of the mustard
plant, and to the corn lands of the Thames valley.   The
jam industry of Dundee is due to the proximity of the
fertile Carse of Gowrie, whilst that of London arises
from the nearness of the fruit-growing counties of
southern England.

The Iron Industry.

The fortunate occurrence of coal and iron near
each other has been referred to before.   Iron-smelting
and the manufacture of iron and steel goods (including
ships) constitute one of our greatest industries.   The
great smelting districts are lowland Scotland, Cleveland, Furness, the Black Country, and South Wales.   In
the Scottish lowlands the most important iron towns
are Glasgow, Airdrie, Falkirk (with the Carron Ironworks near by) and Hamilton.   Glasgow, Port Glasgow,
Renfrew, and Greenock are all shipbuilding centres, and
the Clyde, with its safe estuary, forms the natural exit
for their products.

Belfast in N.E. Ireland is similarly engaged, and imports coal, with which to smelt its iron, from S. Scotland and Cumberland.   Barrow-in-Furness has great shipbuilding yards, its haematite iron ore also

A Launch at Govan, on the Clyde

being smelted with Cumberland coal.   Great steel-works exist at Elswick, near Newcastle, where heavy guns are made.   An important iron-working region is situated on the Northumberland-Durham coalfield, especially along the lower courses of the Tyne and

Wear, where Newcastle, Jarrow, and Sunderland specialise in the manufacture of ships and marine machinery.

Guisborough and Middlesbrough smelt the iron of the Cleveland district of N. Yorkshire. The busy manufacturing towns on the Yorkshire and Lancashire coalfields, *e.g.* Leeds, Manchester and Sheffield, make machinery suited for their particular industries. The rise of the cutlery trade in Sheffield is due to the proximity of coal, iron, and stone suitable for making grindstones.

The South Staffordshire coal and iron field not only smelts iron, but manufactures it into machinery and all kinds of hardware. Towns lie thickly in this region, and each has generally specialised in some one branch. Thus we have nails from Dudley, screws from Wednesbury, bolts from Smethwick, and miscellaneous iron goods from Birmingham. The latter town is sometimes spoken of as the 'toy shop,' for much of the iron goods produced in the Black Country is of a small type, since lack of sea or river communication raises the cost of carriage.

The nearness of Birkenhead to the Mersey coalfield and to Liverpool has made it a great shipbuilding centre, but London and Southampton, in spite of lack of coal and iron, have become similar centres by virtue of their geographical position. Merthyr, on the S. Wales coalfield, smelts much ore brought from Spain, its situation near the coast accounting for this.

Textile Industries. (*a*) **The Woollen Industry.**

The woollen industry arose originally in the sheep-grazing districts of Yorkshire, the Scottish uplands, Norfolk, Wales, Cumberland, Gloucester and Wilts. Another determining factor was the presence of a water suitable for dyeing the material. At the present day, however, we find that the industry has largely migrated to those places possessing coal supplies in addition to the above-named advantages. Further, foreign wool, imported to augment the home supply, is carried by rail

A Witney blanket factory

to these more favoured districts. The main woollen
manufacturing towns are :

> (i)   Scottish : Hawick, Bannockburn, Kilmarnock,
>   Aberdeen and Galashiels.
>
> (ii) English : Bradford, Halifax, Huddersfield,
>   Leeds, and Wakefield (Yorkshire) ; Welsh-
>   pool, Montgomery, and Newtown (Wales) ;
>   Stroud, Bradford, Frome, and Trowbridge
>   (West of England).

The Welsh towns specialise in flannel, the Scot-
tish in tweeds.   Blankets are made both in Yorkshire
(Wakefield and Dewsbury) and Oxfordshire (Witney).
Leicester manufactures woollen hose, as also does
Hawick in Scotland.   The woollen industry of Norwich
has been transferred to Yorkshire.

(*b*)   **The Cotton Industry.**

The cotton industry depends upon a suitable humidity of the atmosphere as well as upon the presence
of coal and iron, and upon a favourable situation with
respect to the port of supply.   We can thus understand Belfast, Glasgow and Paisley, and the numerous
Lancashire towns being engaged in cotton spinning and
manufacture.   Liverpool's position as the great cotton
port is due to its geographical situation.   The plentiful
supply of water from the Pennine streams is another
reason for the supremacy of Lancashire in cotton
manufacture.   The chief towns engaged in this industry
are Accrington, Ashton, Blackburn, Bolton, Burnley,
Bury, Manchester, Preston and Rochdale (Lancs.),
Stalybridge and Stockport (Cheshire).   Lace curtains
and cotton hosiery are made in the districts round
Derby and Nottingham.   The curtains are sent to
Nottingham in the ' brown ' or unfinished condition.

(*c*)   **The Linen Industry.**

The linen differs from the cotton industry in that
much of the raw material is raised at home.   Since flax
thrives in cool, moist climates we find linen centres in

the more northerly part of our islands : Scotland, Ulster, and Durham. The geographical position of Arbroath, Dundee, Dunfermline, Forfar, Kirkaldy and Montrose opposite our Baltic and Dutch sources of supply must be taken into consideration. Darlington, Barnsley and Leeds also manufacture linen goods, and a whole group of Irish towns in the province of Ulster (Belfast, Londonderry, etc.) are similarly engaged.

(*d*) **Other Textile Industries.**

Associated with the linen manufacture on the east coast of Britain is that of sailcloth, canvas, and other coarse textiles. This is largely because we obtain hemp as well as flax fibre from the Baltic.

Silk manufacture is a declining British industry. It was introduced into this country by refugees in 1685, and became established in places where the water was suitable for dyeing. Coventry makes silk ribbons. Congleton, Macclesfield, Chesterfield, Derby, and Bethnal Green and Spitalfields in London are the only places in England where the trade is of any importance.

Other Industries.

The presence of salt and coal has brought about the glass and chemical manufactures of Newcastle, and similar considerations account for the manufactures of St Helens, Bristol, Widnes and Runcorn. It should be noted that the chemical industry is largely subservient to those of cotton and wool, dyes and alkalies being needed in the manufacture of these textiles.

Western ports situated near coalfields naturally have sugar-refineries and tobacco factories. Towns possessing a good supply of water containing common salt, gypsum and chalk become brewery centres ; Burton-on-Trent, Cork, Dublin, and London are good examples. A water rich in dissolved mineral matter will promote the growth of inland watering places, such as Bath, Cheltenham and Leamington. Occurrence of particular kinds of clay gives rise to the pottery industries of N. Staffordshire,

Burslem, Hanley, and Stoke, and of Derby and Worcester. Favourable situation on the coast causes the population to be concentrated in particular places, either seaside resorts, ports and packet stations, or fishing centres. Stonehaven, Wick, Aberdeen, Grimsby, and Yarmouth are among our most important fishing centres.

Position of Towns.

One of the most interesting functions of Geography is to account for the position of a town. In some cases the nucleus of the town has existed from very remote times. Winchester and Colchester, for example, are thought to owe their positions to the flints and clay found respectively near them; these being the materials required by rude races for weapons and pottery. The names of these towns show their Roman occupation, and in many cases sites were chosen as of strategical importance. Chester and Dorchester, the one commanding N. Wales, the other lying in a gap between the Dorset hills, are good examples. Many commanding sites, especially if partially protected by the sweeping curve of a river, gradually grew into towns ; *e.g.* Edinburgh, Stirling, Carlisle, Durham, Conway, and Warwick.

Since rivers were early natural lines of communication, we find towns upon them, especially at their confluences and mouths. York marks the limit of navigation of the Ouse. Gloucester and London lie at the lowest bridge or ford level of their respective rivers ; but the position with respect to the continent and the presence of a tidal estuary have also done much to encourage the phenomenal development of London. A broad rolling plain suitable for military manœuvres has decided Aldershot's position and importance, whilst the situations of Berwick and Carlisle at the extremities of the Cheviots explain themselves from a military point of view.

Internal Communications.

These have been by track, river, road, canal, and railway successively, but the last-named has largely superseded the others owing to its greater speed.

Rivers have been improved in navigability by dredging, canalisation, and the building of docks at their mouths. Canals naturally only traverse the flatter parts of the country, the cost of construction in hilly districts and of the upkeep of many locks being relatively great. They are especially suited for the transport of non-perishable goods ; hence their development in the 'mineral areas.'

Railways.

The British Isles possess a network of railways, and it is impossible in a book of this size to do more than mention the main routes of the various lines. Railways radiate from London as the spokes from the hub of a wheel.

(*a*) **English Railways.**

(i) *The London and North Western* (Euston Station) passes through Rugby and Stafford to Crewe, and thence northwards along the west coast to Carlisle, where it joins the Caledonian line. It sends a branch line to Birmingham, whilst from Crewe other branches pass to Holyhead, Manchester, Leeds and Liverpool. Its Irish traffic, and also that with the great cotton, woollen, hardware and pottery districts should be noted.

(ii) The *Great Central* (Marylebone) crosses the central plain through Aylesbury, Rugby and Leicester, passes east of the Pennines through Nottingham to Sheffield, where it joins the older part of the line —the *Manchester, Sheffield and Lincoln* Railway. It has fish and wool traffic with Grimsby and the West Riding manufacturing towns.

(iii) The *Midland Railway* (St Pancras) also traverses the central plain and the West Riding, the chief towns on this part of the route being Bedford, Leicester, Nottingham, Sheffield and Leeds. The line crosses the Pennines at the relatively low Aire Gap and then passes on to Carlisle where it joins the Glasgow and South-Western line. The locomotive works are at Derby, from which town branches pass to Manchester and Bristol. A branch terminus at Heysham on Morecambe Bay feeds a line of steamers running to Belfast.

(iv) The *Great Northern* (King's Cross) runs due north to Peterborough, and then north-east to Newark, Retford and Doncaster. The last-named town is an important junction with branches to Hull and the 'woollen towns,' and from it the *North-Eastern* line continues through York, Darlington, Durham and Newcastle to Berwick, where the *North British* line begins. Both Great Northern and Midland lines have heavy mineral traffic, especially coal for London's use.

(v) The *Great Eastern* (Liverpool Street) has two main routes ; one through Cambridge and Ely to Lincoln, the other along the east coast to Yarmouth. Fish from Yarmouth and agricultural produce from the eastern counties constitute its principal goods traffic. Harwich connects by steamer with the Hook of Holland.

(vi) The *Great Western* (Paddington) passes due west from London to Bristol, the main towns on the route being Reading, Swindon and Bath. A branch from Didcot passes north-west to Oxford, Warwick, Birmingham, Wolverhampton and Chester. Another branch from Bristol crosses the Severn by means of a tunnel, and thus the boat express can reach Fishguard, via Cardiff and Swansea. The main line of the G.W.R. passes south-west from Bristol to Taunton, Exeter, Plymouth, Falmouth and Penzance.

(vii) The *London and South-Western* (Waterloo) main line links London and Plymouth, passing through Basingstoke, Salisbury and Yeovil. Portsmouth and Southampton are reached by branches through Basingstoke and Guildford. These branches take advantage of gaps in the Downs.

(viii) The *South-Eastern and Chatham* (Holborn, Charing Cross, etc.) is an amalgamation of the old

South-Eastern, and *London, Chatham, and Dover* lines.
It taps the agricultural districts of Kent and Sussex,
and runs to the watering places and ports of the south-
east coast.

Other lines are (*a*) the *Lancashire and Yorkshire,*
(*b*) the *London, Tilbury, and Southend,* (*c*) the *London,
Brighton, and South Coast.*

(*b*) Scottish Railways.

(i) The *North British* links the North-Eastern line
with Edinburgh via Dunbar. Branches radiate from
Edinburgh; westwards through the coal and iron
district to Glasgow, southwards through the 'tweed'
region to Carlisle, northwards across the Forth Bridge
through Dunfermline to Perth, and eastwards to the
coast towns as far north as Montrose, the Tay bridge
being on the last-named route.

(ii) The *Glasgow and South-Western* passes from
Carlisle to Dumfries, and thence by two branches to
Glasgow, one up the Nith Valley direct to Glasgow
via the Sanquhar coalfield and Kilmarnock, the other
rounding the south-west coast through Stranraer, Ayr
and Paisley.

(iii) The *Caledonian* links Carlisle with Glasgow,
Edinburgh and other lowland towns. It serves the towns
upon the Clyde estuary, and from Stirling a western
branch passes to Oban, the great tourist centre, whilst
a north-eastern branch goes to Aberdeen, via Perth,
Forfar, and Stonehaven.

(iv) The *Great North of Scotland* has Aberdeen
as its centre, with branches radiating to Ballater, Elgin,
Banff, Fraserburgh, and Peterhead.

(v) The *Highland* sends branches from Inverness
to Elgin, Perth, Strome Ferry and Loch Alsh (for
Stornoway), and to Wick and Thurso in the far north.

(*c*) Irish Railways.

These have Dublin as their starting-point.

(i) The *Dublin, Wicklow, and Wexford* runs along
the east coast to the towns which give it its name.

(ii) The *Great Northern* passes north to Belfast, through Drogheda, Dundalk and Newry.

(iii) The *Midland Great Western* branches at Mullingar (*a*) to Galway via Athlone, (*b*) to Sligo via Longford and Carrick-on-Shannon.

(iv) *The Great Southern and Western* serves S. and S.W. Ireland. The main routes are to Cork and Limerick. A southern branch links Limerick, Tralee and Killarney with Waterford and Rosslare, the port for Fishguard.

The magnitude of the railway traffic in the United Kingdom can be seen from the official figures for 1905 : mileage 22850, passengers 1200 millions, receipts over £113,000,000.

The Commerce of the United Kingdom.

In 1910 our imports were more than £600,000,000, including food and drink £254,000,000, raw materials £261,000,000, and manufactured articles £156,000,000. Our exports, exclusive of re-exported goods, were £430,000,000, of which food and drink had a value of £24,000,000, raw materials £53,000,000, and manufactured articles £343,000,000. We see from the above figures that we are mainly a manufacturing nation, dependent upon others for much of our food, and for the raw materials required in our manufacturing processes. The following are the chief imports and exports with their values for the year 1910, expressed in millions sterling:

Imports.

Grain and Flour	77	Timber	26
Cotton	71	Fats and oils	37
Meat and Animals	48	Other textile materials	12
Metals and Metal Goods	56	Ores and metals	9
Wool	37	Leather	12

Exports.

Cotton yarn and goods	106	Chemicals	18
Metal goods	89	Linen	8
Woollen yarn and goods	37	Apparel	12
Coal and fuel	37		

An interesting comparison to show the variation in
our foreign trade in recent years can be made from the
following table:

Year	Foreign Trade (Millions sterling)	Year	Foreign Trade (Millions sterling)
1902	812	1908	970
1904	852	1909	1002
1906	983	1910	1109

The commercial supremacy of the United Kingdom
is largely due to her geographical position in the centre
of the land hemisphere, her unfrozen seas, her mineral
wealth, her extensive Empire, and the maritime and
trading instincts of her people. Raw materials are
gathered to Britain as to a focus, and the cheapness
of ocean carriage renders her position with respect to
Europe particularly favourable. It will be well to
note here the ports around her coasts. A considerable
coasting trade is carried on between all the ports in
the Kingdom, in addition to their carrying trade to
and from all parts of the globe.

East Coast Ports.

Thurso is the port for the Orkneys. *Wick* has a
large herring fleet. *Inverness* has principally a coasting
trade. *Aberdeen* exports granite, is largely engaged
in fishing, and does trade with Norway and the Baltic.
Kirkcaldy and *Dundee* receive fibre for their linen and
sailcloth industries from the Baltic and from India.

Leith, Granton, Bo'ness, and *Grangemouth* export
minerals and manufactured goods from the Scottish
lowland plain. Grangemouth should be noticed as
being the terminus of the Forth and Clyde canal.
Much Baltic trade is done from these ports. Lines
of steamers run regularly from Leith, the port of
Edinburgh, to the ports at the mouths of the Rhine,
Elbe and Weser. *Newcastle* exports coal, machinery

London: Royal Victoria docks

and chemicals. A whole group of towns share this export trade of coal and iron goods (*e.g. North* and *South Shields, Sunderland, Hartlepool*). Steamers bring iron ore and timber from the Baltic, especially from Sweden.

Hull has a large trade with the Baltic and Low Countries, the Mediterranean and the East Indies. The chief exports are cotton and woollen goods, and the chief imports grain, wool, timber, sugar and leather. Much wheat is obtained from S.E. Europe, and wool from Russia, South America, and Australia. *Grimsby* and *Yarmouth* export fish in great quantities. *Harwich* is a packet station for Rotterdam, Antwerp and Hamburg. The Great Eastern trains run in direct connection with the line of steamers owned by the same company. *Tilbury* and *Queenborough* are packet stations for the continent. They lie respectively on the left and right banks of the Thames estuary.

London, the greatest port in the world, has miles of docks and wharves which are suitable for every class of vessel. The magnificent liners of the Peninsular and Oriental (P. & O.) and Orient lines start here for Asia, Australia and New Zealand, and those of the Castle line for the Cape. The General Steam Navigation, Batavier, and numerous other companies also send their vessels regularly from London to European ports. Manufactured goods of every description leave this port, the vessels on their return bringing grain, wood, wool, wine, tea, and innumerable other commodities.

South Coast Ports.

Dover, Folkestone, Newhaven, and *Southampton* are packet stations for Calais, Ostend, Boulogne, Dieppe, Havre, and the Channel Islands. *Southampton* is favourably situated for trade with the Cape and America. Continental liners call here on their way to America. *Plymouth* and *Falmouth* have a considerable coasting trade. The British and Irish Co.'s steamers call here on their way to Dublin.

West Coast Ports.

Bristol trades with America and Ireland. It has
not the importance it used to have in the days when
it was the great port of trade for the west coast
of Africa and the West Indies. Still, large quantities
of tobacco, timber, grain, sugar and cocoa are brought
to this port. *Cardiff* is now the third port of the
Kingdom. It exports anthracite coal, and the metal
goods manufactured on the S. Wales coalfield. Irish
provisions and dairy produce are brought here from
Cork, Waterford and Dublin, as well as to the neighbouring ports of Bristol, Swansea and Pembroke.
Swansea receives iron and copper ores from Spain,
as does also Cardiff. It is the centre of the tinplate
industry, for which it receives vegetable oils from
W. Africa. *Milford* and *Pembroke* receive foodstuffs
from Ireland, whilst the Great Western has developed
Fishguard as a mail station. Fast steamers carry the
mails from Fishguard to Rosslare near Wexford. The
ships of the Cunard Line now land passengers and
mails at Fishguard for rapid transmission to London
by the G.W.R. *Holyhead* is but 4 hours' journey
from Kingstown. The mail trains cross from Wales
to Anglesey by the famous tubular bridge.

Liverpool and *Birkenhead* lie in a most favourable
position for American trade. There are regular sailings
to Canada, U.S.A., South America, West Africa, West
Indies, and the near and far East. Cotton, grain, provisions, timber, meat, sugar, wines, wool and fruit are
but a few of the many imports. The chief exports are
cotton, woollen and iron goods, soap and chemicals.
Much trade is done with Belfast, Drogheda, Dundalk,
Dublin, Wexford and other Irish ports. Liverpool is
the second port of the United Kingdom.

Fleetwood, Heysham and *Barrow* are ports for the
Isle of Man and Ireland. *Whitehaven* exports coal to
the linen district of Ulster. *Stranraer* is the port for
Larne on the Irish coast opposite.

Glasgow and the other towns on the Clyde estuary are engaged both in coasting and foreign trade. Atlantic liners from Glasgow make *Moville*, on the north Irish coast, their first port of call, just as those from Liverpool make use of *Queenstown* in S. Ireland. Much trade is done with America and India. The large sugar refineries of *Greenock* depend upon West Indian supplies. The Clyde ports form the western outlet for the metals and manufactures of the Scottish lowlands. *Oban*, *Strome Ferry* and *Loch Alsh* have already been mentioned.

Government and Administration.

Our government is a limited monarchy, consisting of the King, Lords, and Commons. Our present king George V. succeeded to the throne on May 6, 1910. The House of Lords consists of hereditary peers, those created by the king, bishops of the Established Church, Irish peers elected for life, and Scottish peers elected to sit for one parliament. Legislation is largely the work of the House of Commons, whose members are elected by ballot to represent the counties, boroughs and universities. About one-sixth of the population are electors.

The King is the nominal head of the government, but the responsibility belongs to the Cabinet which consists of the premier and eighteen ministers, who hold direct responsibility for their different departments.

Local government must be carefully distinguished from the above. Each administrative county has a lord-lieutenant, sheriff, and other officers. The lord-lieutenant nominates the justices of the peace or magistrates. County, district, and parish councils are the machinery for local government, except in the large towns, where it is vested in a mayor and corporation. Such municipal corporations have received their power and being by royal charter. Scottish mayors are called provosts, and the aldermen are called bailies.

France.

Position and Size.

France is our nearest continental neighbour. Its
sea boundaries are the English Channel, the Bay of
Biscay, and the Mediterranean, whilst it touches Belgium,
Germany, Switzerland, and Italy on the east, and Spain
on the south. Its boundaries are easily defended, except
on the north-east where a line of fortresses is necessary.
The country stretches between 42° and 51° N. lat., and
from 7° E. to 5° W. long. Its area is about twice that
of the British Isles.

Surface and General Features.

Much of the surface is a level plain. This rises in
the north-west and culminates in the ancient uplands of
Brittany, which recall by their slate and granite masses
the corresponding Cornish peninsula. The plain also
rises eastwards to the wooded slaty plateau of the
Belgian Ardennes, and southwards to the central
plateau of Auvergne. The latter consists of ancient
rocks, and many extinct volcanoes are found in the
district. This plateau ends on the east in the Cevennes
mountains, which overlook the Rhone valley. One peak
of the Auvergne—Mont Dore—reaches a height of
6000 feet.

The Ardennes and Auvergne plateaux are connected
by the limestone plateau of Langres, which occupies
much of the Champagne district. Limestone hills flank
also the northern edge of the Central Plateau, and the
Jura mountains separating France from Switzerland
are of a similar type. North of the Jura lie the
richly wooded Vosges, which are 4000 ft. high, whilst
to the south the Alps, with their mighty peaks, Mt.
Blanc (15,776 ft.), Mt. Cenis and Mt. Viso, form the
boundary between France and Italy. The Pyrenees
(with Mt. Maladetta, 11,988 ft.) separate France from
Spain on the south-west and form a natural boundary.

In the Pyrenees

Watersheds and Rivers.

The Seine, which from a navigable point of view is the most important French river, derives its waters from the Ardennes, the Langres, and the Central Plateau. The Loire, with the Allier its chief tributary, flows northwards from the Auvergne group. After their junction, the main river traverses a hilly limestone district before turning westwards at Orleans. The Auvergne plateau also sends westwards the river Dordogne and several tributaries of the Garonne. The last-named river, as also the Adour, flows northwards from the Pyrenees before turning towards the Bay of Biscay. The Rhone is the only river flowing southwards. Its valley has already been noted as lying between the Alps and the Cevennes. The Alps send to it the Isère and Durance, whilst the Saône joins it at Lyons, after flowing southwards from the neighbourhood of the Vosges mountains. The rapidity of the Rhone lessens its commercial value. On reaching the tideless Mediterranean, it forms a delta with shifting mouths.

Coast.

The compact land-mass has a relatively short coast-line with comparatively few good harbours. The coast scenery is not striking, except in Brittany and the Riviera, where majestic views are associated with the older rocks. Salt lagoons fringe the coast in the Landes district south of the Gironde.

Capes Gris Nez, la Hague and Ushant project from the north and west coasts into the English Channel. Here are also the Channel Islands, the sole remnant of our formerly extensive possessions in France. The Bay of Biscay forms the western boundary of the country, and several islands are found along this coast. The island department of Corsica lies in the Mediterranean, and more than one-half of the southern coast of France is washed by the Gulf of Lions, a part of this inland sea.

Climate.

France lies in a lower latitude than England and so
enjoys, on the whole, a warmer climate ; but nearness of
the sea on the west and south, the adjoining continental
mass of Central Europe, elevation, and the direction of
the prevalent Atlantic winds all modify the climate, so
that in January the warmest parts of the country are
the west and south coasts, whilst in July there is an
increased temperature from north to south. This corresponds in the main to what we found in England.
The port of Nantes is seldom visited by frost ; Paris on
the other hand has frequent frosts. Marseilles on the
Mediterranean has an average January temperature
8° higher than that of Paris. Its July temperature
is 72° on the average, that of Paris being 65° F.

The rain-bearing winds from the Atlantic spread
fanwise over the country, blowing from the south-west
along the Channel shores and from the north-west
along the Bay of Biscay. The general disposition of
the highlands towards the *east* of the country is favourable to agriculture, for the winds thus lose their moisture
gradually as they pass over the land. The mean annual
rainfall is about 29 inches. The mountains and plateaux
are the rainiest spots—a rainfall of 60 and 70 inches occurring in the Vosges and Pyrenees as contrasted with
22 inches at Reims. The Mediterranean coast receives
its rain mainly in winter, Marseilles having about $\frac{1}{2}$ inch
of rain in July and $3\frac{1}{2}$ inches in October. Paris, on the
contrary, has its rainfall very evenly distributed throughout the year.

Plants and Animals.

Extensive forests of beech and other deciduous trees
clothe the uplands, with pine woods on the higher slopes
and also in the sandy Landes. Climatic differences favour
the growth of a great range of cultivated plants. Bears,
chamois, and wolves are found, but only in the wooded
or desolate mountainous regions.

Agriculture.

Agriculture is practised with great care and labour, particularly by the numerous peasant proprietors. Barley, wheat, beetroot and flax are grown in the north and north-east. Orchards are widely planted in Normandy. The vine is cultivated very extensively south of a line drawn from Belle Isle to Reims, particularly along the river valleys. The warmth of summer and autumn is essential for the proper ripening of the grapes. Maize, together with tobacco, is grown in the Garonne basin, the latter crop being also found in the Rhone district. South France has groves of mulberry, orange, lemon, and olive. Sheep feed on the poorer pastures of the hills and central plateau, and cattle are found in the moister north-west region.

Fisheries.

Dunkirk and Nantes are the two chief fishing ports, although much fishing is carried on by the coast dwellers of Normandy and Brittany. Cod, herring, mackerel, and sardines are the chief fish caught in the Atlantic. Tunnies are obtained from the Mediterranean, especially round Corsica.

Minerals.

The two chief coalfields lie in the north and round St Etienne. They are more important than the other coalfields because iron is found not far away at Nancy and Le Creuzot. Building stone is quarried in Normandy at Bayeux and Caen ; plaster is obtained round Paris, and Corsica and the Pyrenees yield good marble. Salt is largely obtained by evaporation in the lagoon district on the west coast.

Industries and Manufactures.

Wine-making is the great agricultural industry. In 1909 the quantity of wine produced was nearly 1200 million gallons. The great wine-producing districts are

Champagne (Châlons, Reims, Epernay), Burgundy (the Saône valley with Dijon and Châlon), the valley of the Garonne where claret is made (Bordeaux), the Loire valley (Tours), and Languedoc.   Brandy is made round Cognac, and millions of gallons of cider are the product of the orchards in the north-west.   Beer is brewed in the north-east of the country, where hops and barley are grown.   Provence manufactures much olive oil, and

Marseilles: Grand Harbour

exports typical Mediterranean fruits from Marseilles. Lille and Bordeaux have large beet-sugar factories. Butter, cheese, and other dairy products are made in Normandy and Brittany.

The silk industry is so large that raw silk has to be imported, and this notwithstanding the fact that over five tons of silkworm eggs are incubated yearly.   The Rhone valley is largely engaged in the production and manufacture of silk, with Lyons and St Etienne as important centres. Cotton, woollen, and linen goods are produced on the northern coalfield. Raw cotton is conveyed to Rouen, Nancy and other northern towns by river and canal. Wool from the Ardennes is supplemented by wool from abroad to supply the looms of Dunkirk, Reims, Amiens, Lille, and Roubaix.

Valenciennes competes successfully with Nottingham in the lace trade, and Lille has a large linen industry dependent upon home-grown flax. Ironworks and engineering industries centre round Lille, Nancy, St Etienne and Le Creuzot, the two latter places making firearms and ordnance. The presence of suitable clay beds has given to Sèvres and Limoges their porcelain and pottery trades.

Communications.

The high roads of France, being a legacy from the Romans, are exceptionally good. Full use is made of the rivers for goods traffic, and a splendid system of canals links up the rivers, especially in the north, thus adding to their commercial value. The Marne-Rhine canal joins the Seine to the Rhine system of streams. Another canal—Canal du Midi—connects the Garonne, near Toulouse, with Cette upon the Mediterranean coast. Railways radiate from Paris in all directions:

(i) The *Western* to Dieppe, Havre, Cherbourg and Brest.

(ii) The *Northern* to Boulogne, Calais, Lille, and northern manufacturing towns, with connections to Belgium, etc.

(iii) The *Eastern* to Nancy, with connections for Germany and Austria.

(iv) The *Paris, Lyons and Marseilles* sends branches to Switzerland and to Italy via the Mt. Cenis tunnel and the Riviera. The journey from Paris to Marseilles occupies 12 hours.

(v) The *Orleans* runs south-west from Paris to Bordeaux.

Bordeaux, Bayonne, Toulouse, and Cette are served by the *Southern Railway.*

Commerce and Ports.

The chief exports from France are textiles, wine, chemicals, metal goods, leather, and dairy produce. Her imports include wool, coal, raw silk and cotton, oil seeds and timber, hides, and coffee. Raw materials comprise 66 % of her imports, and manufactured goods form more than one-half of her exports. She receives goods from Great Britain to the annual value of £31,000,000, and sends us goods to the value of £47,000,000.

Calais, Boulogne, Havre, and Dieppe are seaports. Havre has a large American trade. St Nazaire is a rising port, which has deprived Nantes of much commerce. Bordeaux is a great wine port and Marseilles trades largely with the East via the Suez Canal. Cherbourg, Brest, Lorient, Rochefort and Toulon are naval stations.

People.

The original Celts and Iberians were conquered by the Romans, whose language they adopted. In later times the Franks and the Danes invaded the country so that the present race is a mixed one. Teutonic characteristics appear in the north of the country, whilst Roman or Italian stature and temperament are found in the south. Education is free, and military service is compulsory. The bulk of the people are Roman Catholics, and although there is now no state church, all religious beliefs are tolerated.

There are about 39 million people in the country. Paris has a population of 2¾ millions. The industrial population is mainly grouped about the northern coalfield, and around Paris, Marseilles, Lyons, and St Etienne, and there is a tendency for country people to migrate to these centres. The average population is 188 to the square mile.

History as determined by Geographical Considerations.

Proximity to Italy by land and sea, combined with the fertility of the soil and the military spirit of the Romans, led to the invasion of France by the latter people before 60 B.C.   This conquest had good results, for it gave to the Gauls both civilization and security. The inhospitable north drove the Northmen to this country, and was primarily responsible (through William the Conqueror) for the close connection between France and England until 1450.   The narrow strait separating the two countries offered no great bar to this connection. After gaining much importance under the Bourbons, France under Napoleon guided for a time the destinies of Europe.   At a later time (1870) a war with Germany caused the loss of Alsace and part of Lorraine, thus throwing the boundary back from the Rhine to the Vosges.   The Belfort gap, between the Vosges and Jura, has consequently become of great strategic value, since it lies at the junction of French and German territory and possesses no great elevation.

Administration, Divisions, and Towns.

The Republic of France is governed by the Chamber of Deputies and the Senate, who together elect the President for the time being.   The French provinces are divided into 86 departments, and these are subdivided into arrondissements and communes.   Prefects, sub-prefects and mayors are placed respectively over these administrative divisions.   Many of the departments are named after the rivers which flow through them.

Paris, the capital, has extensive manufactures, fine public buildings, squares, and boulevards, and fortifications.   *Marseilles* is a famous seaport.   *Lyons* has silk industry.   *Bordeaux* is a wine port.   *Lille*, a fortress, is famous for its textiles, machinery, sugar, and chemicals.   *Toulouse* has tobacco factories. *St Etienne* has manufactures of hardware and silk ribbons.   *Havre* and *Nantes* are ports.   *Nice* is a winter resort.

Belgium.

Position and Size.

Belgium, one of the smallest European countries, lies to the north of France, and has Germany and Holland upon the east and north. It is only one-tenth the area of the British Isles and stretches through 2° of latitude and 4° of longitude.

Surface and General Features.

The surface is flat except in the south-east where the wooded slopes of the Ardennes rise to a height of 2000 feet. In the north is a marshy district (the Kempen), which is being made more productive agriculturally. The soil is in general sandy, but has been greatly improved by careful cultivation. The flat sandy coast is only 42 miles long, and dykes are necessary in some places to keep out the sea. The two chief rivers are the Scheldt and the Meuse. These run through Belgium for only a part of their course. The Meuse offers fine scenery to tourists in its course through the Ardennes, Dinant being the centre.

Climate.

Brussels has the same mean temperature as London (50° F.). Extremes of climate are only found in the higher Ardennes, the country in general having a cool and equable climate. This is due to the nearness of the sea and the prevalence of westerly and south-westerly rain-bearing winds. The Ardennes receive more rain than other parts of the country. Rain falls in Belgium on approximately half the days of the year.

Agriculture, Animals, and Plants.

Forests cover about one-sixth of the surface and in these live the only large wild animals, the deer and boar. Sheep are largely fed upon the poorer pastures of the

Ardennes, and horse-breeding is an important industry in Flanders.

In Belgium agriculture is carried on with the greatest care. The country is essentially one of peasant proprietors, who till their small holdings with the spade, and reap an excellent reward for their industry. Rye, oats, wheat, beet, potatoes, flax, hemp, clover, colza, madder, and chicory are the main plants grown, none of these demanding great warmth or extreme dryness.

Fishers from the coast towns join in the cod and herring fishery upon the North Sea banks.

Minerals.

These are found in the elevated district of the southeast. Coal, iron, zinc, and lead occur quite near each other in the Ardennes ; and of these minerals, coal and iron are much more important than the others. The Meuse valley is the chief mineral area. Grindstones and black marble are obtained from the same district.

People.

The Belgians are a mixed race, derived from German, Dutch, and French stocks, and although French is the official language, Flemish, Walloon, and German are spoken in different parts of the country. The majority of the people are Roman Catholics, but the state gives monetary aid to Protestants and Jews as well. The people are most industrious and thrifty, and their country is the most densely populated of Europe. There are seven million people in this small land, or, on an average, 600 to the square mile. The bulk of these are crowded together in the busy manufacturing towns, but the agricultural population is relatively dense as well. The Ardennes pastures support the scantiest population in the country.

Belgium, like Holland, with which it was for some time connected, has had a chequered career, having belonged in turn to Burgundy, Spain, Austria, and France. It has formed a separate kingdom since 1830.

Its small size and its easily crossed frontiers prevent it from defending itself against the Great Powers, who have declared it to be neutral territory, so that Belgium is free to develop industrially without the burden of maintaining a huge army.

Industries, Communications, and Commerce.

The main industrial areas lie along the Meuse and Scheldt. Mons, Charleroi, Namur, and Liège all manu-

Antwerp

facture iron goods. Lace is a staple industry at Brussels, Bruges and Mechlin. Linen and cotton goods are made at Ghent, where there is a supply of good water for bleaching purposes. Liège has a most important manufactory of firearms, and Verviers manufactures woollens, and Tournai hosiery and carpets. Charleroi and Namur have glass and chemical works, and the province of Hainault has beet-sugar factories.

The navigable rivers are connected and supplemented by a network of canals, two of which run from Ghent to the sea. Brussels is the natural centre of the railways, and most of these are owned by the state. For its size, Belgium has the longest railway system of the world, and Brussels is directly connected by rail with Paris and Cologne.

Belgium sends to us annually goods valued at £27,000,000, and receives from us £10,000,000. She imports wheat, wool, timber, hides, chemicals, coal, and metals, whilst her exports include iron, machinery, grain, coal, flax, wool, hides, zinc, glass, chemicals, firearms, and rubber. She does much transit trade with Germany and France, her ports being Antwerp and Ostend, which have a daily service to London and Dover.

Administration and Divisions.

The king has responsible ministers, and there are two houses of parliament, the Chamber of Representatives and the Senate. The country is divided into nine provinces and these are subdivided in a way similar to the French departments. *Brussels*, the capital, is a city about as large as Manchester. Its beauty and gaiety have gained for it the name of 'Little Paris.' It has considerable manufactures of carpets, gloves, lace, and ribbons.

Holland.

Position and Surface.

Holland lies to the north of Belgium, having Germany on the east and the North Sea on the west. Amsterdam has the same latitude as Yarmouth. The country is low-lying and flat, $40\,^0/_0$ of its surface being below sea level. Sand hills and dykes protect the coast from invasion by the sea, and practically the whole land consists of recent deposits brought down by glaciers from the north during the ice age, and by the Rhine and Maas from the south. Much land has been reclaimed and now forms rich meadows. The sediment of the slowly flowing rivers has raised their beds many feet above the general level and they are embanked by dykes to prevent flooding. Constant drainage of the

A Dutch windmill

land is necessary, and windmills are used to drive pumping machinery for this purpose. Holland has no rivers entirely her own, but the mouths of the Rhine and Maas are of great commercial importance. Texel and Walcheren are the two most important islands. The two great inlets, Zuyder Zee and the Dollart Zee, are due to inroads of the sea in the Middle Ages.

Climate and Natural Productions.

The climate is moist and equable, although sudden changes of temperature are common. The mean annual rainfall is 28″, and there are more than 200 rainy days in the year, fogs being prevalent as a result of the moist atmosphere. Buckwheat, potatoes, and rye are grown on the drier sandy soils, and chicory, beet, flax, hops, tobacco, and wheat are also important crops. Bulb culture is an extensive industry especially around Haarlem. The moist meadows of the polders (tracts of land reclaimed from the sea) are particularly well suited for cattle rearing, and dairy-produce forms a valuable export. Many horses are bred in Friesland. The Dutch fishermen obtain cod and herring from the North Sea. Oysters are also farmed off the coast.

Minerals are practically absent. There is a little coal in the east, and clay supplies the pottery industry of Delft. The lack of coal makes Holland an agricultural and commercial, rather than a manufacturing country.

The People and their history.

The Dutch are a Teutonic people, extremely clean, thrifty and stolid. They belong mostly to the Lutheran church and have always set great store by their religious opinions. Their small country, with its peaceable people, has, like Belgium, belonged in turn to Burgundy, Austria, and Spain. It became a separate kingdom about 1840. There are two houses of parliament, which meet at The Hague.

Industries, Communications, and Commerce.

Margarine, butter, cheese, leather, tobacco, spirits, and sugar manufactures are all dependent on the agricultural and pastoral pursuits. Glass is made at Maastricht, and Amsterdam does the world's diamond cutting. The flat nature of the country has favoured the development of an intricate system of canals, which take the place of roads. The Dutch have always been a great commercial people, and much of their trade to-day consists of German transit trade and the storage and re-shipment of spices, coffee, tobacco, drugs and other products of their own extensive colonies. Amsterdam and Rotterdam are the chief ports. Flushing is the packet station for Queenborough and Folkestone, and the Hook of Holland for Harwich.

Administration and Towns.

The 11 provinces are divided into 1100 communes, each with its own mayor or burgomaster. *Amsterdam* and *Rotterdam* are both connected with the sea by canals. *Utrecht, Leyden, Amsterdam,* and *Groningen* possess universities. *Schiedam* manufactures 'Hollands.' *Leeuwarden* is a noted cattle market; and practically every town is a centre for agricultural produce.

Germany.

Position and Size.

The German Empire occupies a large part of Central Europe. It stretches from the Alps to the Baltic, and from Russia to France and the Low Countries. It is 1¾ times the size of the British Isles and occupies 17° of longitude and 8° of latitude. It has both Baltic and North Sea coasts, whilst its land boundaries are formed by Russia, Austria, Switzerland, France, Belgium, Holland, and Denmark.

Surface and General Features.

The northern plain of Germany gradually rises towards the south to meet the central highlands. The latter have an average height of 5000 feet. The Harz Mountains may be taken as their northerly limit, and they cover all the country lying north-west of a line drawn from

Harz Mountains : summit of the Brocken

Basel to Dresden. The rift valley of the Rhine lies in the west of these uplands, flanked by the Black Forest and the Vosges. The German portion of the Danube basin has an elevation of about 1500 feet and is enclosed by the German Jura, the Böhmer Wald and the Alps. The limestone Alps form Germany's southern bulwark and attain in places a height of over 9000 feet.

Watersheds, Rivers, and Lakes.

The southerly position of the highlands gives a northerly direction to the rivers and there is a marked parallelism in their courses. The Niemen and Vistula reach Germany from Russia, and bring down much flax, grain, and timber from that country. The Oder flows north-west through the mining district of Silesia before crossing the lower agricultural plain. The Elbe, which rises in Bohemia and cuts its way through the Erz Gebirge, traverses Saxony and Prussia before reaching the North Sea. It is navigable as far as Prague in Bohemia, and is of very great importance commercially. The Weser and the Ems rise in the central highlands, but the Rhine is fed by Alpine glaciers, deep in the heart of the continent. Its depth and constant volume are largely due to increased melting of the ice during the drier summer months. It is in succession a Swiss, German, and Dutch river, but the Germans fondly look upon it as their own.

It rises in Mont St Gothard and flows north-east to the lake of Constance, where much sediment is deposited. Next, it forms the boundary between Germany and Switzerland as it flows westwards to Basel, on reaching which it enters Germany, flowing between Baden and Alsace. Its tributary, the Main, enters at Mainz, and the most beautiful Rhine scenery lies between it and Coblentz, at the mouth of the Moselle. Although its beauty is lost below Bonn, its commercial value is increased, for it passes through the Ruhr coalfield, one of Germany's busiest districts. It gains the sea after traversing Holland, where it has built up a huge delta.

The German lakes are found in North Prussia, comparatively near the sea. In the eastern part of the country they are of irregular shape and relatively deep. Along the coast are a series of *haffs*, brackish lagoons almost enclosed by narrow sandy spits. The Baltic rivers discharge into these haffs.

Coast.

The coast is uniformly low and flat. Dykes are necessary round the mouths of the Weser and Ems to protect the low-lying land from sea encroachment. They are also built along this coast in places where there are no sand dunes.

Climate and Rainfall.

The rise of the ground from north to south tends to neutralise the effect of latitude upon the temperature, and the average July temperature for the whole country lies between 65° and 72° F. The July isotherms run slightly towards the north-east, owing to the presence of the larger continental mass on the east. The eastern Baltic coast has a warmer summer climate than that of the North Sea. In winter the genial effect of the westerly and south-westerly breezes from the Atlantic produces a warmer climate in the west of the country. The Baltic ports are frozen, but those of the North Sea remain ice-free. The low-lying valleys of the Rhine and its tributaries are sheltered, and so have less rigorous winters. The January 32° isotherm passes through Bremen, Brunswick, and Munich. Its southerly direction recalls that of the 40° isotherm through England, and for the same reason. The greatest extremes of climate are found in East Prussia.

Rainfall decreases from west to east (27″ to 20″) and increases from north to south (27″ to 40″), the latter being mainly the result of greater elevation. The average annual rainfall for the whole country is about 28″.

Plants and Animals.

Red deer, boars, and occasionally the elk, are found in the forests which cover one-fourth of the country, and chamois range the high Alps. These are the only wild animals of large size.

The forests are mainly of coniferous trees such as the fir, spruce, larch, and pine, and by careful forestry the area occupied by these is being increased at the expense of the oak and other deciduous trees. The main forest regions are the central highlands and the Black Forest, but pines are also grown on the colder northern plain. The Baltic islands have large beech forests.

Agriculture.

Half the land is under cultivation, and agriculture occupies 40 % of the people. Cereals are grown practically all over the country, but the kind of grain varies according to the climate and the soil. The drier soils north of latitude 50° are used mostly for rye and oats, the cooler climate also being suitable for these cereals. Much wheat and barley are grown on the alluvial soil of the middle Rhine valley and in the states to the east.

Potatoes are a general crop, the Rhine valley and the eastern half of the country being especially productive. The light, sandy soil favours both this plant and beetroot. The latter is obtaining a much larger acreage, in consequence of the increasing sugar industry. It is widely cultivated round the lower Rhine, in the valley of the upper Elbe, in the district between that river and the Weser, in Mecklenburg, and throughout eastern Germany, especially in Silesia.

Hops and barley are cultivated in Bavaria, Baden, and Würtemberg, and much flax is grown in Saxony and the Baltic states.

Latitude 52° may be taken as the northern limit of vine culture. Summer warmth and unclouded autumn skies are essential for proper ripening. Vine cultivation is practised most extensively along the valleys of the Rhine and its tributaries, the Main and the Moselle, the hill slopes being terraced for this purpose. Tobacco is also grown in the valley of the middle Rhine.

The broad northern plain and also those of Bavaria are well suited for horse-breeding. Cattle are kept on the farms in most parts of the country, but especially in the moist regions named above. They are increasing in numbers, being more profitable to rear than sheep, for the importation of wool from Australia and Russia has made sheep-rearing a less profitable industry. Of course sheep still predominate over cattle in the upland parts of the country and also in the drier north-east. Home-grown wool at one time entirely supported the weaving industries of Saxony and Silesia, but now the supply is insufficient to meet the increased demand, which has arisen through the use of coal and machinery. There is a similar state of things in England. Pigs are largely kept ; one district—Westphalia—has long been noted for its hams. Goats replace cattle upon the mountains, being kept for milking purposes. They can thrive on a wiry grass upon which cattle would starve.

Fisheries.

Salmon is found in most of the rivers. The sea fisheries include the cultivation of oysters on the North Sea coast and a little deep-sea fishery farther afield.

Minerals.

Like her rival, Great Britain, Germany possesses large supplies of coal and iron in close proximity. These are found skirting the central highlands ; the three great coalfields being found in the valleys of the Ruhr, the upper Elbe and the upper Oder (in Westphalia, Saxony and Silesia respectively). Copper, silver, lead, and zinc are also mined in the highlands. Germany produces more silver and zinc than any other country in Europe. Central Germany is also rich in sodium and potassium salts. Such mineral wealth has brought Germany to the forefront of manufacturing nations.

The German People.

The Germans are a Teutonic people; Bavarians, Franks, Frisians, Hessians, Saxons, and Swabians all have Teutonic ancestors. When the German tribes migrated south-west to the Rhine district and beyond, Slavonic peoples (Lithuanians, Prussians, and Wends) entered the country from the east, and were conquered and absorbed by the Germans on their return. Thus we find Celtic and Slavonic descendants in south and east Germany to-day. A further admixture of peoples is found on the margins of the country. Danes, Poles, and French are found in the north, east, and west respectively, and speak their own languages.

The numerous dialects of the German language fall naturally into two groups: High German and Low German. These roughly correspond to the upland and lowland areas of the country. The Frisians speak Low German in its purest form, their language being much like our own. The literary language, and that taught in the schools, is High German. This has been developed from Low German by tribes living further south.

As a people the Germans are honest, frugal, hardworking and loyal. They are deeply attached to home and country. The climate, soil, and position of their country have had much to do with the development of these characteristics.

In the 16th century the various peoples followed their princes in the matter of religion, and as a result we find to-day neighbouring states professing different religions. The ratio of Protestants to Roman Catholics is about two to one, North Germany being mainly Protestant. Education is compulsory and is in a state of high efficiency. There are 21 universities and

numerous technical, commercial, and agricultural schools.
The population numbers 60 millions, but these are
specially aggregated in the industrial districts (*e.g.*
Saxony with 658 persons per square mile) and along the
course of the Rhine. The average density of population
for the whole country is 290 per square mile. Germany
thus comes next to Italy and Great Britain among the
large European countries as regards density of population.

History explained by Geographical Position and Considerations.

The southern mountain barrier of the Alps, the
remoteness and barren nature of the country, together
with the warlike character of the Teutonic tribes prevented the Romans getting a firm grip upon Germany.
It later formed a part of the great Frankish empire
of Charlemagne who was crowned at Rome 800 A.D., but
in 870 France was separated from this domain, so that
the Eastern empire embraced Germany, the Low Countries, Austria, Switzerland, and a portion of Italy. This
empire was overthrown by Napoleon in 1806 when he
made Joseph and Louis Bonaparte kings of Naples and
Holland. The struggle between Prussia and Austria
for supremacy over the numerous German states led
to the latter's withdrawal in 1866, but the welding of
a united German empire was not effected until 1871,
after the Franco-German war. At this time Alsace-
Lorraine was annexed. The inclusion of a part of
Poland had taken place towards the end of the 18th
century. In each of these cases it will be noticed
that no great geographical barrier stood in the way
of annexation.

Industries and Manufactures.

During recent years Germany has been rapidly
changing from an agricultural to a manufacturing
country. Some of its industries are dependent upon
its agricultural products (*e.g.* the spirit, sugar, and wine

manufactures). Wine is made chiefly in the basins of
the Rhine and Moselle. Beer is brewed at Strassburg,
Munich, and generally throughout the country. The
areas where beet and potatoes are widely grown
determine the localities of sugar and 'brandy' manufacture. Forestry, which is diligently supervised by
the government, provides lumber for the Rhine rafts
and for the woodcarving and wares of Thuringia. The
Black Forest region is especially noted for these.
Berlin, Hamburg, and Strassburg have tobacco factories.
Leather goods are made in the Rhine valley and at
Berlin.

The iron and textile industries, on the other hand,
have been attracted to the coalfields, Saxony and
Westphalia being the two most important districts.
The iron trade is centred round Aix (Aachen), close to
the Belgian frontier, Essen, where Krupp's steelworks
are situated, Berlin, Breslau, Chemnitz, Carlsruhe, and
Mülhausen. Düsseldorf, Elberfeld, Barmen, and Crefeld
make woollen, cotton, and silk goods. Chemnitz is
similarly engaged in Saxony. Magdeburg has linen,
sugar, and iron manufactures.

Communications.

Internal communication by rail, river, and canal is
exceedingly well developed. Railways radiate from
Berlin, Hamburg, Cologne, Strassburg, Munich, Frankfort, Leipzig, Hanover, Dresden, and Breslau. The high
value of the gently flowing rivers in the lowland part of
the country is increased by their connection by means
of canals. The Oder is connected with the Elbe by the
Friedrich-Wilhelms canal, and with the Vistula by the
Bromberger canal. The Rhine is connected by canals
with the Elbe, Rhone, Danube, and Marne. The Kiel
canal places the port in direct communication with the
North Sea.

Commerce and Ports.

Germany is the second commercial country in the world, the annual value of her commerce exceeding £700,000,000.   She imports raw cotton, hides, grain, coal, coffee, copper, eggs, and tobacco.   Her principal exports are textiles, iron and iron goods, coal, leather, sugar, copper, and hides.   She sends Britain nearly £38,000,000 worth of goods and receives nearly £33,000,000 worth annually in return.

Hamburg, at the mouth of the Elbe, has a world-wide trade.   Its wharves stretch three miles along the river. Coal, coffee, iron, grain and petroleum are the chief imports.   It has a large emigration traffic with America.   The city has chemical, liquor, tobacco, metal and paper manufactures.   *Bremen* has lost its importance as a port by the silting of the Weser, and *Bremerhaven*, lying nearer the sea, has taken its trade.   Tobacco and sugar factories employ many hands.   *Danzig*, a strongly fortified town at the mouth of the Vistula, exports much grain.   *Stettin* has engineering and shipbuilding works, also breweries and potteries.   Its out-port is *Swinemünde*.   *Königsberg* exports fibre and timber.   It is strongly fortified.

Administration and Divisions.

The German Empire is a confederation of states, each of which, whilst retaining its own form of government, sends representatives to the central government and acquiesces in its decisions.   The central governing body consists of the Emperor and two houses of parliament (Bundesrath and Reichstag).   The King of Prussia is Emperor of Germany and in this position he is commander-in-chief of the army.

There are four kingdoms, six grand-duchies, five duchies, seven principalities, and three Free Towns.

Towns.

Berlin has a population of more than two millions, and five other towns have each a population of half a million or more.

Berlin, the capital of Prussia, is also the seat of the imperial government. Its central position on the European plain has made it a great railway centre. It is one of the principal money markets of Europe, and has extensive printing, chemical, and iron industries. *Munich* in Bavaria has renowned art galleries and libraries. Its wood, bronze, and glass manufactures are of high artistic merit. Much beer is brewed at this city. *Dresden* on the Elbe in Saxony has large foundries, and makes musical and scientific instruments. *Meissen,* a neighbouring town, manufactures Dresden china. *Leipzig* on the Saale, a tributary of the Elbe, is the centre of a large book and chemical trade.   These, together with furs, wool, leather and linen, are disposed of at its great fairs, held three times yearly. *Breslau* on the Oder has similar fairs. Its woollen, paper, and iron industries are important. *Cologne* on the Rhine is an important railway centre and river port.   Large quantities of sugar, timber, wine, and textiles are sent down the river. *Frankfort,* on the Main, is a great banking centre. Leather, books, and jewellery are largely sold at its half-yearly fairs. *Nüremberg* makes toys and lead pencils. *Düsseldorf* has coal, iron and cotton industries. *Hanover* produces cotton and iron goods, and has an important leather trade. All the above-named towns have a population of more than 250,000.

Denmark.

Position and Surface.

Denmark consists of the northerly projecting peninsula of Jutland and the neighbouring Baltic Islands. It has the same latitude as central Scotland.   Its area is about twice that of Wales, the country being smaller than Switzerland.

Jutland is bounded on three sides by the sea and there is no place situated more than forty miles from the coast. The Skaw projects into the Skager Rak on the north, and a little further south the peninsula is bisected by Liim Fjord. Its north-west portion is very low and sandy, large tracts of heath-clad moors covering its surface. The greatest elevation (600 ft.) is found in the south-east. The Baltic islands are hilly, Bornholm having granite rocks and fine cliff scenery. Otherwise the whole country is covered by recent rocks, thus closely resembling its neighbour Holland. Iceland and the Faeroes are also reckoned as part of Denmark. Iceland is mountainous, with an extreme elevation of 6000 ft. It is characterised by volcanic activity, and possesses geysers and extensive ice-fields. The Faeroes are a group of basaltic islands. The low sandy western coast of Denmark has dunes, dykes and lagoons. The eastern coast provides safe harbours for small craft.

Climate and Natural Productions.

Copenhagen has average winter and summer temperatures of 31° and 63° respectively. The low level of the country, its nearness to the sea, and the prevalence of westerly winds give it a mild moist climate. The winters are more rigorous on the east, owing to the frozen Baltic and the easterly winds. The amount of rainfall corresponds to that of eastern Scotland. Fogs are frequent.

Five per cent. of the country is covered with beech forests, arable land and pasture making up the remainder in about equal portions. Oats, barley and rye are the chief cereals grown upon the small Danish farms. Poultry farming is of considerable importance and millions of eggs are exported annually to England.

The moist meadows are Denmark's greatest asset. Cattle breeding and dairy farming are very important industries. Denmark has more cattle for its size than any other European country.

Fishing is carried on to a fair extent, and constitutes the main industry of the distant Atlantic isles. Skagen is the northern fishing port. Denmark has few minerals. Bornholm produces clay and a little coal. Iceland exports spar and sulphur. Peat is largely used for fuel.

The People and their History.

The Danes number about 2½ millions, and belong to the Norse branch of the Teutonic family. They profess the Lutheran religion, and in character are thrifty, honest, and peaceful. Formerly their kingdom included Norway and South Sweden, whilst the power they exerted over Britain will be easily recalled. Norway was separated from Denmark in 1814. The slightness of the obstacle presented by the narrow sea-passages of the Baltic explains the Scandinavian-Danish union of past years. The German-speaking district of Slesvig-Holstein was annexed by Prussia in 1864.

Industries, Communications, and Commerce.

Gloves, brandy, and pottery are the most important of the few manufactures. Butter-making is the great industry. Railways connect Frederikshaven with Kiel and Hamburg. Roads are good, and canals compensate for the lack of rivers. The Agger canal connects Liim Fjord with the Kattegat. Till 1857 Elsinore collected passage dues from ships using the Sound; the passage is now free, Denmark having received £3,500,000 as compensation. The Sound may remain ice-free throughout the winter, but sometimes it is blocked for two months.

Denmark's annual commerce is valued at over £73,000,000. She exports butter, eggs, cheese, pork, barley and live-stock. Her principal imports include textiles, coal, hardware, coffee, tea, and sugar.

Administration and Towns.

The government is in the hands of the King and two legislative chambers, and the country is divided into seven districts for administrative purposes.

D.

Copenhagen, the capital, possesses the only deep harbour. Its manufactures comprise gloves, spirits, sugar, iron goods, porcelain, and glass. Almost all the towns export dairy produce ; *Elsinore*, *Odense*, and *Aarhuus* are the chief. *Reykjavik* in Iceland is merely a village.

Scandinavia.

Position and Size.

The peninsula of Scandinavia occupies north-west Europe. It is bounded on the west by the Atlantic Ocean, on the south by the Skager Rak and Kattegat, on the east by the Baltic and northern Russia, and on the north by the Arctic Ocean. It stretches through 27° of longitude and 16° of latitude ; Stockholm has the same latitude as the Orkneys. Scandinavia is $2\frac{1}{2}$ times the size of the British Isles.

Surface and General Features.

The mountainous axis lies near the western coast, Sweden being mainly occupied by a more gentle slope to the Baltic. This slope is largely covered with gravels, clays, and sands brought down by glaciers from the western mountains during the Ice Age. Norway's ancient mountain masses consist of the Kiolen Mountains and the barren granitic Hardanger, Sogne, and Dovre Fjelds. Many glaciers occur, and bleak, snow-covered moors are found in the centre of the country. A low plateau occupies part of Gothland in south Sweden.

Rivers and Lakes.

The Norwegian rivers are short and rapid ; those of Sweden being much longer and slower. The only river of importance in Norway is the Glommen, and its valley is traversed by the railway running north from Christiania.

Many of the Norwegian rivers have falls of great height and beauty.   The Swedish rivers are remarkable for the parallelism of their courses and for the numerous ribbon lakes through which they flow.   The large Swedish lakes—Vener, Vetter, and Mälar—lie in a depression corresponding to that of the Skager Rak.

Norwegian fjord

Coast.

The low Swedish coast, with its sandy islands, cannot compare in beauty with the rugged grandeur of the rocky Norwegian coast, with its innumerable islands and its winding fjords of majestic scenery, possessing mountainous shores of 4000 feet elevation.   The capes Nord Kyn and North Cape project into the Arctic Ocean, whilst the Naze forms the southernmost point of Norway.   The Lofoten Islands form a rich fishing ground.

Climate and Rainfall.

The high latitudes of the northern parts of the country lead to the phenomenon of the midnight sun, and to days of one or two hours' length in midwinter. Norway is cooler in summer and warmer in winter than Sweden, as a result of Atlantic influence and the rain-bearing winds which blow from the south-west both summer and winter. The western coast is traversed by the 32° winter isotherm and by the 57° in summer. Norway's rainfall corresponds to that of western Ireland and Scotland. Passing from west to east of the peninsula, the mean annual rainfall decreases from 35″ to 13″. The Kiolen Mountains deprive the winds of their moisture to such an extent that their eastern slopes have less rain than central Europe. Speaking generally, the climate on the west coast is mild and moist ; and though the Baltic shore is frozen for nearly half the year, yet it has the same average July temperature as Yorkshire.

Natural Productions.

The poor soil and its high altitude and latitude render much of the land useless except for timber. Forests of pine, with ash, oak, and beech in more southerly parts cover half the surface of Sweden and one-fourth that of Norway. Scandinavia supplies half the timber exported from Europe. The south-east portion of the peninsula is the most fertile, and crops ripen, thanks to the longer days. Barley, rye, oats, flax, and hemp are the principal crops grown. There is no agriculture worth mentioning in Norway. Cattle raising is important, and horses and sheep are also bred in large numbers.

The wild animals include the reindeer, elk, bear, wolf, and beaver. Wild fowl live in millions on the western islands, and eagles are found in the more desolate parts of the country. Salmon-fishing in the Norwegian rivers is rented by wealthy English sportsmen, whilst sea-fishing for whale, seal, cod, and herring is one of Norway's main industries.

Both countries have various minerals, but suffer from a lack of coal. Copper and silver are found both in Norway and Sweden, the latter also having supplies of iron, lead, and zinc.

The People and their History.

The Scandinavians are a Teutonic people, simple in their mode of life, honest, thrifty, and hardworking. In common with their brethren, the Danes, they profess the Lutheran religion. The two countries, Norway and Sweden, although now under separate kings, have had a history bound up with that of Denmark. Norway has been the more under Danish influence, and her present king was chosen from the Danish royal house. Sweden has three times the population of the sister country, which is the most sparsely peopled country in Europe, there being but 18 persons per square mile. About one-fifth of the people are town-dwellers, the remainder being scattered over such parts of the country as admit of cultivation or forestry.

Industries, Communications, and Commerce.

Lumbering (with its dependent trades, the manufacture of matches, wood-pulp, and joinery) is an industry common to both countries. Water-power is largely used in these occupations. Every town on the Norwegian coast is a fishing port, whilst Sweden's iron and steel industries are well known. Railways are comparatively few, being best developed in the south. An important line of communication—the Gota canal—joins the great lakes to the sea.

Commerce consists mainly in the export of timber, fish, metals, and animals, and the import of food and clothing. The chief ports are Christiania, Göteborg, Stockholm, Bergen, and Malmö.

Administrations and Towns.

Each country has its own king and parliament. Götaland, Svealand, and Norrland are the Swedish provinces, and Norway is divided into northern, southern, and western districts.

Christiania is the Norwegian capital. It has a busy trade, especially in timber. Other Norwegian towns are : *Bergen*—a fishing town, *Trondhjem*—a tourist centre and railway terminus, *Christiansund, Tromsö*, and *Hammerfest*—fishing towns, *Drammen* and *Frederikstad*—timber ports.

Stockholm, the capital of Sweden, is built on islands connected by numerous bridges. It exports iron and timber, and has textile and leather manufactures. *Göteborg* has similar industries and exports timber, pitch, and metals. Other Swedish towns are *Upsala*—a university town, *Norrköping*—a port with ironworks, *Falun*—with copper mines, *Karlskrona*—a naval station, *Malmö* and *Helsingborg*—ports for Denmark.

Russia in Europe.

Position, Size, and Surface.

Russia is the largest European country. It has an area 18 times that of the British Isles, and it extends from Germany to Asia, and from the Arctic Ocean to the Black Sea. It measures 2000 miles from north to south, and from east to west. The greater part of the country is one vast plain with the low Valdai Hills forming the central watershed. The Urals on the east and the Crimea in the south have an elevation of 5000 ft., but the Caucasus range, important, as we shall see later, from the climatic point of view, is of very great height, its highest peak, *Mount Elburz*, being higher than Mont Blanc.

On account of their great length and low initial elevation the rivers are very slow. They vary, however, in commercial importance. The northern rivers flow to the Arctic Ocean, where Archangel, the chief port, is ice-free only for three months in the year. The Neva

(frozen four months) is the outflow of Lake Ladoga—
one of 5000 lakes found in Finland and west Russia.
The Duna, Niemen, and Vistula bring timber and grain
from the interior to the Baltic, whilst the Dniester,

Barge on the Volga

'Father' Dnieper, the shoaly Don, and 'Mother' Volga
flow southwards to the Black, Azov, and Caspian Seas.
The Volga (2200 miles) is Europe's longest river and
is navigable for steamers for three-fourths of its course.

Climate and Rainfall.

A great land-mass like Russia, lying close to that of Asia, having a great extent from north to south, and but little coast-line or variation in altitude to moderate its climate, naturally experiences extremes of heat and cold.

Cold winds from the north can sweep unchecked over the country, whilst in winter the Caucasus keep off warmer winds from the south.

Severe winters and hot summers are the rule, and the climate becomes more continental as one proceeds eastwards, for the January isotherms run south-east and the July isotherms north-east. It should also be borne in mind that, as a result of latitude, there is a warmer temperature in the south than in the north. Lake Ladoga is frozen for one-third of the year, yet cotton is grown in the south of the country.

Russia is a country of little rainfall, for the winds have already been robbed of their moisture. Most rain falls in summer, more evaporation taking place from the rivers and lakes during this season ; thus Moscow has 3″ rainfall in August and 1½″ in February. As a result of their elevation the Caucasus Mountains receive more rain than any other part of European Russia.

Natural Productions.

Frozen swamps and forests of conifers cover much of northern Russia. Mixed forests, with clearings for the growth of rye, flax, hemp, beet, and potatoes occupy the centre, and south of this the exceedingly fertile wheat lands, the 'Black Earth' district, run from the Dnieper to the southern Urals. Grass steppes are found in the south-east and support thousands of sheep and cattle. The richer parts of the steppes are now being devoted to cereal culture. Around the Black Sea and on the southern slopes of the Crimean highlands the olive and the vine are cultivated. The region to the north of the Caspian consists of barren salt steppes.

Since forests cover one-third of the country, the bear, wolf, and lynx are found in Russia. Arctic foxes, reindeer, and polar bears inhabit the frozen north. The beaver formerly abundant is now only found in scattered localities. Salmon and sturgeon live in the northern rivers and the Volga respectively. The river fisheries of Russia are more important than those of the sea.

Coal and iron are found together in Poland, the southern Urals, and at Tula, south of Moscow. An important coalfield also exists at Kharkov in the Donetz valley. Precious metals and stones are mined in the Urals, where other metals are also obtained. Baku, on the Caspian shore, has large petroleum wells, and marble is quarried from the rocks of Finland and the Crimea.

The People and their History.

The Slavs are an Asiatic race, which has spread over the vast plain as far as Servia and Bulgaria. The Russians of to-day comprise as many as thirty races, having absorbed amongst others the Finns, Lapps, Poles, Tatars, and Kalmuks.

They belong mainly to the Orthodox Greek Church, but the Finns and Poles retain their Lutheran and Catholic religions. The lower classes of the people are intemperate and ignorant, elementary education being badly provided for. The upper classes are well educated and, as a rule, very good linguists.

The land is thinly populated, bearing on an average about fifty persons per square mile. The districts around Kieff and Warsaw have the densest population (about 300 per square mile). Tradition points to the former town being the original centre of Slavonic expansion in the ninth century. Hemmed in by a frozen sea upon the north and by hostile peoples on the west, Peter the Great built St Petersburg as a western outlet in 1703. To-day the Russians have extended their empire eastwards to the Yellow Sea and are pressing towards a Mediterranean outlet.

Industries, Communications, and Commerce.

Before the development of her coal mines Russia was mainly engaged in lumbering, agricultural, and pastoral pursuits, together with the dependent distilling, leather-making, and home weaving industries ; but now she is rapidly developing her iron and textile manufactures upon the coalfields and at St Petersburg. Poland and Moscow have considerable cotton trade, and Tula is the great iron-working centre in Central Russia.

As a result railways have been built to these parts, Moscow forming the natural centre. From this town lines radiate in all directions. Canals connect the divergent rivers, and incidentally the Black and Baltic Seas. The value of the rivers is lessened by winter frost, and in the case of southern rivers by the diminution in volume caused by summer heat and ruthless clearing of forest lands. Roads are very bad, but winter communication by sleigh over the frozen country lessens this disadvantage.

Much trade is done by means of fairs, as at Kharkov, Nijni Novgorod and many large towns, and a large proportion of Russian commerce never touches the sea. Warsaw, for example, has a large trade with Germany, with which almost half of the foreign trade is done. Cereals, timber, eggs, and flax are the chief exports, and machinery, woollens, coal, and cotton the chief imports. St Petersburg, Riga, Odessa, and Archangel are the great ports.

Administration, Divisions, and Towns.

The Tsar is an absolute monarch, but in 1905 a representative parliament (or Duma) was convened for the first time. The country is subdivided into Governments and Districts. Local affairs are managed by the Zemstvos or 'District Councils.'

St Petersburg, the capital, is a handsome city with much export trade, and with china, glass, and weaving industries. *Moscow*, the old capital, is most famous for

Archangel

its citadel, the Kremlin. English firms have foundries in the city. *Warsaw*, a trade centre on the Vistula coalfield, has fairs for live stock. *Odessa* is a grain and wool port on the Black Sea. *Riga* exports cereals, fibre, and timber from the Duna basin and beyond. *Kharkov* is a rising manufacturing town on the Donetz coalfield. *Kieff* has an arsenal, and leather and sugar manufactures. *Kasan* and *Orenburg* do much Siberian trade. *Ekaterinburg* is a mining centre in the Urals. *Slatoust* and *Tula* are iron-working towns. *Lodz* is a Polish town with cotton and woollen factories.

Austria-Hungary.

Position, Size, and Surface.

Austria-Hungary is twice the area of the British Isles, and occupies a very central position in Europe. It lies in much the same latitude as France and there is a fair degree of resemblance between the vegetable products of the two countries. It has only 500 miles of coast-line upon the Adriatic; on the other sides it is closed in by Italy, Switzerland, Germany, Russia, Rumania, and Servia. Its surface varies greatly: the Eastern Alps cover the west of the country and are prolonged into a mountainous border running parallel to the Adriatic. Another continuation strikes northeast to Vienna and thence, as the Karpathians, encloses the Hungarian plain ; the mountain-encircled plateau of Bohemia lies to the north-west.

Austria-Hungary has no river of its own, although it has a great part of the Danube and its feeders within her territory. An immense amount of river traffic is carried on along this river, which is navigable to the German town of Ratisbon. Many lakes of great beauty lie among the mountains of the Tirol ; Lake Balaton or Platten See is a large Hungarian lake not far from Budapest.

Climate and Natural Productions.

As we should expect from its land-locked position, the climate of Austria-Hungary is continental.   Practically the whole of the country has two months' winter frost, yet with the exception of Bohemia, it lies south of the July 70° isotherm.   Rainfall is heaviest in the Tirol (80″), Karpathians, and S.W. mountains.   On the other hand, the Central Hungarian plain has less than 25″ and is subject to summer drought.   The Adriatic region has a typical Mediterranean climate with hot, dry summers.

Forests of oak, ash, beech and pine cover a quarter of the country and much timber is exported.   The northern and upland districts grow rye, barley, oats, flax, and beet, whilst wheat is the main crop of the Hungarian plain.   The warm, dry climate also suits maize, which is extensively grown throughout the Empire.   The vine is cultivated in Hungary (especially in the Theiss valley) and on the warmer southern Alpine slopes.   Olives, plums ('prunes'), oranges, and mulberries grow along the Adriatic and in the Tirol.

The grassy plains support thousands of horses and cattle.   Sheep feed on the slopes of the encircling mountains and provide for the local woollen industry. Many herds of pigs find food in the beech-mast and acorns of the Hungarian forests.

Minerals are associated with the Eastern Alps, the Karpathians and the Bohemian ranges.   They include precious metals as well as the more useful ones.   Bohemia and Moravia have much coal ; indeed, some is exported from the former country to Germany by barges along the Elbe.   Salt deposits occur in the west at Salzburg, and in the north around Cracow.

The People and their History.

The people are of mixed race : German in the north-west, Slavonic in the east, Latin in the south-west, and Hungarian in the middle.   Eight languages are spoken in various parts of the country, and whilst Protestants and Greek Catholics are found in the east, the west is mainly peopled by Roman Catholics. Population is most dense along the middle Danube and in Bohemia.

Many of the Danube towns owe their origin to Roman fortresses. The western half of the country was peopled by German tribes on the fall of the Roman Empire. These largely came via the Danube and Elbe. Austria formed part of Charlemagne's great empire. Later it came into the hands of the Hapsburg dynasty, who gained Hungary in 1526, and after a 200 years' struggle drove out the Turks.

Industries, Communications, and Commerce.

The pursuits of the people are mainly agricultural and pastoral. Much wine is made in Hungary, silk in southern Austria, and paper from the wood pulp of the numerous forests, which also furnish wood for the Austrian chair industry. Bohemia is celebrated for its glass ware, and possesses iron and textile industries. Both Vienna and Pilsen are renowned for their breweries. The north-west is the chief manufacturing district.

Vienna is the natural focus of trade routes and railways, from Italy to Russia and from Germany to the Black Sea and the Balkan peninsula. Trieste and Fiume are seaports upon the Adriatic Sea, but fully one-half of Austria's trade is done with neighbouring countries overland. The value of the annual trade is nearly £200,000,000. Wood, woodwork, sugar, eggs, lignite, woollens, and glassware are the chief exports ; and cotton, coal, wool, and machinery are the principal imports. Germany is Austria's best customer.

Administration and Towns.

The two countries have separate parliaments, but acknowledge the same monarch, the Austrian emperor being king of Hungary. Austria annexed in 1908 the small states Bosnia and Herzegovina, over which the Sultan of Turkey had previously nominal control.

The Danube at Budapest

Vienna, capital of Austria, has nearly two million inhabitants. Its silk, glove, iron, and leather trades are important. *Budapest*, Hungary's capital, is the centre of the Hungarian milling trade. *Grätz*, south-west of Vienna, is a mining centre; *Innsbruck*, in the Tirol, is a tourist centre. *Prague* in Bohemia has a great iron trade. *Carlsbad* has mineral springs. *Pilsen* has important coal mines. *Debreczin*, near the Theiss, has horse and cattle fairs. *Brünn* manufactures woollens. *Szegedin* lies in the centre of the Hungarian wheat district.

Rumania.

This country, which is less than half the size of the British Isles, has the Karpathians and the Danube as two of its boundaries. It shares the marshy Danube delta with Russia, and the eastern part of the country is a continuation of the Russian plain. Cold winter winds sweep across the low-lying frontier and excessive cold results. The climate is very continental, and the hot summers favour wheat and maize cultivation upon the clayey plains. Rainfall here is not great, since the Karpathians cause precipitation before the winds reach the lower land. Agriculture is the one great industry, and although primitive methods are employed, the country is one of the granaries of Europe, grain forming more than $70\,^{0}/_{0}$ of the exports. The Karpathians are thickly wooded, but the lower hill-lands are given up to sheep-rearing, and to fruit and vine cultivation. As the name of the country implies, the people are of Latin race, being perhaps Roman colonists who entered the country from the south. Rock-salt and petroleum are the only minerals worked ; these are found near the Karpathians. There are no important manufactures.

Rumania gained its independence and became a separate kingdom in 1878. *Bukarest* is the capital, and *Galatz* the chief grain port.

The Balkan Peninsula.

Position and Surface.

The Balkan Peninsula is bounded on the north by the Danube, and has the sea as its other boundary. The narrow Bosporus and Dardanelles separate it from Asia, and the wider Strait of Otranto from Italy. The

On the Bosporus

broad northern half is occupied by Servia, Bulgaria and Turkey, whilst Greece embraces the narrow southerly portion, which ends at Cape Matapan. The eastern coast is flatter than the western, which has the Dinaric mountains and their continuation running down it.

The whole peninsula is mountainous, the Balkan Range being a continuation of the Karpathians. The

D.   10

Shar Dagh in the centre of the country has an elevation
of 10,000 ft. The valleys of the Morava, Vardar, and
Maritza form natural lines of communication. The old
roads along these valleys are now supplemented by
railways.

Climate and Natural Productions.

The broader part of the peninsula has an extreme
climate, whereas Greece and its islands have their climate
modified by the sea and by rain-bearing winds. Greece
has a warmer climate, both summer and winter, than
Turkey. The western half of the peninsula has more
rain than the eastern, and more rain falls in winter
than in any other season. Owing to the dry Mediterranean summer and its low latitude Greece shares with
Cyprus the hottest European summer temperature.
Hence tobacco, cotton, figs, and currants are among
the vegetable products. Much maize and wheat are
grown in the north of the peninsula. Sheep, goats,
and cattle are fed on the mountain slopes. Mining and
manufacturing industries are practically absent.

The People and their History.

Numerous races and religions are found here, for
the Slavonic Servians and Bulgarians, who had driven
the Greeks southwards to their mountains and islands,
were conquered by the Turks, who overran the country
in the 15th century. Moslem oppression and misrule
resulted in the formation in 1878 of the kingdom of
Servia, the principality of Bulgaria, and the separation
of the 'Austrian' provinces of Bosnia and Herzegovina.
Turkish misgovernment has hindered civilization and is
largely responsible for the religious and racial strife in
the peninsula to-day.

Communications, Commerce, and Ports.

Inland communication is poorly developed. Roads
are bad, and but few rivers are navigable. From
Belgrade a railway passes up the Morava valley, thence

to Constantinople along the Maritza valley, and to Saloniki via the valley of the Vardar. Athens is connected by rail and ship canal with the west coast.

The Greeks have always been great sailors, and they do most of the trade of the peninsula. Corn, wool, fruit, sponges, olive oil, and wine constitute the chief exports; manufactured goods form the imports. Constantinople, Saloniki, Varna, Piraeus, and Syra are the chief seaports.

Administration and Towns.

Turkey is now a constitutional monarchy, and it is to be hoped that the ills of the old absolutism will disappear under the new order of things. Bulgaria has also undergone a change, her prince being now an independent monarch or Tsar.

Constantinople, the capital of Turkey, has trade by caravan with Asia, and with Europe by rail and sea. *Athens*, the capital of Greece, has many splendid remains of ancient Greek art. *Piraeus*, its seaport, has cotton, iron and glass industries. *Belgrade*, the capital of Servia, exports grain down the Danube.

Switzerland.

Position, Size, and Surface.

Switzerland lies in Central Europe, bounded by the four Great Powers—France, Germany, Austria, and Italy. It has no coast-line and its area is only one-eighth that of the British Isles. Mountains cover three-fourths of its surface, and an idea of the build of the country is best gained by starting from the St Gothard peak, from which radiate four ranges of mountains enclosing the valleys of the Rhine and Rhone. North of these stretches the Alpine foreland, or Swiss sandstone plateau, as far as the Juras, which form roughly the north-west boundary. The southern mountain barrier comprises

Zermatt and the Matterhorn

the Pennine, Lepontine, and Rhaetian Alps; these contain the highest peaks.

Switzerland is a country of great beauty; a land of snow-capped mountains, glaciers, rushing torrents, and narrow lakes. Of such lakes, Constance, Geneva, Neuchatel, Zurich, and Lucerne are the largest. They lie along the courses of the rivers Rhine, Rhone, and Aar, which are also fed by numerous tributaries as they flow outwards from the country.

Climate and Natural Productions.

The climate of Switzerland is greatly modified by its altitude, and this in two ways: both the higher and the northerly slopes are colder than the others. The Alpine foreland has an average temperature of 29° in January and 65° in July. The rainfall is heavy, being 60″ to 90″ on the mountain slopes which catch the rain, yet some of the valleys have but a moderate amount. The hot *fohn* wind (which becomes warm by precipitation of its moisture) is characteristic of the valleys into which it descends, and is responsible for much clearing of snow from the *alps* or mountain pastures.

Only about one-tenth of the land is capable of cultivation, and thus agriculture cannot be of great importance. Sheep and cattle rearing (with dependent glove and milk industries) occupy many of the people. Zurich, Bâle, and St Gall have silk and cotton manufactures. These industrial towns are situated upon the plateau. Watches are made in Geneva and the Jura district. The wealth of the country has greatly increased by the use of water-power from the numerous streams. Tourists visiting the country form one of its chief sources of income.

The People and their History.

At the time of the Norman Conquest Switzerland was part of the German Empire. In the 14th century Austria made an unsuccessful attempt to obtain the country, and about 1350 eight cantons united and freed themselves from their German masters. The cantons now number 22. The people are a mixed race, for Germans, Burgundians, and Goths defeated the Celts and settled in their land. In general the Swiss speak the language of the 'Great Power' to which they are nearest. The population numbers about 210 per square mile.

The mountainous character of the country and the relative poorness of its soil have developed in the Swiss frugality, industry, activity, and a love of country and freedom. They are mostly Protestants.

Communication, Trade, and Administration.

Swiss roads are good, but the rivers are of little use because of their rapidity. Railways run along the valleys, connecting the towns of Switzerland with one another and with Italy and France. Bâle and Geneva are the great outlets of Swiss trade, but much is also carried on via the Simplon and St Gothard tunnels. The annual value of trade done is £100,000,000. Food, raw fibre, and minerals are the chief articles imported. Silk goods, lace, textiles, watches, milk and cheese are exported in large quantities.

The government is a republic, having a president and two houses of parliament. Each canton has local government, besides sending representatives to the central body.

Italy.

Position and Size.

Italy lies to the south of Switzerland and Austria, between the 37th and 47th north parallels. This narrow country is the second of Europe's three southern peninsulas. It has the Adriatic Sea upon the east, and the Mediterranean upon the south and west. If Sicily and Sardinia be included, its size is nearly that of the British Isles.

Surface and General Features.

The northern or continental portion consists of the basin of the Po—fertile soil brought down by glacier and river from the neighbouring mountains. It is flanked by the Alps on the north and west, and the Apennines on the south. The Po receives tributaries from both these ranges, those on its left bank having picturesque Alpine lakes in their upper courses.

Vesuvius

The peninsular portion of the country is traversed by the parallel ranges of the Apennines—the most recently uplifted European mountains. These are, in general, nearer the Adriatic than the Mediterranean shore. They act as the main divide or watershed, sending rivers (notably the Po and the Tiber) north-east and south-west to the sea. The comparatively recent geological changes which have gone on in Italy manifest themselves in the volcanic phenomena of the south (Vesuvius, Stromboli, and Etna). The disastrous earthquake of 1908 caused the death of 77,000 people.

Climate and Natural Productions.

Italy's low latitude, her nearness to the sea, and the presence of the Alps upon the north—a barrier against cold winter winds—give her a warm and equable climate. The Apennines receive most rainfall. The Lombardy plain has its rainfall more uniformly distributed through the year than have the more southerly parts of the country. Naples, for example, has a rainfall of 4″ for each winter month, yet not 1″ for July.

Italy is subject to the hot, sand-laden *Sirocco*, which blows northwards from Africa.

Constant irrigation has brought much of the land to a high state of fertility. This is done in the Lombardy plain by a system of canals from the Po and its tributaries. Maize, wheat, and rice are the chief cereals. Lombardy and Apulia are great wheat-growing districts. Cotton, the vine, olive, mulberry, and fruit trees are found generally.

Sulphur from the volcanic districts and marble from Carrara are the two chief minerals exported. Metal working suffers from lack of coal and metallic ores.

Sheep and cattle are bred, especially in the north. The goat is the common domestic animal. The fisheries are well developed—tunny, mackerel, sardines, and anchovies being caught in the Mediterranean. Coral and sponge are also obtained from this sea.

The People and their History.

The original Italian tribes, conquered by the Romans, have had a great admixture of foreign blood, as a result of Rome's extensive empire. The fall of the latter in the fifth century was due to invasions of northern Teutonic tribes. Italy became part of Charlemagne's dominions in 772, but the geographical barrier of the

Alps eventually caused her separation.   The rival Italian states acknowledged Victor Emmanuel, King of Sardinia, as king of United Italy in 1860.

By temperament the people are excitable, mirthful, and fond of gay colours.   They are mainly Roman Catholics.   The peasantry are poor, frugal, and, on the whole, badly educated.   Northern Italy is one of the most densely populated parts of Europe.

Industries, Communications, and Commerce.

Silks and other textiles are woven in the north, but agriculture (with the production of wine and olive oil) is the national industry.   Railways enter the country via the Brenner, Simplon, St Gothard, and Mt Cenis tunnels, traverse the northern plain, and then skirt both east and west coasts.   Our annual trade with Italy amounts to £18,000,000.   She exports raw silk, silk goods, cotton goods, dried fruits, olive oil, wines, and cheese.   Her chief imports are raw cotton, coal, machinery, raw silk, iron and steel, timber, wheat, wool, and cured fish.   Venice, Genoa, Naples, and Palermo are the most important seaports.   Brindisi is the port of embarkation for the Suez Canal.

Administration and Towns.

The government is under the King and two Houses of Parliament.   The members of the Upper House are nominated by the King.   *Naples* is the largest town. It has a beautiful situation upon the bay of the same name.   *Rome*, the capital, is full of ancient relics of the bygone Empire.   It contains the Vatican and St Peter's, the latter being the largest church in the world.   *Milan* is famous for its white marble cathedral ; it also has silk factories, and a trade in wine and oil.   *Turin* has industries of the same kind.   *Palermo* exports wine, oranges, and marble.   *Genoa* is the leading seaport, having surpassed its old rival *Venice*, the city of gondolas and canals, which lies at the head of the Adriatic.   Venice makes glassware and lace.   *Florence* is noted for its articles of *vertu*, straw plait, and silk goods.

The Iberian Peninsula.

Position, Size, and Surface.

This, the most westerly European peninsula, lies between parallels 36° and 44°, and occupies the south-western portion of the Continent. The Bay of Biscay, the Atlantic, and the Mediterranean wash its three shores. In area it is twice the size of the British Isles.

The bulk of the country is a high plateau traversed by parallel ranges (or *sierras*) and rivers. This plateau is a crust-block of ancient rock, flanked to the north-east and south-west by the valleys of the Ebro and Guadalquiver. Beyond these valleys lie the Pyrenees and Sierra Nevada ranges. The rivers are as a rule rapid and valueless, except for irrigation purposes. They vary greatly in volume at different times of the year.

The country is of a very compact shape and there are few indentations of coast-line. The coast is bold wherever the mountains approach the sea. A glance at a physical map of the country will show how the mountains have determined its outline.

Climate and Natural Productions.

From its latitude Spain should have a warm climate, but its compact form gives it an almost continental one. The coastal mountains deprive the interior of rain, so that the latter is dry and barren. The rain-bearing winds from the Atlantic strike the country on the west in winter, and on the north in summer, owing to the Atlantic region of high pressure lying to the west of Portugal. From this it follows that the northern and western coasts receive much more rain than the interior. The destruction of forests has added to the dryness of the climate, and irrigation must be practised in order to produce crops. Madrid has a very extreme climate. Its mean temperatures for January and July are 38° and 76° respectively.

The vine, wheat, fruits, olives, and maize are the principal plants cultivated. The *huertas* of the Mediterranean coast are devoted almost entirely to the growth of oranges, pomegranates, and grapes.

Vast numbers of merino sheep feed upon the poor grasses of the highlands in summer. Cattle are raised

Portuguese wine carts

chiefly upon the moister grass lands of the north and north-west. Swine are kept in the middle of the country, where the forests of evergreen oak supply them with food.

Minerals are very plentiful and large quantities of lead and silver are produced. Almost one quarter of all the copper found in the world is raised near Huelva on the Rio Tinto.

The People and their History.

Both Spaniards and Portuguese are of mixed race, for Iberians, Celts, Romans, Goths, and Moors have held the land in turn. The Moors invaded the country in 713 and many traces of their occupation remain. The Alhambra at Granada is a notable example. A Burgundian duke expelled them from Portugal and became its king in 1139. Ferdinand and Isabella did a like service for Spain in 1492. Thus Spain and Portugal are separate countries occupying the same peninsula.

The Spanish people are poorly educated and very backward in comparison with other European nations. The pride of the ruling classes has resulted in their country sinking from the leading position it once held. The prevailing religion is Roman Catholicism.

Industries, Communications, and Commerce.

The production of wine (especially of port and sherry) is an important industry.

Agriculture employs two-thirds or more of the people. Barcelona has textile factories. Silkworms are reared along the Mediterranean coast. Alicante and Burgos make woollens. Seville has tanneries and a Government tobacco factory, but these industries are small in proportion to the size of the country.

Communication by river, road, or rail is bad. Railways connect Madrid and Lisbon with the chief towns only. The chief articles exported are wine, ores, fruits, wool, and rubber. Textiles, grain, machinery, coal, sugar, and tobacco are included among the imports. Barcelona, Malaga, Cadiz, Lisbon, and Oporto do most of the trade.

Administration and Towns.

Spain is a constitutional monarchy, possessing a government by monarch and parliament. Portugal became a republic in 1910. *Madrid*, the capital of Spain, stands in the centre of the table-land. *Barcelona*, the chief seaport, has important manufactures. *Seville*, on the Guadalquiver, is a river-port engaged in the orange trade. *Cadiz*, an old Roman town, exports sherry. *Valencia*, in a carefully irrigated district, produces raisins and oranges. *Lisbon*, at the mouth of the Tagus, is Portugal's capital and chief port. *Oporto* exports the port wine made in the Douro valley. *Coimbra* manufactures salt and has sardine fisheries.

CHAPTER V

ASIA

Position and Size.

The continent of Asia embraces one-third of the land surface of the world. It is more than four times as large as Europe, which adjoins it on the west. On three sides it is washed by the ocean (the Arctic, the Pacific, and the Indian). The Red Sea and the narrow Suez isthmus separate it from Africa, and the Mediterranean and Black Seas form part of its western boundary, of which the Ural Mountains approximately form the remainder.

Surface and General Features.

As we should expect in a land-mass stretching from the Equator almost to the North Pole the surface is extremely varied. It is a land of great plateaux and mountain ranges, of immense plains and rivers, of extensive depressions and salt lakes.

The Pamir plateau may be taken as the central mountainous group of the whole continent. This is a plain with an elevation greater than that of the Alps, and with ranges and peaks towering upwards from it for another 10,000 feet. A continuous mountain system stretches north-east from the Pamirs to the Bering Strait upon the Arctic circle. This includes the Tian-shan, Altai, Yablonoi, and Stanovoi ranges. It separates the northern Siberian plain from the Chinese Empire, in which lie the Tarim basin and the Gobi desert.

The Himalayas : Mount Everest

These two regions are bounded on the south by another series of mountains running north-east from the Pamir plateau : the Kuen-lun, Sun-shan and Kingan ranges which end in Manchuria at the Amur river. The noble Himalayas branch south-east from the Pamirs. They vary from 200 to 400 miles in breadth and have a length of 1500 miles. Their peaks are the highest in the world, have perpetually snow-capped summits and numerous glaciers, with scenery of majestic grandeur. The plateau of Tibet occupies the triangular region between the Kuen-lun and the Himalaya ranges. On the east it breaks up into the Pe-ling, Nan-ling, and other parallel ranges of China, whilst to the south the Indo-Chinese and Malayan mountains stretch to beyond the Equator.

West of the Pamirs lies the Aralo-Caspian depression, bordered on the south by the mountainous northern edge of the Iranian plateau. This plateau, including Persia, Afghanistan, and Baluchistan, has for its eastern boundary the Hala Sulaiman and Hindu Kush ranges, which branch southwards from the Pamirs. The Caucasus and Elburz mountains are on its northern side, whilst the Mesopotamian depression and its continuation, the Persian Gulf, flank it upon the south-west. The Arabian and Asia Minor plateaux lie to the west and north-west of this depression. Peninsular India is occupied by the Dekkan plateau.

The most extensive plains are those of Siberia, China, N. India, Turan, and Mesopotamia.

Rivers and Lakes.

The Altai-Stanovoi range sends the Obi, Yenesei, Lena, and numerous other rivers to the Arctic Ocean. These finish their northerly courses over frozen tundras at the icebound sea and are useless for commerce with Europe. The Amur flows eastwards from the Mongolian plateau. The Hoang-ho and Yang-tse-kiang take their flow from the eastern slope of the Tibetan table-land, and with the Si-kiang drain the whole of China proper.

The Mekong, Menam, Salwen, and Irawadi flow south-wards, whilst the Himalayas give rise to the mighty Bramaputra, Ganges, and Indus. The Tigris and Euphrates enter the head of the Persian Gulf by a common mouth.

A remarkable feature of Asia is its large number of internal basins. In these, rivers drain not to the sea but to an inland lake. These lakes are usually salt, and are diminishing in area and volume as a result of excessive evaporation. The Ural, Tarim, Jordan, Amu Daria, and Syr Daria, are rivers of this type, and the chief lakes fed by streams of this kind are the Caspian, Aral, Balkash, Seistan, Lob, and the Dead Sea. Lake Baikal differs from these in being a fresh-water lake, for it possesses an outlet, the Angara, a tributary of the river Yenesei.

The Coast of Asia.

The northern coast is flat, monotonous, icebound, and of little value commercially. Bering Strait on the north-east has a width of 36 miles and separates the continent from North America. The eastern coast has a series of seas (Okhotsk, Japan, Yellow, China) enclosed by fringing archipelagoes (Kurile, Japan, Philippine, Malay) which run along the whole of this side of the continent. The mountainous peninsulas of Kamchatka and Korea partially enclose the Seas of Okhotsk and Japan. The former sea is frozen for part of the year, and icebergs are common off the island of Sakhalin.

Borneo, Sumatra, Java, and Celebes are the largest islands of the Malay Archipelago. Sumatra is separated by the Strait of Malacca from the long, narrow Malay Peninsula.

The Bay of Bengal and the Arabian Sea wash the east and west shores of India. They are parts of the Indian Ocean. The large island of Ceylon lies to the south of India. The marshy Sandarbans lie at the head of the Bay of Bengal, where the Ganges and Bramaputra have

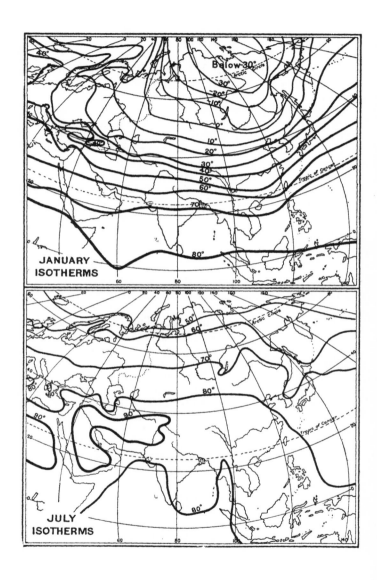

built up a huge delta. At the head of the Arabian Sea, the Gulf of Oman leads into the Persian Gulf, and at its western end the Gulf of Aden forms the entrance into the Red Sea. Both the Arabian and Red Seas have rocky shores where the edges of the Dekkan and of the Iranian and Arabian plateaux lie close to the coast. The Suez Canal leads from the Red Sea to the Mediterranean, the eastern part of which is called the Levant. Syria and Asia Minor also have mountains close to the sea, so that the Asiatic shores of the Mediterranean and of the Black Sea are rocky and have but few ports of any value.

Climate. (a) Temperature.

The great extent of Asia from north to south, its regions of great altitude, its compact shape, its immense size and relative remoteness from the influence of the sea, combine to make the climate one of extremes.

The January isotherms run in a south-easterly direction, curving again northwards towards the east of the continent as a result of the warming influence of the Pacific Ocean. They range from below − 30° F. to 80° F., and latitude 30° N. may be taken as the southern limit of places having a temperature of freezing point throughout January. Yakutsk and Verkhoyansk in Siberia have a January temperature of 45° below zero. Yet at the same time of the year the southern Asiatic peninsulas have an average temperature equal to that of our hottest summers (80°).

The July isotherms range from 50° to 90° F. In general they curve first slightly northwards from Europe and then dip southwards towards the Pacific, both these regions acting as cooling agents in summer. One important exception must be noted : the 90° isotherm is a closed curve, embracing much of the Arabian, Iranian, and Pamir plateaux. These regions are the hottest parts of the continent in summer, making due allowance for elevation as already explained. They are hotter than the Malayan islands which are situated on the equator itself. The July average for India, China, and the south-east is about 80° F.

These countries have but slight range of temperature compared with the Verkhoyansk range of over 100° F. Japan has a range of 40°, China of 30°, England of 20°.

(b) Rainfall.

The rainfall of Asia is chiefly confined to the Mediterranean border and to the south-eastern part of the continent. As a consequence of the winter cold, an area of high pressure exists over central Asia (Mongolia). The outward clockwise movement of the air from this district results in north-west winds bringing rain to Japan, north winds bringing it to the Malay archipelago, and north-east winds bringing it from the Bay of Bengal to the Nilgiri Hills and Ceylon.

In summer the air over the heated continent forms a low-pressure area north of India. The air circles inwards in an anti-clockwise direction. These are the great rain-bearing winds which strike Ceylon, India, Burma, Malaysia, and the Philippines from the south-west, and China and Japan from the south-east. South-western Arabia also benefits from these summer winds.

These periodic winds are known as *Monsoons*. In India the winter winds are termed the north-east monsoons, the summer rain-bearing winds from the Indian Ocean being called the south-west monsoons. At the change of the season there are sudden storms of great violence. These are known as *Cyclones* in the Indian Ocean and *Typhoons* in the China Sea. They frequently do great damage to shipping in the harbours.

Plants and Animals.

The Arctic region of the tundras has bog-mosses, lichens, dwarf shrubs, and flowering bulbs. The surface only of the ground is thawed during the summer. The chief animals are the reindeer, arctic fox, and wild goose. The Siberian region has a forest belt of larch, birch and deciduous trees in the north, and steppe lands (with

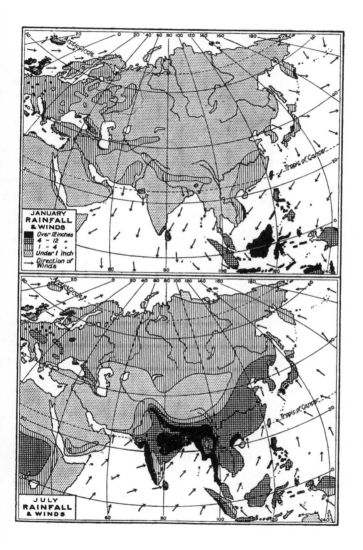

JANUARY
RAINFALL
& WINDS
Over 12 inches
4 – 12 "
1 – 4 "
Under 1 inch
→ Direction of
Winds

JULY
RAINFALL
& WINDS

pasture, and stretches of desert land) in the south and south-west. The forests harbour bears, foxes, sables, and other fur-bearing animals. Wolves are found in packs on the open plains of the steppes.

The monsoon district grows both temperate and tropical plants. Millet, wheat, rice, cotton, poppy, tea, coffee, flax, jute, and indigo are the main crops. Bamboo, coconut and other palms and teak are plentiful, both here and in Malaysia. The latter islands include camphor, sago-palm, and spices among their vegetable products. The animals of this part of Asia include the tiger, elephant, leopard, rhinoceros, crocodile, and many snakes. The silk-worm is widely cultivated.

The plateaux have but scanty vegetation and animal life. The date-palm grows in the Arabian desert and much coffee and fruit are produced in south-west Arabia near the Gulf of Aden. Sheep, goats, and horses are largely kept, and the yak is used for transport purposes across the mountain passes. The camel is the beast of burden in south-west Asia.

Minerals.

Asia is rich in minerals but as yet they are little worked. Siberia possesses a large store of both precious and useful metals in her mountains ; the development of these will accompany that of the country. Precious stones are found there as well as in Burma and Ceylon. China, India, and Japan have large coalfields, but China has scarcely touched her coal up to the present time. Malaysia has both tin and petroleum ; the latter is also found in Further India, and on the shores of the Caspian.

European enterprise and capital have been used to obtain mining concessions from Asiatic potentates. When Asia's mineral wealth has become accessible, she will come to the forefront of the continents, but now she depends almost entirely upon agricultural and pastoral pursuits.

The Peoples of Asia and their Religion.

The Malays, one of the four great Asiatic races, seem to have originated in the Malay Peninsula, and later to have peopled the neighbouring islands. On the other hand, the Mongols, Aryans, and Semites appear to have spread from the Pamirs; the Mongols to the east and north-east to occupy China, Japan, Tibet, and Further India; the Aryans to the south to people Iran and India, and a later band westwards from the Pamirs to become the inhabitants of Europe; and the Semites to the south-west to occupy Asia Minor and the plateau of Arabia. The chief religions are Mohammedanism in the south-west, Brahminism in India, Buddhism throughout the monsoon countries, Confucianism in China, and Shintoism in Japan; but the inhabitants of the northern half of the continent are mostly heathens.

The distribution of the population depends upon the character of the soil and to a great extent upon the distribution of rainfall. The northern plain, the Aralo-Caspian depression, the Kirghiz steppes, the Tibetan and Mongolian plateaux and deserts, and the Arabian interior are the most thinly peopled parts of the continent. The density here is less than one per square mile. The fertile monsoon lands present the opposite extreme; India, Cochin China, China, Japan, and the Philippines having more than sixty-four persons per square mile. These countries, especially India and China, form remarkable instances of the great supporting power of well-tilled land, when fertilised by the regularly recurring rains brought by the monsoons.

Industries and Manufactures.

The steppe dwellers are nomads, producing wool, hides and tallow from their flocks. Weaving is important in Kashmir (shawls), and in Persia and Asia Minor (rugs and carpets). Wood and ivory carving and metal filigree work are typical Indian occupations, whilst silk culture and weaving are common from India to Japan. China gave her name to better class pottery, being the home of this industry. Japan however is by far the most important manufacturing country of Asia. The slight possibility of agricultural development, and the fact that she has plentiful coal-deposits, have been two reasons for the great strides she has made recently as an industrial country. Her chief manufactures are pottery, textiles, metal goods, lacquer ware, cement, and glass.

Internal Communications.

The great length of the rivers renders them slow and well adapted for communication, especially in Siberia, China, and India, but from time immemorial well-marked caravan routes have been a means of communication. Caravan routes are well developed in Arabia, Syria, Persia, N.W. India, and across Siberia from Ekaterinburg to Vladivostok. These routes follow the easiest path and the railways are naturally being laid along them at the present time.

The Siberian railway is Russia's great military and colonising highway, and in the future will become of great commercial value. It starts at Samara on the Volga, and crossing the Urals passes Omsk, an agricultural centre, goes near to Tomsk, the university town, then through Krasnoyarsk, a mining town, to Irkutsk and Lake Baikal. It skirts the southern rim of this lake and soon enters Manchurian territory. At Harbin it branches to Vladivostok and Port Arthur. The latter terminus, together with part of the line, is now under Japanese control. Russia has also pushed her railways to Tashkent and Andijan in Turkestan, and to the frontiers of Afghanistan and Persia.

The British, urged by military as well as trade considerations, have connected all the chief Indian towns by rail ; and a railway passes up the Irawadi valley from Rangoon. China's railways are increasing. The capital, Peking, is already connected with Newchwang and Hankau, thus being placed in communication with the Manchurian line and the Yangtse-kiang valley.

Commercial Routes and Ports.

The Siberian railway gathers up wheat, tea, metals, and wood-pulp from that vast region, and the Transcaspian line forms the outlet for wool, hides, tallow, cotton, and tobacco from Turkestan, but the bulk of Asia's foreign trade is done by sea.

The main route is via Suez and the Red Sea. From the Gulf of Aden the steamship routes diverge to the Persian Gulf for wool, dates, and pearls, to Karachi for wheat, to Bombay for cotton, and to Colombo for tea, and coffee ; thence northwards to Madras, Calcutta, and Rangoon for coffee, sugar, rice, and indigo ; and eastwards to Singapore for tapioca, tin, teak, and spices.

North of Singapore numerous Chinese ports are available for tea, silk, sugar and camphor (*e.g.* Hong-Kong, Canton, Shanghai, and Tientsin), whilst the Japanese ports of Yokohama, Nagasaki, and Osaka export textiles, copper, tea, rice, and coal.

Russia in Asia.

Position and Size.

Russia in Asia occupies the northern half of the continent. It is more than forty times the size of the British Isles, its area being five million square miles. It stretches from the Urals to the Pacific, and from the Arctic Ocean to the heart of the continent. Persia, Afghanistan, and the Chinese Empire form its southern boundary, which in one place is only fifty miles from that of our Indian Empire.

Surface and General Features.

We are apt to look upon Siberia as one vast plain sloping northwards from the great southern mountain barrier, but this is only true of the western half. That part of the country lying east of the Yenesei river is mountainous, culminating in peaks of upwards of 15,000 feet in the volcanic range of Kamchatka near the Pacific. The Altai-Yablonoi range sends the great rivers Obi, Yenesei, and Lena northwards to the Arctic Ocean, the Yenesei being partly fed by the overflow from Lake Baikal—Asia's largest sheet of fresh water. These rivers are frozen for half the year, and the Amur, which forms part of the boundary between Siberia and Manchuria, has its mouth ice-blocked for fully nine months.

The Kirghiz steppes occupy the south-west portion of Siberia, and to the south of these lies the Aralo-Caspian depression, which in part is below sea level. The Turanian desert occurs here, and covers an area more than twelve times that of our islands. The only fertile parts are along the rivers, which are fed by the icy snows of the Pamirs and the Tian-shan range. The most important of these rivers flow into the Sea of Aral. They are the Syr Daria and the Amu Daria, the latter of which waters the fertile oasis of Khiva.

Transcaucasia, reckoned by the Russians as part of their European dominions, consists largely of the southern slopes of the giant Caucasus range, where several peaks exceed Mt. Blanc in height.

Climate.

The Siberian winter is so rigorous that the soil is frozen to a great depth. The absence of any great mountain barrier on the north allows the cold Arctic winds to sweep over a wide stretch of country. On the other hand, the summers are as warm as parts of central Europe lying 10° further south. Rainfall is not great, and more rain falls in summer than winter.

Central Asiatic Russia has very dry hot summers and a wide range of temperature. Turkestan has 55° range of temperature compared with Japan's 40° and Britain's 20°. The southern valleys of Transcaucasia have a warm genial climate.

Plants and Animals.

The valueless Siberian tundras give place on the south to forests of conifers. Similar forests clothe the slopes of the Altai-Yablonoi range. Between the two forest belts, and especially to the south-west, are vast grassy plains, which, by virtue of their rich black earth, must sooner or later develop into a granary similar to the Canadian plains. The southern steppes are incapable of such development ; their grazing value is already utilised by the nomad tribes. The oases in Turkestan and Khiva, and the irrigated region around the Amu Daria and Syr Daria are already producing cotton, corn, tobacco, and fruit. Beech, mulberry, and walnut trees are plentiful in Transcaucasia, where cotton, sugar, vine, and typical Mediterranean fruits are also grown.

The dog and reindeer are the Siberian beasts of burden. Large numbers of fur-bearing animals (bear, fox, marten, mink, ermine, sable) live in the forest zone. Sheep, camels, horses, goats, and cattle are bred upon the steppes and constitute the main source of wealth. The yak and camel provide means of transport in the cold and dry parts of the country respectively.

Minerals.

Transcaucasia includes silver, copper, coal, and salt among its minerals. The petroleum industry round Baku on the Caspian shore is of very great importance. Steamers and railway engines use this fuel instead of coal. Siberia's minerals are found in the Urals and along the southern mountainous border. Vast supplies of gold and silver, as well as of useful metals and graphite, lie in these mountains. Baikalia has a large coalfield as well as metallic ores, and is a most promising mining district.

The People and their History.

Mongolian races occupy the greater part of Siberia. In the steppe regions we find the nomadic pastoral Kirghiz tribes and warlike Turkomans, whilst Aryan races (Circassians, Georgians, and Armenians) live in Transcaucasia. The country is thinly populated, many parts having less than one person per square mile. Frozen tundras, parched deserts and thick forests present great barriers to human habitation, and grassy steppe lands have but little supporting power. In the near future the colonisation of Siberia along the line of the railway will lead to a great increase in population. At present, fertile Transcaucasia is the most densely peopled area.

Russia has been steadily pushing her boundaries eastwards during the last fifty years. She obtained Syr Daria, and control over Bokhara in 1868 and 1873. One year previously the Khanate of Khiva practically passed into Russian hands. Some people see in these extensions a sinister design upon India, where only the Hindu Kush range separates Russian from British territory. Without doubt it is the natural expansion of a great people towards an outlet situated upon an unfrozen open sea.

Industries, Communications, and Trade.

The silk and wine industries of Transcaucasia, and the leather and carpets of Turkestan are the only manufactures worth mentioning. The Siberian rivers are the natural highways in summer, and the fast-developing railway system will do much to bring agricultural and pastoral produce to Europe. In addition to the trans-continental line, Russia has built two railways to serve the Aralo-Caspian region. These diverge from Moscow, one passing to the north of the Sea of Aral, the other being a continuation of the Baku line east of the Caspian. This passes eastwards through Merv and thence onwards to meet the first line at Tashkent. Wool, tallow, hides, cotton, tobacco, and tea are carried westwards by these lines, which not only serve Turkestan, but are in touch with the caravan trade of the Far East via the Tian-shan mountains.

Chief Towns.

IN TRANSCAUCASIA : *Tiflis*, on the Kur river, has silk, shawl, carpet, and wine manufactures and a considerable caravan trade. *Batum* and *Baku* are Caspian ports for petroleum. *Kars* and *Vladikavkaz* are military stations.

IN TURKESTAN, ETC : *Tashkent*, the capital, has fairs and a large caravan trade in silk, cotton, carpets, precious stones, spices, and dyes. *Merv* and *Khiva* are situated in fertile oases. *Andijan* has cotton manufactures. *Samarkand* contains the tomb of the great prince Tamerlaine or Timurlane, immortalised by Marlowe.

IN SIBERIA : *Omsk* and *Tobolsk* are trading and agricultural towns on tributaries of the Obi. *Tomsk* is a university town on the Obi. *Yakutsk* on the Lena has a large trade in furs. *Irkutsk, Tchita*, and *Nerchinsk* are mining centres of increasing importance.

The Empire of Japan.

Position, Size, and Surface.

The Japanese Empire lies close to the Pacific coast of Asia, which it fringes from 50° N. latitude to the Tropic of Cancer. The principal islands are Yezo, Hondo, Shikuku, and Kiushiu, but the empire includes also the Liu-Kiu Isles, and Formosa on the south, the isthmus of Korea on the west, and the Kurile Isles and the south of the island of Sakhalin on the north. The area is about the same as that of our own islands. The islands are in general mountainous, the highest peak—Fujiyama, on Hondo—being a volcano.

Fujiyama

It is snow-capped for ten months of the year ; one may frequently see it as the background of Japanese pictures. The islands are very liable to earthquake shocks.

The coast-line is relatively long and consequently the rivers are short, rapid and not of great commercial value. The sea of Okhotsk is frozen during the winter, and the Sea of Japan to the west is not always ice-free.

Climate and Natural Productions.

When we contrast the above with the tropical climate of Formosa—Japan's most southerly island—we see that the climate is exceedingly varied. Hondo, the largest island, has a temperate climate. Tokyo, upon this island, has a winter like London and a summer like the Mediterranean. Thus Japan has a more extreme climate than we have, but this does not apply to the sub-tropical isle of Formosa, which has its days almost always of equal length and a small range of temperature (20°) in consequence. A warm current of the Pacific—the Kuro Siwo—washes the south-eastern shore of the archipelago and tempers its climate as it passes northward to Kamchatka. Both summer and winter monsoons bring rain to the country from the Pacific and the Sea of Japan respectively. Typhoons do great damage to property and shipping towards the end of summer and are specially formidable in the Formosa Channel.

One-third of the land is covered with forests, the chief trees being the lacquer tree, camphor laurel, paper, mulberry, wax tree, sago-palm, as well as the pine, cedar, maple and others familiar to us. The bamboo, a gigantic grass, grows freely and is utilised in innumerable ways. Tea plantations occupy the slopes in the south.

Only one-eighth of the land is capable of cultivation, but this is done most thoroughly by spade work, so that good crops of wheat, rice, millet, tobacco, cotton, and indigo are obtained. Japan can never be a great agricultural country by reason of its mountainous surface. There is very little pastoral industry, for the people are but slight flesh-eaters. They obtain large supplies of cod and shell-fish from the neighbouring seas, whilst the rivers abound in salmon and trout.

Japan is singularly rich in coal, iron, sulphur, and copper. She exports coal as far as Bombay. Sakhalin, Yezo, and Kiushiu have the most important coalfields. Precious metals are also found in the empire.

Tea and rice fields, Japan

The People and their History.

The Japanese are a Mongolian race, and, like the Chinese, long resisted any intercourse with western nations. They abolished their feudal system in 1871, and for the last forty years have eagerly embraced Western ideas, so that to-day they constitute the 'great power' of Asia. Formosa entered the empire after the struggle with China in 1895. The protectorate of Korea followed the war with Russia in 1905, and its annexation was completed in 1910.

The towns and people present a curious mixture of 'east' and 'west.' The people retain their ancient religions, Buddhism and Shintoism—the worship of ancestors.

The population, of which three-fourths live upon Hondo, is about the same as that of Great Britain.

Industries and Communications.

Japan is rapidly developing her manufactures upon Western lines. She has coal and iron, together with the humid atmosphere suitable for cotton spinning. Other manufactures are lacquer ware, silk goods, paper, glass, cement, porcelain and bronze. As a land where labour is cheap she has long been famous for small articles of artistic merit.

All her lowland towns are connected by railway. The Korean line terminates at the seaport of Fusan. Land journeys for short distances or through hilly country are performed either in jinrikishas or chairs. Flat-bottomed boats are used for coasting purposes and for lower river traffic.

Commerce and Ports.

The commerce reaches an annual value of £86,000,000. This is four times the value of trade twenty years ago. Raw silk, silk goods, copper, cotton yarn, coal, tea, and matches are the chief exports. Japan imports raw cotton, iron and steel, engines and boilers, rice, sugar, and petroleum. Osaka, Yokohama, Kobe, and Nagasaki are busy seaports open to foreigners.

Administration and Towns.

Before 1889 the country was an absolute monarchy with the Mikado as its head. Now it has a constitution, the monarch being assisted in the government by two houses of parliament.

Tokyo, the capital, has a university and manufactures blankets, silk goods, and lacquer ware. Its port is *Yokohama*, seventeen miles distant. *Osaka* is a city of canals, with shipbuilding and cotton industries. It is the centre of the tea district. *Kyoto* makes bronzes and porcelain, as does *Nagasaki*, a centre for wood and ivory carving. *Tamsui, Keelung*, and *Tainan* export camphor and tea from Formosa.

The Chinese Empire.

Position, Size, and Surface.

The Chinese Empire is roughly triangular in shape, being wedged in between Siberia on the north, British Asia and Annam on the south, and the Pacific on the east. It includes Manchuria, Mongolia, Chinese Turkestan, and Tibet, as well as China proper, thus forming a vast realm, thirty-five times as large as the British Isles. In latitude it stretches from 50° N. to the Tropic of Cancer.

On the north and west lie the plateaux of Mongolia, Turkestan, and Tibet, with the vast desert of Gobi and the Tarim system of internal drainage. The fertile Manchurian plain lies near the sea in the north-east and to the south of it is another plain—that of the Hoang-ho—of incredible productiveness. The Hoang-ho plain is covered with porous, yellowish earth called *loess*, which is exceedingly fertile when properly irrigated. The Hoang-ho is too fast and shallow a stream for commerce, thus being a contrast to China's longest river, the Yang-tse-kiang, which is navigable for 1000 miles. Both rivers are subject to sudden changes of level and disastrous floods often occur.

The Pe-ling range separates the plains of these two rivers, and the parallel Nan-ling range in the south marks off the basin of the Si-kiang, the third great river of China. This river flows through the hottest, moistest part of the country (*i.e.* the chief tea-producing district).

Climate and Natural Productions.

China is a typical monsoon country, but the summer monsoon wind blows from the south and so the south-eastern part (*i.e.* China proper) receives most rain. The Si-kiang valley has more than 70″ rainfall annually, the Hoang-ho plain 25″ and the table-lands of the interior only 10″. The temperature is tropical only in the south, although the whole country has an average July temperature of over 80° F. The coastal region is the most equable, extreme climates being experienced in the north and west of the country.

Agriculture is the all-important industry and is practised with extreme care, although with primitive implements The cereals grown include wheat, maize, millet, and rice. Rice is grown along the Yang-tse-kiang plain, and in the damp south-east, where plenty of water is available for its germination. The hill slopes are irrigated by manual and bullock labour, and tea and mulberry shrubs cover many miles. Tobacco, cotton and sugar are also widely grown. The province of Yunnan is the chief seat of opium culture.

Sheep and goats are bred in the thinly-peopled provinces of the interior, but the pastoral industry is unimportant in China itself. The larger wild animals —the bear, elephant, tiger, leopard, and rhinoceros— inhabit the interior provinces. The Chinese are skilful fishermen. They use the cormorant to help them in their river fishery.

The northern mountains have many metallic ores, and vast coalfields occur, especially in the provinces of Shan-si and Szechuan. China clay and salt have been mined in China for centuries.

The People and their History.

The Chinese are Mongols, and reached a high state of civilisation several centuries before the Christian era. They spread eastwards along the parallel valleys of the Chinese rivers, and have peopled these fertile regions with a dense population. Until 1911 political

power was entirely in the hands of the Manchus, the
nomad Mongols who conquered the empire and assimi-
lated its civilisation in the 17th century.   China proper
has the enormous population of 400 to the square mile,
whereas the western part of the empire has a density
of less than 10.

Silkworms feeding on mulberry leaves

It is estimated that in China there are at least 100
towns with more than 100,000 inhabitants.   The people
are hardworking, frugal, and conservative.   They dislike
foreigners, but have in recent years opened over thirty

ports to foreign ships. Hongkong was ceded to the British in 1842. Confucianism is the state religion, but there are also many Buddhists and Mohammedans.

Manufactures, Communications, and Commerce.

Porcelain and paper-making have been Chinese arts for long ages. The cultivation and weaving of silk is another of her old industries, and Nankin gave her name to 'nankeen' cotton goods. With the above exceptions there are no manufactures of any importance.

Internal communication by road is bad. The great rivers are the natural highways for traffic, and in Turkestan practically all the trade is done by caravan— Kashgar and Yarkand being the chief centres. China possesses about 4000 miles of railway. Peking is connected by rail with Port Arthur, Nankin, Shanghai, Canton, and Yunnan. French and British railways connect Yunnan with Mandalay and Tongking. The Chinese telegraph system is well developed.

Commerce has an annual value of over £89,000,000 ; the chief exports are silk and silk goods, tea, beans, cotton, hides, and straw braid ; and the imports cotton goods, opium, rice, sugar, oil, and metals. Hongkong, Shanghai, Canton, Tien-tsin, Fuchow, and Amoy are important ports.

Administration and Towns.

The Emperor is an absolute monarch. He appoints governors or viceroys to the various provinces, who are responsible for collection of the revenues.

China however is now following the lead of Japan in embracing Western ideas. In 1911 a great revolution was successfully organised against the Manchu dynasty and the future development of China is of the first importance to the civilised world.

Peking is the capital. *Shanghai* has cotton and woollen mills. *Canton* has an enormous river population. *Hankow* and *Nankin* are centres of cotton and silk industries, and *Fuchow* of tea cultivation.

South-Eastern Asia.

Position, Size, and Surface.

South-eastern Asia lies wholly within the Tropics. It consists of (*a*) the peninsular portion occupied by Annam, Siam and Lower Burma, and ending at the equator in the long narrow Malay Peninsula; and (*b*) the numerous islands to the east and south. These include the Philippines, Moluccas, and Sundas. This is a region of wide extent; for example, Sumatra and Borneo are each as large as the British Isles, and Java is as large as England.

The surface in general is mountainous, sloping to the sea where the lowland coastal plains are frequently swampy. A mountainous backbone traverses the whole length of the Malay Peninsula and the islands of Sumatra, Java, and Borneo. Mt. Ophir in Sumatra is nearly 10,000 feet in height, and Kinabalu in Borneo is 13,698 feet. This is a region of great volcanic and earthquake activity. The volcanic island of Krakatau in Sunda Strait, between Sumatra and Java, was half blown away in a terrible eruption in 1883. Many of the islands owe their great fertility to their volcanic soils.

The peninsular region is well watered by the Irawadi (which is navigable to Bhamo—a distance of 900 miles), the Mekong, and the Menam ('Mother of Waters').

Climate and Natural Productions.

The temperature is tropical but equable. The mean annual temperature is 80° F., yet the range of temperature is only about 5° F. This remarkable result is due to the low latitude, whereby the sun shines nearly vertically for almost equal times each day in the year, and to the great rainfall brought by both monsoons. This region is one of the wettest in Asia. The summer monsoons bring most rain, for they have traversed a greater stretch of water. Typhoons are prevalent in the China Sea, especially at Manila harbour, but do not reach the Southern Philippines.

Altitude has here a great influence on climate : regions with an elevation of more than 4000 ft. have a cool climate, whilst those below 2000 ft. are purely tropical. These conditions have a great effect upon the character of the vegetable productions. The slopes are peculiarly suited to the growth of tea, a plant requiring a well-drained soil, but also frequent moisture. The wet, hot lowlands are great rice-producing regions. The tropical forests supply teak, ebony, camphor, india-rubber, pepper, cinchona, and cacao. Many varieties of palms flourish here, including the sago and coconut palm. Other products include cloves, nutmegs and their surrounding mace, cinnamon, tobacco, cotton, indigo and coffee. The growth of vegetation is exceedingly rapid owing to the favourable conditions of moisture and temperature. The tropical forests are extremely luxuriant and in many places impenetrable, and the chief agricultural difficulty consists in keeping the plantations clear of rank growths.

Both peninsula and islands are singularly rich in animal life. 'Wallace's Line,' passing through the Strait of Makassar and between the islands of Bali and Lombok, separates the islands having Asiatic and Australasian forms of life respectively. The larger wild animals of Asia are found to the west, whilst marsupials, including the kangaroo, inhabit the islands east of that line.

The seas are rich in fish, many of which are of remarkable form and extraordinarily brilliant colour. Java has anchovy fisheries, and fishing for pearls is a well-established industry throughout Malaysia.

Great variety of minerals occurs both in the peninsula and archipelago. Tin is the most important mineral, and its production has affected the Cornish mining industry. Coal is widely found, and precious metals and stones are obtained in Indo-China.

The People, Manufactures, and Trade.

The Malays, a brown race, people the islands and the southern part of the peninsula, but mixed with these are darker, more primitive tribes, and settlers from China and India. Mongol races inhabit the broader northern part of the peninsula, which may be considered as an extension of the Chinese territory. Buddhism is common throughout Indo-China, but in the islands there are many Mohammedan and heathen tribes.

The native industries, in addition to mining, agricultural and forest pursuits, comprise the carving of wood, ivory and metal, and are only of local importance. Communication is mainly by water by means of junks. The Dutch have built a network of railways from end to end of Java. A French line proceeds from Hanoi northwards to Yunnan, and an English one similarly from Mandalay. Siam has railway communication between Bangkok and the forested mountains. The chief exports are the vegetable and mineral productions mentioned in the preceding section. Singapore, Hongkong, Manila, Bangkok, and Batavia have the bulk of the export trade, and Hongkong is one of the great ports of the world.

Administration.

Apart from the native despotic kingdom of Siam, the district is possessed by the British, French, Dutch, Portuguese, and Americans. Britain occupies much of the western and southern parts of the peninsula, the island of Singapore, and the northern portion of Borneo. France has the eastern border of the peninsula, including the lower plain and delta-lands of the Mekong river. The Philippines passed into the hands of the United States in 1898 after a native revolt against the Spaniards. The Dutch (always a great trading nation) possess practically the whole archipelago. Their export trade from Batavia makes Rotterdam one of the world's coffee ports.

India.

Position, Size, and Surface.

Our Indian Empire occupies the central southern peninsula of Asia. It is twelve times the size of the British Isles and stretches from the 37th parallel of north latitude to within 6° of the Equator; about half the country lies in the torrid zone.

We may divide its surface into three regions: (i) the Himalayas, (ii) the great northern plain, and (iii) the Dekkan table-land. The Himalayas form the great northern mountain barrier stretching more than 1000 miles, with peaks raising their snow-clad summits nearly 30,000 ft. above sea-level. Caravans take more than 60 days to cross the range from north to south. Its lower slopes are covered with forests, and the fever-laden *Terai* jungle forms an almost impenetrable marshy barrier to the south of the range. The great lowland plain of the Indus and Ganges stretches across the country from sea to sea. Its alluvial soil is carefully irrigated, and forms the most densely populated area of India. The Indus runs on the northern slope of the Himalayas. It turns to the south in the mountainous country of Kashmir, and after draining the Panjab by its tributaries, flows to the west of the Rajputana desert, and reaches the Arabian Sea by numerous mouths.

The Ganges receives practically the whole drainage of the southern Himalayan slope. On its right bank it has as tributaries the Jumna (enclosing the fertile Doab region) and the Son, which flows through India's richest coalfield. The Ganges joins with the Bramaputra in building up a large delta at the head of the Bay of Bengal. This district, the Sandarbans, covers an area of several thousand square miles, and is covered with swampy malaria-breeding jungle. The principal mouth of the Ganges is called the Hugli. Each of the three rivers, the Ganges, Indus, and Bramaputra, has a length of more than 1500 miles.

The triangular plateau of the Dekkan lies to the south of the plain of the Indus and Ganges. The Vindhya Mountains form its northern edge, whilst the Eastern and Western Ghats bound it along the coast and meet in the Nilgiri Hills of Maisur. The plateau is a crust-block, the north-west part of which is a lava sheet. Indeed, much of the soil of the Dekkan is volcanic in nature, and is very fertile when properly irrigated. The western rim of this plateau is the higher, so that most of the rivers (Mahanadi, Godavari, Kistna, etc.) flow eastwards.

The Narbada and Tapti, however, take an opposite course, flowing westwards at the northern edge of the plateau. Speaking generally, the Dekkan rivers are difficult to navigate. The majority of them form deltas upon the eastern coastal plain, which is of a greater width than that along the west coast. The surf beats very heavily upon the eastern shore. The mountainous wooded island of Ceylon lies to the south. It is separated from the mainland by Palk Strait, which is only navigable by small vessels. The area of the island is about that of Ireland.

Climate and Rainfall.

India, from its latitude, has naturally a hot climate; and, owing to their great height, the Himalayas present all gradations from tropical to Arctic climates. In January the isotherms follow the lines of latitude, the northern plain having a temperature of 55° to 65° F., *i.e.* about equal to our July temperature, whilst the Dekkan plateau has from 70° to 80° F., a temperature equal to that of South Europe in summer. These figures will explain why wheat can ripen in India in winter.

The July isotherms do not correspond with the lines of latitude. The north-west part of the country is the hottest during that month, having a temperature of over 90°. This district includes the Rajputana desert and much of the Indus valley. The west coast is at this time the coolest region, having an average temperature of less than 80° F. This is largely due to the ameliorating action of the south-west monsoon. The coasts and the south of India have more equable temperatures than the plains, and in summer the eastern part of the Ganges plain is cooler than the western. Kandy in Ceylon has only a range of 5° whilst Sind and Peshawar in the north-west have a range of 40°.

These ranges of temperature are partly dependent on the amount of rainfall and its seasonal distribution, and the rain is brought by the periodic winds or monsoons, the causes of which have been dealt with previously. India's rainy season is from June to October, when the south-west monsoon strikes the country from the Arabian Sea. The Western Ghats cause much rain along the western coast, which during the year receives 200″ rainfall.

Very heavy rainfall is also experienced in the northeast of the country, Upper Bengal and Assam having a greater rainfall than any other country outside the tropics. Much rain falls throughout the country at this season, but it should be noted that the Indus valley benefits least from the south-west monsoon. During the cool months, November to February, the north-east monsoon brings rain to the eastern coast, South Dekkan and Ceylon. This wind gathers moisture in its passage over the Bay of Bengal. North-west India again receives but slight benefit from the monsoon. The annual rainfall of Sind is only 10″.

Natural Productions.

The extensive forests are under the control of the Indian government, and yield teak, ebony, and sandalwood. Coconuts, bananas, and other fruits are produced in abundance. The great variety of cultivated plants is dealt with below.

The forests and swampy jungles are the haunts of large fierce animals, including the elephant, rhinoceros, lion, leopard, tiger, and hyena. Poisonous snakes and other reptiles are common pests. The birds of India are very numerous and brightly coloured. Cattle and sheep are bred on the Dekkan uplands for their flesh,

Drying cacao, Ceylon

wool, and hides. The elephant, ox, yak, mule, and camel are used as beasts of burden. The bullock is in general use for ploughing and draught purposes.

The pearl fishery is an important industry in Palk Strait. Over six million tons of coal are raised from Indian mines yearly. The two chief coalfields lie in the Narbada and Son valleys. Iron, copper, gold, diamonds, and salt are also found in the peninsula, but the last-named mineral is mostly obtained from the Salt Hills of the north-west.

Agriculture.

Agriculture, which directly occupies three-fourths of the people, is the most important industry in the country, and the greatest care is bestowed upon it. It has been estimated that there are more than 30,000 miles of canals for purposes of irrigation. The failure of a crop means famine to millions of people. The scarcity of rain in the Indus basin, and the uncertainty of its extent in that of the Ganges, make irrigation absolutely necessary. It is necessary also in the rich but thirsty soil of the Dekkan. Tea plantations occupy the moist slopes in Assam and Ceylon. The Nilgiris and Ceylon produce also much coffee. Wheat is grown in the dry Indus basin and in the northern Dekkan. Opium and cotton form the chief crops in the Ganges plain, rice and jute being produced in the delta of that river. Rice is also generally grown along the eastern coast plain. Indigo, millet, hemp, pulse, sugar, and oil seeds are widely produced in the peninsula. Usually two crops are grown yearly, the times of sowing being about the end of June and September.

The People and their History.

The Aryan peoples who invaded India from the table-lands of the north-west drove the original inhabitants—a darker skinned race called the Dravidians—to the less hospitable lands of the Dekkan, reserving for themselves the fertile plain of the Ganges, which is now one of the most thickly peopled parts of the country. This plain and the plains of the coast have a population of more than 300 to the square mile. The Dekkan table-land is less thickly peopled, whilst the region with the scantiest population is the dry plain of the lower Indus. About three-fourths of the people profess the Brahmin religion and one-fifth are Mohammedans.

Our connection with India commenced in 1600 when Elizabeth granted a charter to the East India Company, which by the end of the century had founded about half a dozen trading stations upon the coast. French intrigue caused the 'Black Hole' incident of 1756. Clive's work in reforming the Company's abuses led to great increase of territory, and by 1817 Britain controlled, roughly, all India south of the Ganges. The Crown took over the affairs of the Company in 1858. At present, a large part of India is in the hands of feudatory princes. The strategical importance of Baluchistan has led to its recently becoming a British state, thus forming a buffer to the south of Afghanistan. The 'outposts of empire' are Gilgit, Peshawar, Quetta, and Chitral in the north-west, these being points near the Afghanistan border and the sphere of Russian influence.

Manufactures, Communications, and Commerce.

The native manufactures are relatively unimportant. The province of Bengal has most manufactures, including wool and silk goods, carpets, muslins, carved wood, and metal wares.

The natural highway of the northern plain is the Ganges and its tributaries. The British have developed a good system of railways, especially in the north. A main line leads from Calcutta to Peshawar in the extreme north. Another proceeds from Karachi up the Indus valley (with a branch westwards up the Bolan Pass to Quetta) to meet the north-western system at Lahore. Bombay is connected by radiating lines with Allahabad, Calcutta, Masulipatam, Madras, and Goa. These lines are not only useful from the commercial and military, but also from the humanitarian point of view, being a means of rapid distribution of food in times of famine.

Commerce has an annual value of more than £200,000,000. India exports raw cotton and jute, jute goods, rice, hides, seeds, cotton goods, tea, opium, wool, lac, wheat, and dyes. Cotton goods form one-fourth of her imports, the other great imports being hardware, sugar, railway-plant, machinery, oils, silk and woollen goods. Most of the trade is done through Calcutta and Bombay. Other ports are Madras, Karachi, Surat, and Calicut. The overland (*i.e.* caravan) trade is valued at £9,000,000 yearly.

Delhi : The Palace and Lahore Gate

Administration, Divisions, and Towns.

British India is governed by a Viceroy, or Governor-General, assisted by a legislative council. He acts in conjunction with the Secretary of State for India, who is the head of the India Office in London. The various provinces are entrusted to governors and lieutenant-governors, some of whom have councils to help them in provincial affairs. Each native prince has an official British *Resident* at his court, who safeguards British interests.

Delhi, the historic city which became the capital of British India in 1911, is an important railway centre.

Calcutta, the former capital, on the Hugli, has jute, cotton, and iron works. *Bombay*, upon an island on the west coast, is a great cotton and corn port, with cotton factories and dye works. *Madras*, on the surf-beaten Coromandel Coast, exports cotton, coffee, and sugar. *Karachi* is a wheat port on the Indus delta. *Patna*, on the Ganges, is a great centre for cereals, opium, and indigo. *Lucknow* has gold and silver manufactures. *Benares*, a holy city on the Ganges, has bronze and shawl industries. *Cawnpore*, the scene of the massacre in 1857, makes cotton goods and leather. *Allahabad* has a large trade in cotton and corn. *Nagpur* is the capital of the Central Provinces. *Amritsar* has fairs and caravan trade. *Rangoon* exports rice and teak from Burma.

Afghanistan.

Size, Position, and Surface.

The wild, little-known country of Afghanistan occupies the north-east portion of the Iranian plateau. It exceeds the British Isles in area, and is enclosed by Russian territory on the north, Persian on the west, and British on the east and south. The Hindu Kush and Sulaiman Mountains form its eastern bulwark. North and south of the latter range are the Khaibar and Bolan passes, by which the country can be entered from India.

Afghanistan is largely a mountainous desert. It has no navigable rivers. The rivers it possesses, with the exception of the Kabul river which flows eastwards to the Indus, either dwindle and lose themselves in the sands, or drain south-westwards to the salt marshy lake

The Khaibar Pass

D.

13

Seistan—one of Asia's numerous systems of internal drainage, and, like the others, associated with the barren interior of a dry plateau.

Climate and Natural Productions.

The climate is extreme and the summers are the hottest experienced on the continent. Since the country is hemmed in by lofty mountains, the interior is extremely dry. There are but few fertile valleys. One of the chief of these is in the north-west, around the town of Herat. In these valleys, cereal crops of wheat and barley, pulse, and a great variety of fruits (including the date and the grape) are raised. The hill pastures are utilised for sheep, goat, and horse breeding. The more favoured regions produce two crops yearly, the times of sowing being spring and autumn; much of the agricultural work is done by slave labour.

The People and their History.

The Afghans, who number less than the population of London, are, in some parts, a peaceful, agricultural, and pastoral race, and in others fierce, warlike tribes, cunning and cruel beyond other Asiatics. During the past half-century they have been the scourge of north-west India, delighting in plunder and warfare. They include the Pathans, Afridis, and hill tribes, and some of our best blood has been spent on their frontiers. Lord Roberts occupied Kandahar, the key of India, with a British force in 1880.

Owing to the mountainous nature of the country the tribes are very numerous. Practically each village forms a separate clan. There is little cohesion among the different tribes, some of whom openly defy the Amir, their nominal ruler.

Industries, Trade, and Towns.

Silk, felt, and carpet goods, and *postins* or sheep-skin overcoats, are the only manufactures. Trade is done by camel and pony caravans with Bokhara on the north, India on the east and Persia on the west.

Communication is very bad, there being no wheeled traffic in the country, although good roads run through the eastern passes.

The government of Afghanistan is a typically oriental, oppressive, and exacting despotism. The Amir, according to a recent understanding between Russia and Britain, at which the frontiers of the country were agreed upon, is now not to be interfered with by either of the two countries in his government of the land. The chief towns are *Kandahar, Kabul,* and *Herat,* the latter being quite near to *Kushk,* the terminus of the Russian railway on the north.

Persia.

Position, Size, and Surface.

Persia differs from Afghanistan by possessing a coast, for it has the Caspian Sea upon the north, and the Persian Gulf and Arabian Sea on the south. It is five times as large as the British Isles, and extends from Asiatic Turkey on the west to Afghanistan and British Baluchistan on the east.

It resembles Afghanistan in possessing a mountainous border and inland drainage systems of dwindling rivers. The Elburz range, with Demavend as its highest peak, fringes the southern Caspian shore. Parallel ranges of mountains (the Zagros and Koh-rud) cross the country in a south-easterly direction and nearly all the towns lie in the fertile valleys enclosed by such ranges. Fully one-third of the country is covered by a vast salt desert.

Climate and Natural Productions.

The climate, as a result of the build of the country, strongly recalls that of Afghanistan. The mountainous regions have exceedingly cold winters, whilst the summer heat of the interior is unbearable. The rainfall in the north-east is as low as 5″ annually, but the whole country has a scanty fall, less than 14″ per annum.

Moist winds from the Caspian give to the narrow coastal plain the highest rainfall, and the northerly Elburz slopes are pleasantly cool in summer. The south-west of the country benefits slightly by the south-west monsoon, rain-winds travelling north-east from the Persian Gulf.

The scanty rainfall frequently leads to drought and famine, and agriculture is only practised in the irrigated valleys. Unfortunately irrigation is much less used now than it was in the palmy days of the old Persian Empire, when the naturally fertile soil was cultivated to a high degree of productiveness. Wheat is grown in the Ispahan valley, and the opium poppy, tobacco, vine, and rose are the other plants receiving most attention.

The hilly pastures and half-desert plains are used for flocks of sheep and goats. The only large wild animal is the Persian tiger, which roams in the Elburz district. Coal and a variety of metals are found in the north and west. Persia has also supplies of petroleum similar to those of Transcaucasia.

The People and their History.

The Persians are an Aryan race who spread south-westwards from the Pamirs. They were originally fire-worshippers, but now Mohammedanism is the prevailing religion. They are instinctively polite, fond of flattery, and very ceremonious. Their ancient empire stretched from the Aegean Sea to the Indus, but it has dwindled continuously to its present dimensions. The Afghans revolted from Persian rule in the 18th century. The Russians to-day exert great influence over Persia, for their territories touch one another both on the north and north-west. By agreement with Britain, Russian influence is now limited to the northern part of the country, and British to the east, near Afghanistan and Baluchistan.

The population, which numbers about 10,000,000, is mainly found in the fertile valleys of the north and south-west.

Industries, Communications, and Trade.

Persian woven goods (silks, rugs, carpets, and shawls) have been famous from earliest times, and found their way to Europe by caravan. Besides these, there are the manufactures of inlaid swords and metal goods, ornamental pottery, and the famous attar of roses. The bulk of the trade is done by mule caravans. Roads are practically absent and there is no wheeled traffic. Russia is steadily pressing for railway connection with a port on the Persian Gulf. Her railways are already on the Persian border south of Tiflis and near *Meshed*, and a line is now under construction from Baku along the coastal plain of the Caspian to the town of *Resht*.

Administration and Towns.

The Shah was a despotic monarch until 1905, when a single legislative chamber was instituted. Since that date a second 'house' has been formed, but the work of the new parliament has been much hampered by the monarch's attempts to resume his former absolute power. Persia is in a period of transition. Modernising Western influences are at work and doubtless the future will see great changes and improvements in the condition of the country and of the lower classes.

Teheran is the capital. *Kerman* and *Yezd* have weaving industries.

Turkey in Asia.

Turkey in Asia includes Asia Minor and the lands to the south. It receives more rain than the Iranian plateau lying to the east, for winds blow southwards from the Black Sea in winter and eastwards from the Mediterranean in summer. The country is mountainous and mainly pastoral, sheep and goats being the chief animals kept. If irrigation were practised, the land would be very fertile, but the present Turkish misrule causes neglect of both agricultural and mineral wealth.

Wheat is grown near the source of the Halys river, and Mediterranean fruits, tobacco and cotton are exported from Smyrna on the Aegean coast. The chalky ranges of Palestine have forests of oak, sycamore and cedar. *Beirut*, connected by rail with the important caravan centre *Damascus*, and *Jaffa*, which exports silk, oranges, and tobacco, are the chief outlets of Syria.

East of the Syrian desert lies the district of Mesopotamia, once phenomenally fertile and the centre of a great empire, now producing only dates and hardy Bedouin horses. *Basra*, lying among the swampy lands near the head of the Persian Gulf, is the sea outlet for this district.

Arabia.

Arabia, the waterless land, consists of a great desert table-land twelve times the area of the British Isles. In the hot interior rain falls about once in two years. The south-western province of Yemen is the only part possessing perennial streams. Coffee, cotton, and fruits are grown here and exported from *Mocha*. Camels, horses and mules are the chief domesticated animals. There is a great variety of wild animals in the scantily peopled districts. The towns of *Mecca* and *Medina*, the latter being connected by rail with *Aleppo* in Asia Minor, are the great resorts of pious Mohammedans, for these towns have the birthplace and the tomb of the Prophet.

CHAPTER VI

AFRICA

Position and Size.

Africa forms the south-western portion of the largest land-mass of the world. It is separated from Asia by the submerged rift of the Red Sea, and the narrow Isthmus of Suez is its only attachment to that continent. The land-locked Mediterranean separates it on the north from Europe, a continent which it almost joins at Cape Ceuta.

In point of size Africa is intermediate between Europe and Asia. It is three times as large as Europe, but only two-thirds the size of Asia. It extends from 37° north to 35° south latitude, so that fully three-quarters of its surface lies within the Torrid Zone ; consequently it is the hottest of the continents. From Cairo to Cape Town is about 5700 miles, and the extreme width is almost the same distance.

Surface and General Features.

Africa is a very compact continent, and apart from the fact that its southern half is much narrower than the northern, there is very little irregularity in shape. The regularity in build is equally remarkable. If a line were drawn from Cape Negro on the west coast to Suakin on the Red Sea, we should find that it would approximately divide the continent into a north-western region of low elevation, and a south-eastern region having an elevation of more than 3000 feet. Of course this would not be strictly true, for some portions in each region would be exceptional.

In the north-west of the continent are the Atlas Mountains which run from the Atlantic seaboard to a point opposite Sicily. Although their average elevation is about 6000 feet, they attain double that height in Morocco, and become a broad plateau in Tunis.

South of the Atlas is the vast Sahara Desert, which extends from the Atlantic almost to the Nile and has an area as large as Europe. It is an immense sandy waste, devoid of rain and with scarcely any vegetation. Although of generally low elevation, its central region is higher than other parts.

The remainder of Africa consists of extensive plateaux, which reach so near the sea that only a narrow coastal plain is found. The Kameruns (height 13,000 feet) form the edge of the plateau at the Bight of Biafra, and all along the eastern side of the continent is another rim of the plateau. Many parts of this rim are of greater elevation than the Kameruns :—the snow-clad peaks of Abyssinia reach a height of 15,000 feet and Kilima Njaro, Kenia, and Margherita—situated in the lake district of the plateau—are higher still, and are snow-clad even though situated on the Equator. Lying just north of the Tropic of Capricorn is the Kalahari Desert, itself a portion of the plateau. From it successive terraces (the high veld, great Karroo and little Karroo) descend to the narrow coast plain of the south, where the Drakensberg, Zwarteberg, and Lange-berg Mountains form successive escarpments.

Rivers and Lakes.

To the plateau formations of Africa are due the tortuous courses and unnavigable nature of the rivers, the numerous lakes, and the systems of internal drainage so characteristic of the continent. The rivers in many cases flow round the rims of the plateaux and cannot take the shortest way to the sea. Where they break through, they have deep falls which impede navigation,

The Victoria Falls on the Zambesi

and this is the greater drawback to trade, because as a result of the build of the continent, these falls occur comparatively near the sea.

The *Nile* owes its unfailing water supply to the equatorial rains which feed the great lakes Victoria and Albert Nyanza, but it obtains its greatly increased volume in flood time from the increased rainfall in the North Torrid Zone during our summer months. The Blue Nile joins it at Khartum and the Atbara at Berber, both these tributaries draining the well-watered Abyssinian mountains. There are six cataracts between Khartum and Aswan, and the river has been dammed at Aswan and Asiut in order to regulate the amount of water available for irrigation. The Nile enters the Mediterranean by many mouths.

The *Niger* rises relatively near the sea on the northern side of the Kong Mountains, but it flows north-east into the heart of the Sudan, passing the town of Timbuktu, before it is deflected southwards by the rim of the plateau. It reaches the Atlantic at the Bight of Benin, where it forms a marshy, fever-stricken delta covered with dense mangrove woods.

The *Congo* follows an equally tortuous course. It receives the waters of lakes Bangweolo, Mweru, and Tanganyika, has numerous falls in its passage to successively lower portions of the plateau, and enters the Atlantic near Boma. It forms no delta, recalling the Amazon in this respect. Like that river, its waters can be recognised far out at sea. The *Zambesi* and *Limpopo* flow eastwards from the plateau, and the *Orange* river flows westwards. These are the chief rivers draining the southern half of the plateau.

Inland systems of drainage occur in connection with the *shotts* of the Atlas region, lake *Ngami* on the fringe of the Kalahari desert and lake *Chad* in the Sudan. All these lakes are salt, there being no overflow.

Coast.

The regularity of the coast-line has already been mentioned. The Azores and Madeira Islands belong to Portugal, and the Canaries to Spain. These islands, in the main, offer, by their fertility, a strong contrast to the barren desert coast of the mainland, for the Sahara reaches quite to the Atlantic. Cape Verde is the most westerly point of the continent. South of this cape the coast curves to the east, where the Gulf of Guinea forms a large inlet. Marshy unhealthy shores characterise this gulf and its bights (or bays) of Benin and Biafra. The island of Fernando Po is a partially submerged peak of the Kamerun Mountains. The oceanic islands of Ascension and St Helena lie far in mid-ocean. They arise from a ridge which runs roughly from north to south in the Atlantic.

Good harbours are rare upon the African coast, and although Cape of Good Hope has more than 1000 miles of coast-line, she has no really good harbour. Table Bay has been improved by the building of a breakwater. Cape Agulhas is the most southerly point of the continent. Delagoa Bay is the best natural harbour.

The eastern coast of Africa is bolder than the western. The wide Mozambique Channel separates Madagascar (the third largest island in the world) from the mainland. This island has a mountainous centre, descending to the sea in terraces. The Seychelles, Mauritius, and Zanzibar islands all belong to Britain. Cape Guardafui, lying at the head of the Somali peninsula, is the most easterly point of Africa. The Red Sea is reached from the Gulf of Aden through the narrow Strait of Bab-el-Mandeb. Communication with the Mediterranean is made at its northern end by the Suez Canal. The north coast of Africa is low around the Nile delta, but rocky in Tunis, where Cape Blanco projects furthest in the Mediterranean.

Climate and Rainfall.

Africa possesses a very hot climate, since three-fourths of it lie within the Tropics. It is the hottest of all the continents, and, owing to its compact shape, the reduced isotherms have a very regular arrangement. In January, when the sun is over the Tropic of Capricorn, the isotherms in the broader part of the continent range from 50° F. on the Mediterranean coast to 85° F. near the Equator, and follow the latitude parallels very closely. In the narrower portion (which lies in the South Torrid Zone and consequently has the greatest effect of the sun's rays during this season) the interior is the hottest region and experiences a temperature of 90° F., whilst from this heated region to the western and southern coasts there is a decrease to 70° and 65° respectively. The western and south-western coasts are cooler than the eastern, this being partly due to the cold ocean current which flows northwards along the western shore.

Temperature conditions are reversed in July : the Cape experiences a temperature similar to that of the Mediterranean in January; isotherms in the southern half of the continent range from 55° in the south to 80° along the Equator, and run approximately parallel to one another in a south-easterly direction ; whilst the interior of the Sahara forms the heated land-area with a temperature of over 90° F. At this time the Arabian and Iranian plateaux are also experiencing a similar temperature.

From the above we see that the equatorial region, although hot, enjoys an equable climate and this is largely due to the heavy rains which fall throughout the year. These 'convectional rains,' as they are called, are due to the rise of heated moist air and the condensation of its moisture when it reaches a cooler layer of the atmosphere. Owing to the sun's rays having an almost equal power all through the year

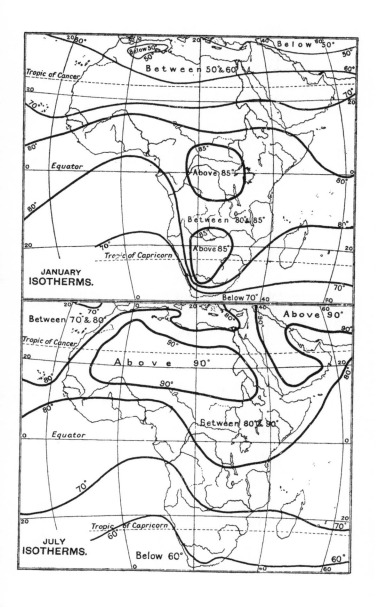

Tropic of Cancer

B e t w e e n   5 0   &   6 0

Below 50

Between 50 & 60

Below 60

Equator

Above 85°

Between 80 & 85°

Above 85°

Tropic of Capricorn

JANUARY
ISOTHERMS.

Below 70°

Between 70° & 80°

Above 90°

Tropic of Cancer

A b o v e   9 0°

Between 80 & 90°

Equator

Tropic of Capricorn

JULY
ISOTHERMS.

Below 60°

rain occurs on the Equator at all seasons, whereas the North and South Torrid Zones experience these rains during our summer and winter respectively.   Two deserts, the Sahara and Kalahari, lie to the north and south of these rainy zones.   They owe their dryness largely to the fact that they are uninfluenced by winds from the ocean, for apart from the convectional rains, only ocean winds bring rainfall to the continent, and the influence of these winds is profoundly modified by the relief of the land.

Thus in winter the northern winds bring rain to the Mediterranean region, but they lose much of their moisture by meeting the Atlas Mountains which lie close to the coast, so that they deposit no rain as they travel southwards over the warmer, lower, inland region.   Again the south-eastern trade winds, which in summer are drawn inland from the Gulf of Guinea by the African-Asiatic region of low pressure, are made much drier by the Kong Mountains of Guinea and by the Kameruns, so that the Sahara gains no moisture from these winds.

The northern half of the east coast gains little benefit from the monsoons, because these blow parallel to the coast.   On the other hand, Madagascar and the southern half of the east coast obtain much rain from the south-east trade winds, and the amount of rainfall here gradually decreases from the eastern to the western coast, East Madagascar receiving most, and the Kalahari least, rain.   The west coast, south of the Tropic of Capricorn, is very dry, owing to the south-east winds blowing away from the coast.   The western part of Cape of Good Hope, however, receives rain from westerly winds only in July (*i.e.* the winter), when the whole wind system has moved northwards with the sun.

If we summarise the rainfall due to ocean winds we find decreased rainfall (*a*) from the Mediterranean and Gulf of Guinea to the Sahara, (*b*) from the Kameruns to the Somali peninsula, (*c*) from Madagascar to Walfish Bay.

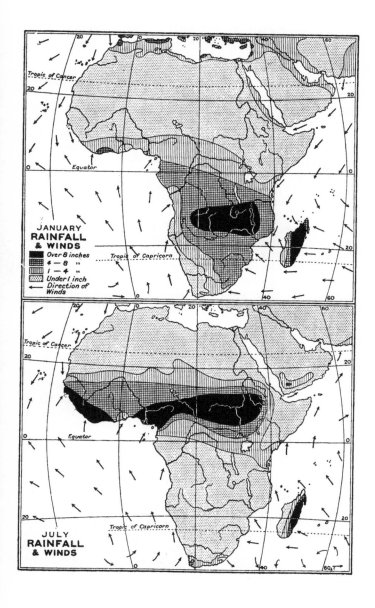

JANUARY
RAINFALL
& WINDS
■ Over 8 inches
▦ 4 — 8 "
▥ 1 — 4 "
▨ Under 1 inch
→ Direction of Winds

Tropic of Cancer
20
Equator
0
Tropic of Capricorn

JULY
RAINFALL
& WINDS

Tropic of Cancer
20
Equator
0
Tropic of Capricorn

Plants.

The distribution and character of African vegetation closely depend upon the temperature and rainfall. Thus the extreme north and south of the continent, which have a Mediterranean climate, have also Mediterranean vegetable products—cereals, tobacco, and fruits ; the moderate winter rains and the warm summers are exceptionally favourable to these plants.

But, as we have seen above, Africa lies mainly in the Torrid Zone and has a high temperature, with excessive rainfall in certain districts. Wherever these two conditions occur, there are dense tropical forests, which resemble the Selvas of the Amazon in their great extent and the tangled variety of their vegetation. These forest areas coincide almost exactly with the regions of heavy precipitation. They are found in Guinea, the Kameruns, the Congo basin, the Zambesi valley, the east coast northwards from the mouth of the Zambesi to the Equator, and the island of Zanzibar.

The oil palm, from the fruit of which an oil useful in soap-making is obtained, is characteristic of the forests of Guinea, and the Congo forests have great supplies of rubber. Mahogany, ebony, and teak are among the valuable woods obtained, and banana and coffee trees are very plentiful. Where the rivers reach the sea, slimy mangrove swamps line the shore, and the estuaries are exceedingly unhealthy. Where clear ground occurs in the forest zone, crops of sugar, tobacco, maize, and millet are easily grown ; for the land is naturally fertile, and climatic conditions favour the most rapid growth of vegetation.

Still lying within the tropics, but outside the forest belt, are the *park lands* or savanas, where the more moderate and intermittent rainfall allows the growth of both trees and grass. The name 'park lands' describes these districts very well, for clumps of woodland are found dotted over grassy plains and

Baobab tree

glades.   They practically cover the continent between
15° N. and 20° S. latitude, with the exception of the
tropical forests.   The baobab or monkey bread tree,
with its massive trunk and pendent fruit, is commonly
found in these regions.   The park lands pass, with
decreasing rainfall, into the steppes or purely grass
lands which become bare and scrubby near the deserts,

African crocodile

but such steppes are few in Africa.   They are found
in the Sudan, the interior of the Barbary States, the
plateau of the lakes, the Somali peninsula, and the
South African interior.   In the deserts drought-
resisting plants, especially the welwitschia, are found.
The date-palm has its home in the oases of North
Africa.   The Kalahari desert has more vegetation

than the Sahara, because it receives more rain. Lack of rain is the great cause of the infertility of the Sahara.

Animals.

Africa is extremely rich in wild animals. The elephant, rhinoceros, hippopotamus, and ape inhabit the land. Lions hunt the numerous species of antelope which live on the park lands. Crocodiles infest the rivers, and pythons and many smaller snakes are found. Birds include great numbers of birds of prey, the ostrich, bee-eater, flamingo, weaver, sun-bird, paradise-finches, and secretary-bird. Many of the insects are harmful to plant and animal life, the tsetse fly is fatal to horses and cattle, and an allied species is the dreaded carrier of the sleeping-sickness, which has killed some hundreds of thousands of human beings.

The two temperate regions are suited for sheep and goat grazing, and cattle rearing is becoming more and more important in our southern colonies.

Minerals.

There are comparatively few minerals which are as yet known to exist in Africa, and these, as usually happens, are found in the mountainous districts. Natal has both coal and iron, and the latter is also found in the Atlas Mountains. Accra and Cape Coast Castle export gold from the 'Gold Coast,' but the greatest supply is now found in the south of the continent, where Rhodesia and the Transvaal possess reefs of rich gold-bearing quartz. Diamonds are mined round Kimberley, where the De Beers Company holds the mines and regulates the output. Salt is obtained from the inland drainage systems of the western Sahara and Lake Ngami. The only other mineral of importance is copper, which occurs in Cape of Good Hope near the mouth of the Orange River.

The Peoples of Africa and their Religion.

The peoples and languages of Africa are numerous and varied, as we should expect from the continent's great extent. The debased Bushmen and Hottentots occupy the south-western corner of the continent, whither they have been driven by more powerful tribes. The Bantu races occupy the narrower portion of Africa as far north as the Great Lakes. Their chief industry is cattle-rearing. All the Bantu languages bear a resemblance to one another, and one dialect—the Swahili—is used as the commercial language of East Africa. A Malayan race occupies the eastern half of the island of Madagascar.

The extremely interesting Pygmy race, whose members fight with poisoned darts, and inhabit the dense forests, is found in the Congo basin. The Negro tribes inhabit Guinea and the southern Sudan, but they are hemmed in upon the north and east by Caucasian races (Arabs, Berbers, Tuaregs, Copts, and Somalis) who have entered the continent from the north-east, and have now spread over the northern half of its surface. Mohammedanism is the religion of the Arabs and their subject races, whereas the native races are usually fetish-worshippers (or idolaters), some even being cannibals.

European races are chiefly represented by the Dutch and British in the south, and by French, Germans, and Portuguese along the coasts.

The population of Africa is estimated at 160 millions, the most thickly peopled regions being the Nile and Niger valleys; the Barbary states, the Lake district, the Lake Chad area, and the coasts of Guinea, Zanzibar, and Natal follow next in order of density of population. The mere enumeration of the above names shows us how important is the supply of rain and river water, in determining the fertility, and consequently the supporting power, of a land area.

Europeans in Africa.

Africa is rapidly ceasing to be the Dark Continent, so quickly are its territories being acquired by European Powers. We notice how Spain holds none of the mainland, for during her palmy days she was too busy with the affairs of South America. The Portuguese, however, took an early part in the exploration of Africa in the 15th century, and they retain to-day possessions upon the east and west coasts.

Cape Town was founded by Dutch refugees in the middle of the 17th century, and this nation gradually passed inwards as far north as the Limpopo river, founding the two Boer republics which are now British provinces. France occupies Algeria, a large part of Sahara, French Congo, Madagascar, and a portion of Somaliland. Belgium has achieved notoriety by the mismanagement of the Congo Free State. Germany holds part of the Slave Coast, the arid lands of the Damaras and Namaquas, and the land lying between the Great Lakes and the sea.

We on our part have not been idle. In addition to four coastal regions in Senegambia and Guinea, with 'spheres' of influence stretching far into the Sudan, we control Egypt proper, and possess the eastern Sudan lying to the south as far as the Great Lakes, where British East Africa continues to the sea-board of the Indian Ocean. Our territory of Somaliland on the Gulf of Aden is separated from our other North African possessions by the mountainous country of Abyssinia.

German East Africa—a length of 600 miles between Tanganyika and Victoria Nyanza—alone separates these regions from our southern system of dependencies, which stretch unbroken from the Cape (S. lat. 35°) to within 8° of the Equator.

The Barbary States and the Sahara.

Position and Size.

The Barbary States (Morocco, Algeria, and Tripoli), which derive their name from the Berbers who peopled them before the Arabs, lie upon the Mediterranean shore and have a combined area of about six times that of our own islands ; whilst the Sahara desert, to which they all extend upon the south, is as large as Europe and stretches as far south as the 25th parallel.

Surface and General Features.

The Atlas range, which runs parallel to the coast in double and sometimes triple ranges, is the most noteworthy feature. It attains its greatest altitude in the west, where a height of 14,000 ft. is reached, but its average elevation is about half that amount. It separates the fertile coast plain from the desert lands of the south, acting, as we shall see later, as a most efficient rain-barrier and so giving fertility and life to the Barbary States.

In Algeria, a very fertile valley, called the *Tell*, lies between it and the coastal range, whilst to the south many lakes or *shotts* are found in the valleys and on the plateau. Tripoli is practically a desert land, watered at certain seasons by parched *wadis*.

The Sahara desert begins immediately south of the Atlas. It is a vast sandy waste, where the level surface is only relieved by sand dunes and low stony plateaux. It is not absolutely barren, for wherever water is obtainable from wells or springs there are fruitful oases, some of which are of considerable area. Towards the south of the Sahara, the plateaux rise to a height of 6000 ft. and form the inland drainage system of Lake Chad in the southern Sudan.

Oasis of El Kantara

Climate and Rainfall.

The northern slope of the Atlas and the coastal plain have a warm temperate climate with a range of temperature approximating to our own, but of course the temperatures actually experienced are warmer owing to lower latitude. The Atlas range provides great variety of temperatures according to the particular elevation, but south of this range a typically hot desert climate is met with. The Sahara is 10° F. hotter than the Equator in July and its daily variations in temperature are extreme. The sand is so hot during the day that eggs may be cooked by burying them below the surface, yet at night the temperature falls very many degrees, there being great radiation of heat into the cloudless sky. This great alternation of heat and cold causes the rocks to expand and contract, and so is responsible for splitting them into fragments. This pulverising action has continued for centuries, and has been aided by the wind driving the sand before it in great *simooms* or sand-storms.

The Atlas range is the climatic barrier as regards rainfall. The rain-bearing cyclonic winds from the Atlantic are made to deposit their moisture to the extent of 40″ annually upon the northern side of the range, with a result that the interior of the country has nowhere a rainfall of 10″ per annum. The coastlands, favoured as regards temperature and rain (which falls mostly in the winter and spring, and so tends to raise the temperature of those seasons) possess the finest climate of the Mediterranean.

Natural Productions.

The vegetation is sub-tropical, and agriculture is carried on upon the lowlands and lower slopes. Tobacco and rice are grown on the lowlands, and cereals, olives, grapes, figs, and oranges on the terraced mountain sides. Dates are an important product, especially in south Tunis and the many oases of the desert. One peculiar crop is an uncultivated one—esparto (or alfa) grass, which covers about ten million acres in the shott region. The export of alfa, however, is on the decline. It is being ousted from the paper market by the great development of the wood-pulp industry of North America and Europe. Forests of cork and other ever-green oaks and cedar are found upon the mountains, the drier grass-lands of which are used as pasturage for goats, sheep, and cattle. The camel is the common beast of burden in the south, and native birds include the brilliant flamingo around Lake Chad, and the ostrich upon the steppe-lands south of latitude 20° N.

The People and their History.

The Berbers are the original race, but they have been driven southwards by the Arabs, who invaded the land from the east in the 6th century. Previous to this, 'Africa'—as the Romans termed their province—had been held in succession by Phoenicians, Greeks, and Romans, and many ruins of ancient civilisation are found scattered about the country. The Arab-Berber peoples usually profess Mohammedanism, but some are without religious belief. Much of the interior of the country is occupied by lawless tribes engaged in cattle-grazing and pillage.

The French have colonised Algeria, which they annexed after the bombardment of Algiers in 1830, in consequence of frequent piracies which had partly stopped the Mediterranean trade. The torture of hapless Christian prisoners led to the French assumption of a 'protectorate' over Tunisia in 1881.

The northern towns of the Barbary States have a fair number of Jews and Europeans, who have settled either for health or trade. The bulk of the population lies to the north of the Atlas Mountains.

Industries and Communications.

The Arabs manufacture pottery, and blankets, carpets, and rugs from the wool of their flocks; these manufactures are the only ones of importance except the brass-work and tanning trade of Fez. Pastoral and agricultural pursuits occupy nearly all the inhabitants, but we must not forget that the Arabs are born traders, and that their caravans of camels regularly journey 2000 miles into the Sahara from Fez, Biskra, Tripoli and other towns to Lake Chad, Ghat, Kano, and Timbuktu, bringing on their return dates, salt, gold, ivory, and feathers. Good roads and railways have been made in Algiers. The railway from the port of Oran passes through Algiers (which has communication with Marseilles by steamer), Constantine, Bona, Tunis and Biskra, the caravan terminus.

Commerce and Ports.

Marseilles receives wine, tobacco, grass, cork, and corn from Algeria ; and Tunis exports olive oil and dates. *Tangier* ships dates, oranges, figs and other fruits to the northern parts of Europe. *Biserta* is used by the French, principally for military purposes.

Administration and Towns.

Marakesh (or *Morocco City*) is one of the residences of the sultan, or absolute monarch of Morocco. Like *Fez* it is a picturesque Moorish town. *Algiers*, the capital of the French colony, has similar character-istics in its older portion ; but the newer town is well built and modern. *Tunis* has the ruins of Carthage situated about twelve miles distant. *Tripoli*, the capital of the Turkish state of the same name, is surrounded by mud-walls. It has a large caravan trade, but its commerce is impeded by the shallow, dangerous harbour upon which it is situated.

The Senegal, Niger, and Congo Districts.

Position, Size, and Surface.

The district with which we are about to deal lies within 15° north and south of the Equator, and to the west of the 30th meridian. It is bounded on the north by the Sahara, on the east by the Lake plateau, and on the south by the Zambesi basin. That we are dealing with an immense district is shown by the fact that the Congo State is seven times as large as the British Isles, whilst the Portuguese territory of Angola has more than half that area.

North of the Gulf of Guinea there is a coastal plain from which the Kong Mountains rise abruptly, whilst their northern slope towards the Sahara is much more gradual. East of the Gulf lies the immense rectangular basin of the Congo, which is separated from the Lake plateau by the giant Ruwenzori Mountains. The Congo is the largest river in Africa—in fact it comes next to the mighty Amazon in point of volume. Its numerous tributaries, thanks to convectional rains, bring down a large volume of water at all times of the year, and Lakes Bangweolo, Mweru, and Tanganyika also help to feed the river. One large expansion of the river deserves special notice: this is Stanley Pool, which occurs in a low-lying part of the basin, and took its name from the celebrated explorer.

In the west the Kong Mountains give rise to three rivers: the Senegal and Gambia flowing westwards, and the great Niger river, which flows as far north as Timbuktu before it begins its seaward journey. Its chief tributary, the Benue, flows from the east and ~reaches it not far from its swampy, unhealthy delta.

Marshy lagoons are very numerous upon the Guinea Coast, and the climate is most unwholesome for Europeans. This coast is also characterised by a lack of good harbours, and a heavy surf which makes landing a very difficult matter. The old names—Grain, Pepper, Ivory, Gold, and Slave Coasts, were applied by traders from the chief commodities obtained in earlier years. A group of volcanic islands in the Bight of Biafra includes Fernando Po belonging to Spain, and St Thomas and Princes Island belonging to Portugal.

Climate and Natural Productions.

The tropical position of the district gives it a very equable, hot, rainy climate; the average temperature is 30° F. higher than that of Britain, and the range of temperature only a few degrees. The rainfall is exceptionally heavy, the yearly average being over 60″, increasing to more than 80″ on the Bight of Biafra and Liberian coasts. Such conditions, although unhealthy for white men, are specially favourable to the luxuriant growth of tropical trees, such as the oil-palm, teak, and mahogany.

Practically the whole Congo basin is covered with such forests, and they also extend for 100 miles inland from the Guinea Coast. Where clearings occur, tobacco, cotton, sugar, and rice are cultivated. The production of cocoa in the island of St Thomas, and of coffee on the slopes of Angola, are fast becoming important industries, but palm oil, ground-nuts, and rubber are still the staple exports of the whole district.

On the savana lands of the southern Sudan, sheep and ostriches provide wool and feathers, which find their way to the coast either down the Niger, or up that stream and down the Senegal.

The country is decreasing in importance as an ivory-producing region, owing to the increased scarcity of the elephant; although this animal, as well as other great beasts such as the hippopotamus, is still not uncommon. The forests are too thick for any but large quadrupeds, yet the larger apes, having different means of locomotion, are very numerous. The streams swarm with crocodiles.

Mineral wealth, as far as we know, is small, if we except the gold dust which gave its name to one part of the coast, and the copper and iron supplies of the Congo interior.

The People.

The Sudanese are of mixed Arab and Negro races. The Arabs are the chief trading and pastoral people, whereas the Negroes, especially in the thickly populated region stretching from the mouths of Niger to Lake Chad, are industrious agriculturists. The least civilised peoples are the forest tribes of the Congo basin, who are heathens and often cannibals as well.

Communications, Commerce, and Ports.

Rivers are the only means of communication through the forest zone, and camel caravans through that of the desert. *Sokoto* and *Kano* are the two chief caravan termini. The Senegal, Gambia, Niger, and Congo are great highways of trade, but unfortunately the Congo is impeded by rapids and falls for about 100 miles near its mouth. This difficulty however has been surmounted by a railway from the port of *Boma* to *Leopoldville* upon Stanley Pool, from which point there is a navigable stretch of 1000 miles. As the various European powers have extended their 'spheres of influence' into the interior, they have constructed railways running for some distance inland from the coast ports, notably *Sekondi* to *Kumasi, Lagos* to *Abeokuta,* and inland from *St Paul de Loanda.* A French railway connects the upper waters of the Senegal and Niger, so that *Timbuktu* has two routes to the sea. The exports from the district are all natural products : wool, ivory, and feathers ; ground-nuts, palm oil, wax, and rubber.

Administration and Towns.

LIBERIA is a native state, founded by the United States for freed slaves.

European powers have obtained possession of the following districts :

BRITAIN : Gambia (*Bathurst*), Sierra Leone (*Freetown*), Ashanti (*Kumasi*) and Nigeria (*Lagos, Kano, Sokoto*). The last-named country extends northwards to Lake Chad, where it meets the French and German 'spheres of influence.'

FRANCE : French Guinea, Ivory Coast, Dahomey, French Congo, and Niger (*Timbuktu*), meeting at Lake Chad.

GERMANY : Togoland, and the Kamerun country as far inland as the same lake.

PORTUGAL : Angola (*St Paul de Loanda*), part of Guinea Coast, and the islands in the Gulf of Guinea.

BELGIUM : Congo Free State (*Leopoldville, Stanleyville, Nyangwe*).

All the towns mentioned in parentheses above are engaged in the collection and distribution of forest products.

The Nile Basin.

Position, Size, and Surface.

The Nile basin, which includes Egypt, the eastern Sudan, and Abyssinia (the ancient Ethiopia) extends from the Equator to the Mediterranean Sea, and practically embraces the whole of north-eastern Africa. Although it has an area more than ten times that of the British Isles, yet its build is comparatively simple : two plateaux (the Abyssinian and Lake plateaux) are found in the south-east and south, a ridge of highland skirts the western shore of the Red Sea, whilst the remaining portion of the district is comparatively flat, and is composed of sandy desert lands—the Libyan desert to the west, and the Nubian desert to the east of the Nile.

The Nile alone gives fertility to Egypt. Its head streams are thought to rise from the glaciers of the Ruwenzori Range and feed the Lakes Victoria, Albert, and Albert Edward. Lake Victoria is the largest of the three, and has a diameter of 200 miles. The heavy equatorial rains ensure a plentiful supply of water to the White Nile, which leaves the plateau on its north-ward journey as a rapid stream with many waterfalls.

About 10° N. lat. it receives the waters of the Bahr-el-Arab and Sobat from the Sudan and Abyssinia. Where these three rivers unite they cause the low-lying marshy district to be repeatedly flooded during the summer rainy season, and as a result the Blue Nile, which enters the main stream at Khartum, brings down more suspended matter (*i.e.* is muddier) than the parent stream ; for the latter has already deposited much of its silt by inundating the country higher up. The upper courses of the Nile are much impeded by *sudd* or floating masses of densely-matted vegetation.

The last tributary of any importance is the Atbara. The town of Berber stands at the confluence. The Atbara, like the Blue Nile, brings water from the Abyssinian volcanic plateau, and this mainly during the summer rainy season. These two tributaries are responsible for the summer rise of the Nile, which begins so regularly in June, and ends by flooding the narrow strip of Nile valley. At Cairo the river rises 27 feet above its normal level, and all along the lower valley the flood-waters bring moisture and fertile silt to a land which is hard and unworkable at other seasons.

The six cataracts of the Nile are worthy of mention. They occur between Khartum and Aswan, and are caused by the river flowing over hard crystalline rocks. From the latter town to the sea the Nile dwindles steadily in volume, for it is traversing a region of high temperature and low rainfall, and, in addition, much of its water is withdrawn for purposes of irrigation. The character of this portion of the country is responsible for the Nile receiving no tributary of note after the Atbara.

The Nile has built up a large delta of very fertile soil at its entrance to the sea. This delta is steadily proceeding seaward, there being no strong tides in the Mediterranean to carry away the suspended matter ; and, as a consequence, dredging is necessary to keep even two of the many mouths open to traffic. The coast of the delta is fringed with lagoons. Not far to the west is Aboukir Bay, where Nelson defeated the French fleet in 1798.

Climate and Rainfall.

The plateaux, being situated within 15° of the Equator, have a hot equable climate modified by elevation. Egypt, on the other hand, has a climate of greater range. For example, the January and July temperatures near the Nile delta are 57° and 82°, whereas the temperature of the plateaux approximates to 80° all the year round. Again, the Middle Nile valley has the hottest summer temperature of the whole region. It is much hotter in summer than the Equator itself.

Rainfall is excessive in summer in Abyssinia, but constant in the Equatorial region. Egypt proper, with the exception of the seaboard, where an annual fall of 8″ occurs, may be classed as rainless. Hence the great importance of the river Nile to the country. Cairo, the capital of Egypt, has an annual rainfall of less than $1\frac{1}{2}$ inches.

Natural Productions.

The Abyssinian valleys possess tropical forests of the usual type ; the plateaux are principally composed of park lands ranged by big game ; and grassy steppes, which have a future before them as wheat-producing regions, are found in the Sudan around Khartum.

Pasturage of goats and sheep is the main industry here and on the slopes of Abyssinia.

Egypt has 10,000 sq. miles of land capable of irrigation and fertilisation by the Nile. The dams of Aswan and Asiut regulate the supply of water so that agriculture can proceed throughout the year, and a similar structure serves the delta lower down the river. As many as

The Nile Barrage

three crops can now be grown in the course of a year. Indeed the barrage of the Nile is one of the finest achievements of civil engineering when it is remembered that it ensures food to ten million people. Rice, tobacco, cotton, wheat, barley, maize, millet, durra, indigo, hemp, and sugar are all grown in the Nile valley and delta. Many fruits, including the banana, fig, and date, are also produced.

Apart from building stones in Egypt and a few metals in Abyssinia and the Upper Nile, the region is very poorly supplied with minerals.

The People and their History.

The Egyptians belong to the Hamite race. The *fellahin* are tillers of the soil, whilst the *Copts*, who profess a debased form of Christianity, usually hold higher positions. Arabic is the language spoken, and Mohammedanism is the prevailing religion. Suakin is the port used by 'the faithful' when they wish to make pilgrimage to Mecca. The internal trade of the country is in the hands of Arab merchants. The Abyssinians are like the Copts in their religion, but differ widely from them in their brutal, martial disposition and love of display.

The distribution of the people along the banks and delta of the Nile is one of the best examples of the strong influence that geographical conditions exert upon the movements of men.

The certainty of inundation and successful crops has made Egypt a *settled* country from earliest times. Once a people departs from the nomadic and purely pastoral life, it advances more quickly towards civilisation, and Egypt was a civilised country thousands of years before Britain. Another great reason for her early development was her position upon the trade-routes from Africa, Asia, and the Levant. The Persians, Greeks, Romans, Arabs, and Turks have in turn occupied the Nile delta. Egypt's important position with respect to the Suez Canal brought rival English and French influences into the country, and the suppression of an Egyptian revolt by the British at Tel-el-kebir in 1883 gave us control over her internal affairs.

Abyssinia. affords a strong contrast. Its remoteness and the inaccessibility of its mountain fastnesses have preserved it from European interference, except when the cruelties of its native ruler Theodore compelled the British to storm Magdala and put an end to them in 1868.

Industries, Communications, and Trade.

Abyssinia has no manufactures, and Egypt but few, including cotton, linen, and earthenware for home use. The export trade of Egypt consists of hides and the vegetable products of the basin—rice, sugar, lentils, and grain. Cotton and linen goods, machinery and coal are largely imported. "Alexandria has the bulk of the trade. The French port of Jibuti is being connected by rail with the capital of Abyssinia. Cairo has railways to Rosetta and Damietta at the principal mouths of the river, to Ismailia on the Suez railway which runs from Port Said to Suez, and to Aswan situated higher up the Nile. A continuation of the line southwards avoids the cataracts by running in a straight line from Wady Halfa to Berber, whence branches link up Suakin on the Red Sea and Khartum, the capital of the Sudan.

Caravan routes join the fertile oases to the nearest Nile towns, and the river itself has always been the great natural trade route from north to south. Its current is extremely slow in its lower parts, and navigation is aided by prevalent northerly winds. The cataracts are no obstacle to the passage in times of flood. We have yet to speak of the Suez canal, which runs through the Bitter Lakes from Port Said to Suez—a distance of about 90 miles, and saves a journey of several thousand miles in going to the far East from Europe. It cost £20,000,000 to construct, and possesses an average depth of 28 feet and a varying width of from 144 to 213 feet. Great Britain holds the largest number of shares in the canal company, and the greater number of ships using the waterway sail under her flag. By international arrangement the canal is never to be closed to any navy in time of war.

Administration and Towns.

Egypt proper is under Turkish rule, but the real control of the country rests in British hands, for the Khedive acts agreeably to British advice. Britain has complete control of the Sudan, but Abyssinia is an independent country. Its native ruler is called the Negus.

Cairo, the capital of Egypt, is situated near the famous Pyramids. *Khartum*, the scene of General Gordon's death, was an old centre of the slave trade. *Aswan* preserves the Nile waters in a lake 100 miles long by its bar, which is more than a mile long. By these means water is saved for use in irrigation during the hot dry Egyptian summer. *Port Said* and *Suez* owe their importance to the canal, *Alexandria* being the chief Egyptian seaport. *Massawa*, an Italian port on the Red Sea, exports coffee and hides from Abyssinia.

The Eastern Plateau.

Position and Surface.

This extends from the Gulf of Aden to the Zambesi river and embraces the region of the great lakes. The northern country of Somaliland is a low-lying part of the plateau, but near the Equator the average elevation is much higher, and gigantic snow-clad peaks occur ; the best known of these are Kilima Njaro, Kenia, and Ruwenzori, the latter two being volcanic in origin. Active volcanoes are found to the south of Albert Edward Nyanza.

The lakes are mostly of the ribbon type occupying rift valleys, and are a very prominent feature. Victoria Nyanza, which comes next to Lake Superior in point of size, is 200 miles in diameter. It stands at an elevation of 4000 feet above the sea, and is studded with islands near the Uganda (*i.e.* the northern) shore. Its shores are possessed partly by the British, partly by the Germans. The long, narrow shape of Lakes Tanganyika and Nyasa has made them convenient boundaries between various European spheres of influence. Tanganyika thus affords a boundary-line for 400 miles.

Climate and Natural Productions.

Latitude gives a tropical climate to the country, but this is greatly moderated by elevation and prevalent winds. The uplands have a climate suited to Europeans, and in this drier interior are large areas of steppe and park lands, where a great variety of big game is found. The narrow coast plain receives summer rains from the monsoon winds, and consequently possesses a tropical forest with oil and rubber trees, and an unhealthy climate for whites. Somaliland has least rain, and here the steppe lands are largest. Uganda is both agricultural and pastoral. Indeed the lake shores, together with the river valleys, are the only agricultural districts. Coffee, sugar, rice, cotton, and tobacco are the chief crops. The island of Zanzibar is the main source of the world's supply of cloves.

People.

The people are principally hunters of Bantu race. Some are Christians, others Mohammedans. The latter religion has been adopted from the Arabs, who have long carried on the ivory and slave trade. Population is most dense along the coast and the waterways, *i.e.* where agriculture prevails over grazing. Uganda has fully 300,000 people.

Administration, Commerce, and Communications.

The district has been subdivided amongst the British, Germans, Portuguese, Italians, and French. The British, French, and Italians have strips of the shore along the Somali peninsula. The French railway from the seaport *Jibuti* towards Abyssinia has been noted in a previous section. British East Africa extends from Abyssinia to Kilima Njaro, and *Mombasa* is the port. It is the terminus of the Uganda railway, the other terminus being *Port Florence* upon Victoria Nyanza, and its increasing trade rivals that of *Zanzibar*.

The latter island, although British, lies off German territory. German East Africa is bounded on the west by Victoria Nyanza, Tanganyika, and the northern half of Nyasa ; Portuguese territory begins at the river Rovuma, and stretches south beyond the Zambesi. *Mozambique* is the chief port. Ivory, rubber, hides, and gum are shipped from the district as a whole, whilst the imports (cotton goods, guns, powder, brass wire, and beads) are indicative of the needs and simple character of the native inhabitants.

British South Africa.

Position, Size, and Surface.

Our possessions in South Africa stretch from the southern end of Lake Tanganyika to Cape Agulhas, *i.e.* from 8° to 35° south latitude—a distance of 2000 miles, and a vast territory eight times as large as our own islands. It is roughly wedge-shaped, having Tanganyika at the northern apex ; yet whilst the greater part lies inland, flanked by Portuguese and German territory, British South Africa possesses the whole of the south coast from the mouth of the Orange River on the Atlantic to Delagoa Bay on the coast of the Indian Ocean.

A great plateau covers most of the country and descends in terraces to the coastal plain. In the Transvaal the plateau has an elevation of 4000 feet, and its surface is diversified by rounded *kopjes* and watercourses. The plateau, which in the southern part of the country is known as the *veld*, ends in a range of mountains, the Drakensberg, running parallel to the south coast. These mountains reach a height of 12,000 feet in the east. On their southern seaward side they descend to form the Great Karroo, a wide plain flanked on the south by more mountains and narrow plains. The Kalahari desert and the inland drainage system of Lake Ngami lie towards the west of the plateau.

The rivers flowing from the plateau vary greatly in volume at different seasons and so are of little use, especially in the south. Neither the Zambesi nor the Limpopo have their deltas in British territory, and the alternately swollen and parched Orange river, which flows westwards to the Atlantic, separates British from German territory in its lower course. As is usual in countries where plateau-rims lie close to the coast, the rivers are impeded by rapids and falls ; for instance the Tugela river in Natal falls through 1800 feet in one district. South African rivers are thus of little value for commerce. Again, their approach from the sea is sometimes obstructed by sandbars, as is the case with the Orange and Limpopo rivers. The coast is also unfavourable to trade, the harbours being few in number and poor in quality. Breakwaters have been constructed, notably at Cape Town, to afford safer anchorage.

Climate and Natural Productions.

Although British South Africa stretches far into the Torrid Zone, it is fortunate that the elevation of the plateau tempers the climate of the northern portion, and also that little British territory lies in the dry hot Kalahari district. The temperature is naturally warmer than that of our own land owing to its lower latitude, but it has greater daily variation. The Cape of Good Hope has a range of about 10° F., and Central Africa is more equable than this ; the annual range on the veld is a little more than that of Britain, and for this its distance from the sea and rain-bringing winds is largely responsible.

The south-east trade winds bring rain, and consequently the eastern part of the country has the greater rainfall. They are stronger and bring more rain during the southern summer, when they are drawn inland by the low-pressure area which exists over the continent

south of the Equator.   Cape Town and its neighbourhood, however, resemble the Mediterranean in receiving
most rain during the winter.   This is brought from the
Atlantic by westerly winds.

The climate in general is warm and dry.   In fact it
is too dry upon the Karroo and veld for agriculture to
become the staple occupation.   This dryness shows itself
in the heath and 'bush' vegetation, as well as in the
grass of the veld and the general scantiness of forests.
We must of course make exceptions of the seaboard,
where grain and vines are grown near Cape Town, and
tropical fruits, tea, sugar, indigo, and spices in Natal.
The latter recall somewhat the vegetable products of
the eastern coast of the continent ; in fact there is a
gradual transition from temperate to tropical products.
The same is seen inland, where the grasses and acacia
of the veld pass into the scrub of the Kalahari upon the
west, and the oil, cotton, and rubber of the Rhodesian
plateau and the Portuguese coast upon the north and
east.

Wild animals are becoming scarce in the south ; on
the veld and Karroo they have given place to herds of
sheep, goats, horses, and ostriches.   In fact we may regard the 'middle terrace' as an essentially pastoral area.

Minerals and precious stones are of exceptional
importance.   Gold is mined both in Rhodesia, and
on the *Witwatersrand* or '*Rand*' of the Transvaal.
Diamonds are obtained from the Kimberley district,
copper near the mouth of the Orange river, and coal
from Natal.

The People and their History.

Various, yet sharply defined, races occupy South
Africa, and the great problem of the future is the
successful blending of these into one people.   We may
neglect the disappearing Hottentots and Bushmen, but
the Bantu races of blacks are of a higher type and
certainly add to the difficulty of the 'race problem.'
But besides these there are the two white races—the

Diamond Fields, Southern Rhodesia

British and the Boers.   The latter are more numerous
than the British.   They are sprung from Dutch colonists
who sought religious freedom in Cape Colony[1], but were
dispossessed of Cape Town by the more strenuous
Britons about 100 years ago.   Some remained in the
neighbourhood, where their descendants form the Cape
Dutch of to-day; others, more dissatisfied, trekked
further inland to found the two Boer states, which
now form the Transvaal and Orange River States
respectively.

These two States have, with Cape of Good Hope and
Natal, a total population of about five millions, yet of
these only about one quarter are Europeans.   This is
but few when we consider the size of the country, but
is explained by the nature of the soil and climate.

Without doubt the presence of gold in the Transvaal
increased the friction between the white races, and led
to the annexation of the Boer states by Britain.   The
gold of Rhodesia is one of the lures which has led the
British prospector northwards towards the Equator,
although more lasting benefits will be obtained from the
development of that region's capacity for grain and fruit-
growing.   Much of the extension of the Empire in South
Africa has been due to the enterprise of 'chartered
companies,' and affords an interesting parallel to the
history of our Indian Empire.

Communication, Commerce, and Ports.

A country of such extent as this, with an interior
devoid of roads and navigable rivers, must necessarily
develop its railways ; especially when we consider that
the mining centres—always 'foci of population'—lie far
from the sea.   A line of rail 1500 miles long runs from
Cape Town to the Zambesi, crossing in succession the
Karoo, veld and high plateau, and linking up in its
course vintage towns such as Paarl, and mining towns
like Kimberley.   Another line begins at Port Elizabeth

[1] The name of Cape Colony is no longer officially used, Cape of Good
Hope being one of the four provinces of the Union of South Africa.

and East London, and sending off side-branches on its way, traverses the pastoral Boer states as far as Pretoria. Branch lines also connect Johannesburg and the gold mining district with the Portuguese seaport Lourenço Marques upon Delagoa Bay.

The total trade is valued at more than £120,000,000, of which more than three-fourths is with the United Kingdom. Gold, diamonds, wool, hides, ostrich feathers, and mohair (from the Angora goat) figure most prominently among the exports, whilst the white peoples require textiles, food, and metal goods. The chief ports are Cape Town, Port Elizabeth, East London, and Durban. Port Nolloth ships the copper mined at Ookiep, and Lourenço Marques exports some of the Transvaal gold.

Administration.

Cape of Good Hope, Natal, Transvaal, and the Orange Free State have a united parliament. These four states have been combined to form the Union of South Africa. The South African or Union Parliament meets at Cape Town, but Pretoria is the seat of government. Each of the four states has its own parliament (or Provincial Council) to deal with taxes and elementary education.

Towns.

In Cape of Good Hope : *Cape Town*, the capital on Table Bay, the harbour of which has been greatly improved by a breakwater ; *Grahamstown*, a pastoral centre ; *Paarl*, in the grain and wine district ; *East London* and *Port Elizabeth* are seaports exporting wool, hides, etc.

In Natal : *Pietermaritzburg*, the capital ; *Durban*, the second South African seaport ; *Newcastle*, in the coal mining district.

In Transvaal and the Orange Free State : *Pretoria* and *Bloemfontein*, the respective capitals ; *Johannesburg, Kimberley*, and *Barberton*, mining centres.

In Rhodesia : *Bulawayo* and *Salisbury*.

CHAPTER VII

AUSTRALIA AND NEW ZEALAND

Australia.

Position and Size.

Australia, the smallest of the continents, lies to the south-east of Asia. It is bounded on all sides by the ocean and is the largest island in the world. Tropical seas—the Timor, Arafura, and Coral Seas—bound it upon the north, and the Pacific, Southern, and Indian Oceans on the east, south, and west respectively. It lies between the 11th and 44th parallels of south latitude and the 113th and 154th meridians of east longitude. In size it approximates to Europe, but is somewhat smaller, having an area of three million square miles.

Surface and General Features.

The most pronounced feature in the build of the continent is the great range which runs roughly parallel to the east coast and is never more than 150 miles from the sea. This range, which is known by different names in various parts, attains its greatest height (7300 feet) in Mount Kosciusko in the south-east, where the peaks are snow-capped throughout the year, but in general its height is only one-third of this. In its northerly half it forms the eastern edge of an elevated region stretching far into the interior.

Two lowland areas—the Eyre and Murray basins—which are separated from each other by a ridge culminating in the southern Flinders Range, lie to the west of the East Australian Highlands; and the western table-land occupies the remainder of the continent.   The highest parts of this table-land are in the centre of the continent and along its western shore.

The nearness of the mountains to the Pacific shore causes the Fitzroy, Burdekin and other eastern rivers to be short and swift.   Those from the western slope are much longer; they comprise the Murray with its tributaries the Murrumbidgee, Lachlan, and Darling, and Cooper's Creek and similar rivers flowing into Lake Eyre.   Speaking generally, Australia is a dry land, and its rivers are frequently dried up during the hot summer season.   Yet this is not true of the Murray and its largest tributaries, for they are fed by the snows of the Great Dividing Range.   The Murray, like other rivers in this dry land, is shallow and unfit for navigation by large craft, although its length (together with that of the Darling) is 1500 miles.

The sources of these rivers are not very high, and as they are situated far from the mouth, there is only a slow current of water.   In many parts of its course the Darling has a fall of six inches only to the mile.   This being the case, floods frequently occur during the wet season, with very disastrous results.   Another reason for the Murray's small value commercially is that it spreads out its waters into a shallow lagoon—*Lake Alexandrina*, an expanse 30 miles wide—before it enters the sea as a turbulent, rapid stream.

On looking at a map of Australia we notice the large number of lakes in the interior.   These are associated with the plateau structure of the continent, a structure which has been aptly compared to a pie-dish or saucer.   One of these lakes, Lake Eyre, has already been mentioned as forming the reservoir of an inland drainage system, but in common with the other large lakes it is shallow, and during the dry season is little more

than a series of pools and marshes.   More than half the
continent has internal drainage.

Australia may be termed a land of large temporary
lakes and short coastal rivers.   The latter are shown
well upon the northern and western coasts as well as
the eastern, but for more than 1000 miles along the
southern coast, no river of importance reaches the sea.
We shall see the reason for this in a later section
dealing with the climate of the continent.

An outer Barrier Reef

The Coast.

Australia has about 10,000 miles of coast-line, but
this is small when its area is taken into account, for
it is one of the most compact continents, and resembles
Africa in this respect.   The two peninsulas of Cape
York and Arnhem Land partly enclose the Gulf of
Carpentaria on the north, and the Great Australian
Bight, with its inhospitable limestone cliff wall, is the
corresponding inlet on the south.   There are relatively

few good harbours in Australia; Spencer and St Vincent Gulfs and Port Philip should be noted upon the south coast, for they are all approaches for commerce; and Port Jackson on the east coast is one of the best and safest openings.

The east coast is rocky as a rule, and for 1400 miles of its length it is fringed by the Great Barrier Reef, built by millions of coral animals. These thrive only in warm, pure waters, and it is notable that gaps appear in the reefs opposite the mouths of the swift eastern rivers. In its southern part the reef attains a width of 70 miles. It acts as a natural breakwater and calm water stretches between it and the coast, though sunken rocks make the passage less used than it would be. The island of Tasmania is separated from the mainland by Bass Strait.

Climate and Rainfall.

We note first that the Tropic of Capricorn almost bisects the continent, so that the northern and southern portions are respectively in the South Torrid and Temperate Zones, and from this it follows that the Australian seasons will be the reverse of ours, *i.e.* winter during our summer and *vice versa*. We may say generally that Australia has hot summers and mild winters. During July the isotherms (reduced to sea level) range from 50° F. in the south to 75° F. in the north. At this time the sun is over the North Torrid Zone, and the continent experiences its coolest season, the isotherms practically following the lines of latitude. A very different state of things is found in summer (*i.e.* about January), for then the interior of the continent experiences great heat and is hotter than the Equator for the time being. This heated central region is bisected by the Tropic of Capricorn and has a temperature exceeding 90° F.

Combining these two conditions we find that, whereas the coasts have an annual range of less than 20° F., the interior suffers greater extremes; *e.g.* the Murrumbidgee has a 30° range, and Lake Eyre a 35° range.

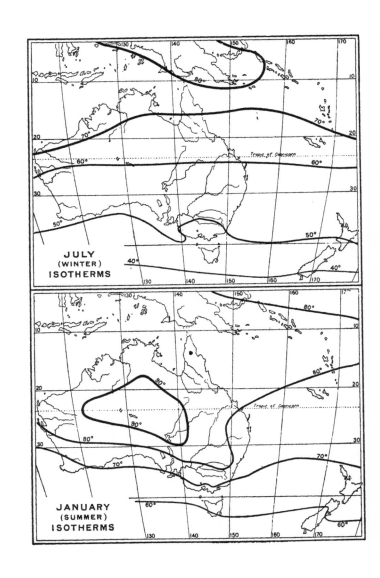

JULY
(WINTER)
ISOTHERMS

JANUARY
(SUMMER)
ISOTHERMS

It has already been said that Australia is a relatively dry continent; it is a continent with much sunshine in consequence, there being an absence of a cloud-screen between the land and the sun. This is of importance in connection with the rapidly developing fruit industry. About half the continent receives less than 10″ of rainfall in the year, and a large area of this district does not receive 5″. Winter (*i.e.* about July) is the dry season of the year, except in the south-west and Tasmania, where westerly winds are prevalent, and along the south-east coast, where the south-east trade winds exert a certain effect. At this season, however, the trade winds do not bring very much rain to the country for two reasons : first, the whole trade wind system has moved northwards with the sun, and secondly, the southern part of the continent is at this time a region of high pressure, so that the tendency is for air to travel seawards.

In January there is the opposite tendency, for the heated interior causes the air above it to be at low pressure, and air is drawn inwards from the sea. This influence is so great that the south-east trade winds are augmented by north-easterly and northerly winds, and a monsoon effect is created, the northern and eastern coasts receiving much more rain than at other seasons. The south coast of Victoria and South Australia benefit, in that a portion of the 'brave westerlies' is deflected northwards over the continent and brings rain to those parts.

Summarising, we find that rainfall is greatest on the north, east, south-east, and south-west coasts, the highlands causing much condensation. It decreases towards the interior, and that part of the continent bounded by 22° and 30° S. lat. and 120° and 130° E. long. may be considered a rainless region. Winter rains occur in the south-west and in Tasmania, the westerly winds retreating somewhat to the south of that island during summer.

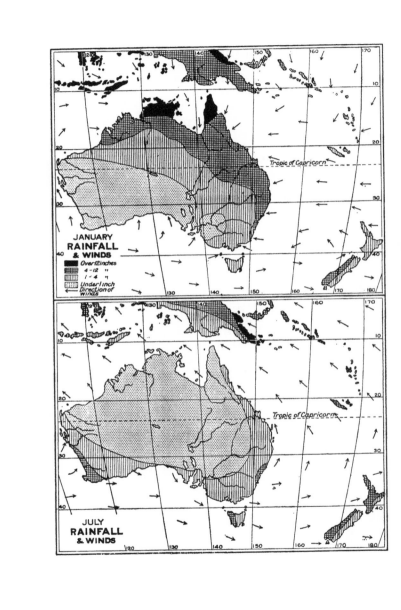

JANUARY
RAINFALL
& WINDS

Over 12 inches
4 - 12 "
1 - 4 "
Under 1 inch
Direction of
Winds

Tropic of Capricorn

JULY
RAINFALL
& WINDS

Tropic of Capricorn

Plants and Animals.

Australia is essentially a land of drought-resisting plants, and the latter avoid loss of water during the hot weather in many remarkable ways : some shed their leaves, others keep them, but always place them edgeways to the sky and heat; some have a thick sap which evaporates slowly, others have resistant leaves of a leathery kind which the heat cannot penetrate. Many have leaves which cannot be recognised as such, and are converted into prickles and spines. There are tropical forests in the north with mangroves and rubber trees, but the usual Australian forest is of a very different kind. Tree ferns and gum trees (eucalypti) are typical. It is said that there are 150 kinds of gum trees in Australia. The settlers call them by characteristic names, such as blue gum, stringy bark, and iron bark. Such trees, as also the native hardwood trees (karri, jarrah—which are extensively used for street-paving and harbour construction) are found only where the rainfall is reasonably plentiful, for all trees give off more moisture than smaller plants.

In drier parts, particularly on the inland side of the East Australian Highlands, are wide grass lands, and these pass inland into impenetrable thickets of dwarf acacias and eucalypti which go by the general name of 'scrub.' Sometimes this scrub is ten feet high, and its multitudes of thorns render it quite impassable. Beyond the scrub lies the stony and sandy rainless desert.

The Australian animals are no less peculiar. The native mammals include the duck-billed platypus, and the ant-eater. It is the marsupials, however, which are the really typical Australian animals such as the kangaroo, opossum, and wombat. Snakes are common, as are alligators in the northern waters. Amongst the birds must be reckoned the emu (or Australian ostrich), the lyre bird, bower bird, black swan, white crow, and numerous parrots and pigeons.

It will be noticed that no milk-giving animal like

the cow, nor any food-giving plant, has occurred in the above lists.   The importance of this will be seen in treating of the native people of Australia.   Yet

Giant Gum Tree, South Australia

Australia by its climate is suitable for the temperate and sub-tropical animals and plants of other countries. This is well seen in the introduction of European cereals, vegetables, and fruits, as well as of sheep, cattle, horses, camels, and that great pest, the rabbit. Climatic conditions determine that Australia shall be of most value as a pastoral country, and one suited for sheep rather than cattle, but agriculture is successfully practised in the moister regions.

Sugar, tea, and cotton are raised on the eastern coast, the cultivation necessarily being in the hands of coolies who have been imported from the Pacific islands for the purpose. Where rainfall is scanty or precarious much has been done by irrigation to improve agriculture, rivers and wells being used as sources of water supply. The clear sunshine of the country has given success to wheat, vine, and fruit culture, and wine and raisin manufacture must now be reckoned among Australian industries.

Fisheries.

Besides mackerel, herring, whiting, and other familiar sea fish, there are pearl fisheries off the north and west coasts (Thursday Island and Shark's Bay), and another industry—one which shows the interdependence of nations—is carried on near the Great Barrier Reef. This is the capture, drying, and curing of the *trepang* or sea slug, for shipment to China, where it is highly esteemed as an article of food.

Minerals.

Australia is exceptionally rich in gold deposits ; indeed she is the second gold-producing country in the world, and the presence of this mineral has given her a larger white population than she otherwise would have had. Silver, coal, copper, iron, and tin are also mined, but not to the same extent as gold.

The People and their History.

The present population numbers more than four millions, but of these only a few are natives or aborigines, and they are fast decreasing in number. They are an undeveloped race, for owing to the nature of their country's animals and plants, they have never adopted a pastoral or agricultural life, and consequently have not the barest elements of civilisation. They

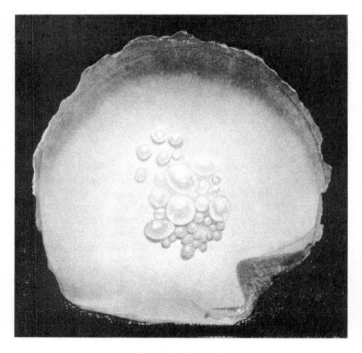

Queensland pearls

hardly know how to build themselves shelters against bad weather, and live on shell-fish, roots, and berries.

The average density of population is little more than one per square mile, and most of the people are to be found in the south-east of the continent, the remainder

being in the other coastal districts. We can understand
this distribution from the following considerations :

(a) The earliest settlements were in the south-
east.

(b) This district has a temperate climate and
moderate rainfall.

(c) The East Australian Highlands proved a bar
to penetration inland.

(d) The discovery of gold in the south-east in
1850.

(e) The later discovery of gold in West Australia.

(f) The barren nature of the interior of the
country.

Industries and Manufactures.

Pastoral, mining, and agricultural industries are pre-
eminent, and although the discovery of gold brought
people to the country, mining has now given place
to grazing as the most important industry. The huge
scale on which sheep-farming is carried on can be
judged from the fact that 240,000 tons of wool were
exported in 1908, whilst butter is being sent out from
the country in an increasing amount every year. The
production of cereals and wine is also increasing at a
rapid rate.

There are as yet few manufactures ; woollens and
machinery are manufactured to a small extent in
Victoria, but such articles are the main imports from
the United Kingdom. A country is never a manufacturing one until it reaches a later stage of its development,
when people are more numerous. Australia's commerce
has an annual value of £116,000,000.

Communications.

Owing to the lack of navigable rivers and good roads,
railways are necessary to bring the produce of the
interior to the ports ; and these lines are best developed, as we should expect, in the south-east and

east. There is a coast line connecting all towns from
Adelaide to Rockhampton. Lines also connect the
eastern coast with the navigable parts of the Murray
and Darling. The Murray is navigable for small
steamers from Albury almost to its mouth ; Bourke
stands at the head of the Darling navigation. West
Australia has railways from the goldfields to the seaports. All the large towns are connected by telegraph.

Administration.

As each state grew to greater importance, it was
allowed a separate parliament by the mother country.
West Australia, the last to gain such recognition,
obtained its parliament in 1890. Each state parliament consists of two houses, and closely follows the
British model. There is also a Governor appointed for
each state.

Victoria, Queensland, New South Wales, Tasmania,
South Australia and West Australia formed a Commonwealth in 1901, *i.e.* they all now send representatives to
a federal parliament which meets at *Dalgety* in New
South Wales. This commonwealth (amongst other duties)
administers the Commonwealth Territory, previously
known as the Northern Territory and governed by
South Australia.

The individual states still retain their original parliaments, which were granted them by charter at the
time of their formation.

Victoria.

Position, Size, and Surface.

The river Murray forms the northern boundary of
this colony, which is about two-thirds the size of the
British Isles, and occupies the south-eastern portion of
the continent. The East Australian Highlands—known
here as the Grampians and the Australian Alps—run

througn the middle of the state, and slope northward
to the Murray basin.   On the south of the range is a
coastal plain about 60 miles in width.

Climate and Natural Productions.

The southern position and seaboard of Victoria give
it the most temperate climate of the island-continent.
Rainfall is heaviest upon the mountains, and the north-
west (or Wimmera) district has the driest climate,
especially in the winter months.   This district has been
freed of its scrub by rolling and burning, and is now a
fertile wheat-growing area.   Oats, barley, and maize are
the other cereals grown.   The great fruit-producing
district lies round *Mildura* on the Murray, where fine
orchards of peaches and apricots are the result of irrigation.   Olives and grapes are also largely produced.

Fully half the colony has fine pastures, and wool
ranks first among the exports.   The colony owes its
origin to the gold rush of 1851, and the quartz reefs
of *Bendigo* and *Ballarat* still supply gold to the value
of £2,000,000 annually.

Commerce and Towns.

The chief exports are gold, wool, live-stock, cereals,
butter, hides, and meat.   The imports are the same as
those of Tasmania.   About half the Australian commerce is done through *Melbourne,* the capital, which
is the largest town in the continent.   It contains about
half the people of Victoria, its population being more
than half a million.   *Geelong* exports wool.

Tasmania.

Position, Size, and Surface.

The island of Tasmania, which is about as large as
Scotland, lies to the south-east of the continent, from
which it is separated by Bass Strait.   It has been called
the 'Switzerland of the South' from its mountains,
valleys, and many beautiful lakes.   There is practically

no coastal plain. Its two chief rivers, the Tamar and
Derwent, flow respectively north and south ; the estuaries of both provide good harbours.

Climate and Natural Productions.

The climate is very equable and healthy, for the
annual range is only about 16° F., and comparing it
with Europe we may say the climate corresponds to
that of northern France. Nearness to the sea and
rainfall in both summer and winter produce the
equability of temperature. The western half of the
island receives more rain than the eastern ; this is
because the rain is mainly brought by the 'brave
westerlies.' Tasmania differs from Australia in being
free from droughts.

The uplands are well wooded, the forests comprising
Huron pine, eucalyptus, and tree ferns. Wheat and
oats are grown, but more attention is paid to the cultivation of temperate fruits (apples and grapes) and hops.
The jam industry is increasing in importance. Sheep
are reared in large numbers and wool is an important
export. The island has coal and tin, but is poor in gold.

Commerce and Towns.

Wool, fruit, timber, and meat are sent abroad in
return for tea, sugar, clothing, and metal goods. The
two chief towns are *Hobart*, the capital, and *Launceston*.
Both are seaports and have small woollen factories and
tin-smelting works.

New South Wales.

Position, Size, and Surface.

This state gained its name from the resemblance
between its rugged coast and that of South Wales. It
shares the eastern seaboard with Queensland, and also
abuts upon South Australia and Victoria. Its surface
presents the same three regions as Victoria, except that
here they extend from north to south instead of from east

to west. The East Australian Highlands are known in this
colony as the Australian Alps, the Blue Mountains, and
the Liverpool Range. The Alps contain Mount Kosciusko (or Townsend) with its snow-covered peak more
than 7000 feet high, and with steep gorges and rushing
waterfalls.

Climate and Natural Productions.

The temperature increases from south to north in
winter, whilst in summer the interior is the hottest
part. It is also the driest, and is subject to droughts.
In 1895 more than ten million sheep perished during
the dry season. New South Wales has more sheep
than the rest of the continent. They feed not only on
grasses but on the dry *salt bush* of the interior, especially
in the region to the west of Bourke, where numerous
artesian wells have been sunk to provide them with
water. The Murray valley around Goulburn is irrigated and produces good wheat crops, but maize,
tobacco, sugar, and fruits are grown on the hot, moist
coastal plain, which varies in width from 30 to 120 miles.
Typical forests of gum trees, wattles, palms and cedars
are found on the damp slopes of the East Australian
Highlands. Gold, silver, and tin constitute the chief
metallic deposits, and the coal mines of Newcastle
employ 10,000 men, some of the coal being shipped as
far as San Francisco.

Commerce and Towns.

The state receives food, drink, textiles, and metal
goods in return for wool, gold, coal, meat, and butter.
Most of the trade is done through *Sydney*, the capital,
a town of over half a million inhabitants, situated
near *Botany Bay* (which saw the beginning of the
colony as a penal settlement), and connected by rail
with raisin-producing *Albury*, wheat-growing *Bathurst*,
pastoral *Bourke*, and the capitals of Victoria and Queensland. Sydney is a naval station and its fine harbour is
strongly fortified. With coal and iron near at hand it will
doubtless develop into an important manufacturing city.

Sydney Harbour

Queensland.

Position, Size, and Surface.

Queensland is twice as large as New South Wales, having five times the area of our own islands. It occupies the north-east of Australia, and has the Commonwealth Territory to the west and New South Wales to the south. The East Australian Highlands are wider here than in the other colonies ; in the south they are known as the Darling Downs.

Climate and Natural Productions.

Queensland is bisected by the Tropic of Capricorn, so it is both the hottest and wettest Australian state, though the rainfall decreases towards the interior. Its temperature is such that field-work upon the coast cannot be performed by whites, but is done by *Kanakas* from the Pacific islands. Rice, sugar, maize and fruits are the principal crops grown. The eastern slopes of the East Australian Highlands which are moister feed large herds of cattle, whilst the drier western parts are devoted to sheep. Forests cover much of the table-land, and it has been estimated that half the colony is wooded. Towards the north the forests are tropical in character. The three goldfields (*Gympie, Charters Towers, Mt. Morgan*) are connected by rail with the coast. Tin and coal are obtained from *Herberton* and *Ipswich*.

Commerce and Towns.

Most of the towns of any importance lie on the coast and are connected by railway. They export gold, silver, copper, tin, coal, meat, hides, tallow, wool, and sugar, the imports being of the usual type. The population numbers about half a million, and the coastal plain supports the greater number of these. *Brisbane*, the capital, does trade with North America as well as with Britain. *Rockhampton* and *Maryborough* both export gold and animal produce. *Ipswich* on the coalfield has woollen manufactures.

South Australia.

Position, Size, and Surface.

Before the administration of the Commonwealth Territory by the Federal Parliament, South Australia extended from the north to the south of the continent and was half as large again as Queensland; but size is no guide to value, for most of the colony is desert land, unexplored to the present day. The coast regions are the only parts fit for habitation; indeed we may say that only the south-east portion of the colony is of much value. Here the limestone plains support sheep, and, by irrigation, grow good crops of wheat and fruits.

Climate and Natural Productions.

The climate is tropical in the north, where heavy rains occur by reason of the monsoons, hot and dry in the central desert zone, and even in the south the country is subject to drought. Wheat, oranges and grapes are grown here, the heat of summer being increased by hot winds which blow from the north. The grass is relatively poor and suited only for sheep, although horses are bred for military purposes to the north of Adelaide, where the rainfall is heavier. Copper and gold are the only important metals, the former occurring at *Wallaroo* in the mountains near Spencer Gulf, the latter at *Pine Creek* in the far north.

Commerce and Towns.

Wool, wheat, copper ore, wine, and raisins form the chief exports. *Ports Pirie* and *Augusta* export wheat and wool. *Adelaide*, the capital, is connected by telegraph with *Port Darwin* in Commonwealth Territory, and it has been proposed to link north and south by a railway also. Part of this line has already been made, but it is doubtful whether such a railway would repay the cost of construction. The products of the northern region are gold, tobacco, maize, sugar, and cotton.

West Australia.

Position, Size, and Surface.

West Australia is the largest of the states ; it is more than eight times as large as our islands, and comprises all the continent lying to the west of the 129th meridian, but much of this vast territory is useless desert. The western and south-western parts alone are peopled. Numerous rivers flow westwards from the interior plateau, but they are short, rapid, and variable in volume.

Climate and Natural Productions.

The south-west coast is the coolest part of this otherwise hot state, which also receives the heaviest rains. These occur mostly in winter, when the belt of westerly breezes is found in lower latitudes. The sandy interior is practically devoid of vegetation, but in the south-west there are forests of jarrah and karri covering an area as large as the British Isles. The western coast is rapidly developing as a fruit and vine-growing district, for the clear, dry summers are especially favourable to fruit ripening. Grazing (both for sheep and cattle) is carried on in the river valleys and on the hill slopes of the west. *Perth* and *Albany* are horse-breeding centres. Gold, whose late discovery accounts for West Australia being the youngest colony, is obtained from the mines of *Kalgurli* and *Coolgardie*.

Commerce and Towns.

Gold, timber, wool, and pearl shells (from the Shark's Bay fishery) are exported. The imports are textiles, food, and manufactured goods. *Perth* is the capital, and its port, *Fremantle*, is rapidly eclipsing *Albany* by reason of its better harbour.

New Zealand.

Position, Size, and Surface.

The islands of New Zealand lie in the Pacific Ocean, about 1200 miles to the south-east of Australia. They have a combined length of 1100 miles and an area about that of the British Isles; but whereas our own islands are situated in the centre of the land hemisphere, New Zealand lies in the centre of the water hemisphere. They stretch from 34° to 48° south latitude, being in about the same latitude as south-western Europe. The chief members of the group are North and South Islands, with the smaller Stewart Island lying further to the south.

Both the large islands are mountainous, but South Island is the more so. Its mountain range, the Southern Alps, runs throughout its length, and is nearer to the western shore. Its highest peak is Mount Cook, which is 12,000 ft. high—as high as the Pyrenees, and the snow-capped summit has glaciers resembling those of the Alps. One of these glaciers is an immense ice-sheet 12 miles long and 2 miles wide. Nestling among the Southern Alps are many narrow ribbon lakes, which also recall those of Switzerland. The largest, Lake Wakatipù, has a winding length of 50 miles and is situated amongst charming scenery. The Southern Alps slope on their eastern side down to the well-known Canterbury plains lying along the east coast.

North Island has volcanic phenomena similar to those of Iceland and the Yellowstone Park, for active and extinct volcanoes (Ruapehu, Tongariro, and Egmont) form the principal peaks in its mountain system ; and north of the large lake Taupo, which is drained by the Waikato river, is a wonderful region of hot springs and lakes, mud volcanoes and geysers.

The Great Geyser, Wairakei

North Island has a less regular coast-line which is broken by numerous bays and inlets. The wildest coast region is in the south-west of South Island, where the Southern Alps lie close to the sea, and fjords with steep sides and picturesque wooded islands stretch inland with winding courses for 20 miles or more. As a result of the narrow extent of the large islands from east to west, no part of New Zealand is more than 75 miles from the sea.

Climate and Natural Productions.

This island group is situated entirely within the South Temperate Zone, and this, together with the insular position, prevents excessive summer heat or winter cold. The annual temperature increases from south to north and decreases with elevation, but all parts of the country enjoy an equable climate. Auckland, the climate of which has been compared with that of the Riviera, has an annual range of only 14° F., and other towns such as Christchurch and Wellington have but 16° and 18° range. Much of this equability is due to the rains which are brought at all seasons by the westerly winds, and, as in Tasmania, the amount of rainfall decreases from west to east. There are no droughts in New Zealand.

As a result of the comparative dryness of the east we find the Canterbury Plains of South Island forming an ideal pasture ground for sheep, there being nearly 20 millions of these animals in the colony. The islands are well wooded, but the gums and wattles of Australia are absent. The typical tree of New Zealand is the *Kauri Pine*, from which gum is obtained for making varnish. Tree ferns form much of the undergrowth in the forests. Another characteristic plant is *Phormium* or New Zealand Flax—a plant something like the aloe —the fibres of which are exported for rope-making purposes. It is found in the hottest part of the country along the course of the Waikato river.

Agriculture is mainly devoted to cereal and fruit culture. Maize, wheat, barley, and oats are widely

Maori Dwelling

produced (the latter two crops in the cooler eastern part of the South Island), whilst the climate is also sufficiently warm and dry to ripen oranges and grapes.

Gold and coal are found in both islands ; Auckland is in the neighbourhood of the richest gold mines, and it has much coal of moderate quality. The best coal is obtained from *Westport* on the west coast of South Island. One curious industry, which employs 4000 men in North Island, is the digging of "fossil gum"—the remains of dead Kauri trees. This kind of gum is prized more highly than that obtained from the living trees.

The People and their History.

The Dominion of New Zealand is sparsely peopled ; it contains less than a million people, and the parts with least population are the interior of North Island and the western half of South Island, elevation and natural features being responsible for this distribution. There are less than 50,000 natives, or Maoris, and these, although much more intelligent and capable of civilisation than the aborigines of Australia, and even sending their own members to parliament, are not increasing as fast as the white population. Till the middle of the 19th century the islands were only places of call for European traders. They were annexed by Britain in 1840 and received power to govern themselves 15 years later.

Commerce and Towns.

All the important towns are connected by railway. The main lines run from Auckland to Wellington and from Christchurch to Invercargill. The annual trade is valued at about £27,000,000, and the chief exports are wool and animal products (meat, tallow, skins, butter, cheese), gold, flax, and gum. The British population of New Zealand require tea, sugar, clothing, drink, and metal goods. Steamers make regular sailings to Auckland and other ports from Britain, Australia, and the United States. Practically all the towns are on the coast and serve as seaports ; the most important are *Auckland, Wellington, Christchurch, Dunedin, Nelson,* and *Napier.*

CHAPTER VIII

NORTH AMERICA

Position and Size.

The North American continent is a great triangular land-mass with an area more than double that of Europe. Its broader end lies within the Arctic Circle, whilst it tapers to the south, almost to the Tropic of Cancer. It has an equally great extent in longitude. The meridian 100° west almost bisects the continent, the eastern and western limits of which are 52° and 168° W. long.

Surface and General Features.

It is a land of magnificent mountain chains, immense plains, fresh-water lakes large enough to be called seas, and rivers of extraordinary length ; it can only be compared with Asia in the magnitude of its physical features.

The *Cordillera* system of crystalline and sedimentary mountain ranges, crust-blocks, and basins, runs as an axis from north to south of the continent, and is continued southwards along Central and South America. These 'Rocky Mountains' have peaks over 16,000 feet high. The date of their upthrust is geologically recent, and although in height they greatly exceed the *Appalachian* or *Alleghany* system which runs in a somewhat similar direction down the east of the continent, the latter is a much older mountain-mass. In common with other districts of recent elevation, the western mountains have volcanic and earthquake phenomena associated with them. The southern part of this range merges into the Mexican plateau.

A vast plain extends between the two highland regions. This plain has two gentle slopes (one to the north, another to the south), from a faint divide or slightly elevated region which roughly corresponds with the southern boundary of Canada from the Rocky Mountains to the Great Lakes. East of the Alleghanies is the Atlantic coast plain, which by comparison is much the smaller of the two. Like Europe, North America has been greatly subjected to glacial action during the Ice Age; indeed, the surface soil of the northern half of the continent consists almost entirely of glacial deposits.

Rivers and Lakes.

Flowing westwards from the Rockies we have the comparatively short Pacific rivers, but the term *short* is only used here relatively, for even the Yukon river which looks insignificant on a map of the continent is navigable for 1000 miles in summer. The other rivers upon this slope—Fraser, Columbia, Colorado—are remarkable for the *cañons* or deep gorges with vertical sides, which they have carved for themselves in their course. This phenomenon is characteristic of very dry districts where no small tributaries break through the banks of the main stream.

The rivers of the northern slope, and the lakes which they drain, lose much of their commercial value by the fact that the frozen Arctic Ocean receives their waters. Even the St Lawrence, which lies nearer to the Equator than Cornwall, has its mouth ice-bound during the winter. Of the five great lakes drained by it, four—Superior, Huron, Erie, and Ontario—form part of the boundary between Canada and the United States ; Michigan lies wholly in United States territory. Superior, the largest fresh-water lake in the world, is as large as Ireland.

The giant Mississippi river with its tributaries, the Missouri, Ohio, Arkansas and Red rivers, drains the whole southern slope of the great American plain—an area more than half that of Europe. The main stream is navigable for 4000 miles, and its value as a highway cannot be over-estimated.

Like Asia, Africa, and Australia, North America possesses systems of inland drainage connected with its plateaux. These are chiefly found in the great Basin lying west of the Rockies. Lake Utah has fresh water, because it sends its surplus water by a stream (the Jordan) to the larger lake, the Great Salt Lake.

Coast.

The Arctic coast, with its numerous islands and straits, is in the grip of ice and snow practically all the year. A passage through Hudson Strait to the bay of the same name is possible only during the short summer. Icebergs from the north render the coasts of Labrador very cold and bleak. The Gulf of St Lawrence is almost land-locked by the large islands of Newfoundland and Cape Breton Island. Cape Race in Newfoundland is the most easterly point of the continent. The narrow Bay of Fundy, lying to the west of the peninsula of Nova Scotia, is remarkable for its tidal rise, which attains a height of 60 feet and a velocity of six miles per hour.

South of Cape Cod the eastern American shore is low and marshy, and the Gulf of Mexico, which is separated from the Atlantic by the peninsula of Florida and the West Indies, has a coast of a similarly uninteresting type. The western coast, on the contrary, has fine bold cliffs owing to the nearness of the Pacific coastal ranges. In the northern portion the fjords and islands recall Norwegian scenery. The two peninsulas of the west—California and Alaska—are long, narrow and mountainous. Bering Strait, which separates North America from Asia, is only 36 miles wide.

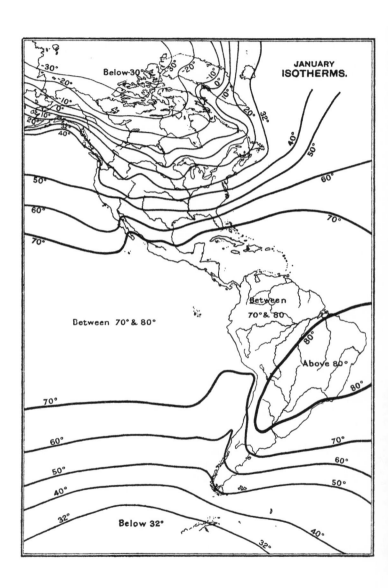

Climate and Rainfall.

The wide extent of the continent from north to south shows its effect on both summer and winter temperatures. A temperature map shows the continent crossed by a series of roughly parallel isotherms, the coldest being in the north. These range from $-30°$ F. to $70°$ F. in January, and from $40°$ F. to $90°$ F. in July. As was seen in Asia, with which continent comparison should be made throughout this section, the winter isotherms curve southwards, and the summer ones northwards, from the eastern and western coasts, from which we see the moderating influence of the sea on each side of the continent.

More than half the area has an average January temperature below freezing point, the southern limit being a diagonal line drawn from the coast at $50°$ N. lat. on the west to $40°$ on the east. The winter in this region is severe and increases in rigour as one proceeds northwards ; the lakes, rivers and seas being frozen. Speaking generally, the American winter is much more severe than that of Europe. New York is colder than the Orkneys, which lie $20°$ further north.

The summers are hotter than those of Europe, the hottest region being found in the great basin towards the west of the United States, where temperature conditions are similar to those of the Iranian plateau and Arabia. The western coast-ranges of mountains shut off the moderating effect of the Pacific Ocean from the interior ; consequently the latter is a region of great extremes, whilst the Pacific border is characterised by an insular climate. On the other hand, there are no great mountain-barriers lying in the north or south, so that Arctic winds in winter, and hot southern winds in summer can sweep the interior for a great distance, and so increase its range of temperature. The blizzard, so typical of the American climate, is an Arctic ice-laden wind sweeping southwards over the country.

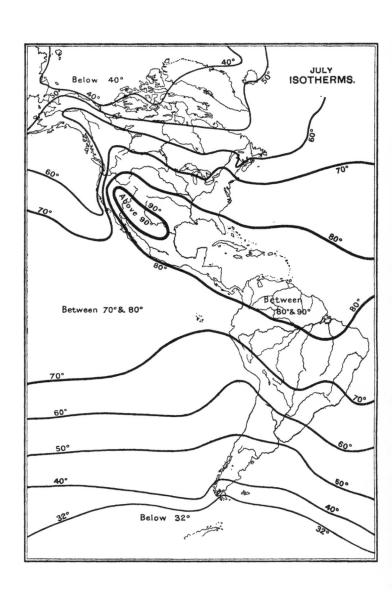

American conditions of barometric pressure strongly resemble those of Asia, for owing to the rapid rate at which the land cools in winter, the air over the centre of the continent has a relatively high pressure, so that winds tend to pass outwards from land to sea. As a result of this, the winter is a dry season, especially in the western interior. On the contrary, an area of low pressure occupies the central region during summer (cf. Asia) and winds from the sea are more common. This is especially true of the eastern half of the continent, which possesses only a moderately elevated mountain-system, and so admits of easy penetration.

The north-western Pacific and the south-eastern Atlantic coasts are the wettest parts of the continent. That this is due to the ocean winds is easily seen from a map showing their directions with respect to the continent.   The northern Pacific coast is under the influence, both in winter and summer, of westerly winds similar to those which exercise so good an effect upon the climate of western Europe.   In Europe the absence of a mountain barrier from north to south allows these winds to deposit their moisture gradually over a very large area, but in America the western ranges are near the shore, so that a narrow belt of wet country results.

Towards the south of the Pacific coast the North-East Trade winds blow away from the country, and this part is dry in consequence.   These winds bring rain to the south-eastern district, and also in summer to the whole eastern coast, for, owing to the existence of a high-pressure area in the Atlantic, they gradually veer round to the north, to form the system of westerly winds which will pick up moisture in their easterly passage across the Atlantic.

Natural Productions.

Latitude and elevation are of the utmost importance in determining the form of the vegetation.   In the far north it is too cold for vegetation, and south of this lies a belt of coniferous forest, which stretches many

degrees further south along the slopes of the Rocky
Mountains. Mixed forests usually occur south of
lat. 46°. The drier parts of the Great Plain are wide
grass lands, but many regions in the Great Basin are
too dry for either pasture or cultivation. The central
dividing meridian 100° W. long. may be taken as the
boundary between the richer and poorer lands, with the
exception of the Saskatchewan river basin in western
Canada. The northerly limit of land capable of cultivation is approximately the 65° July isotherm. In the
eastern half of this cultivable area the great crops are
wheat in the north, maize, requiring more heat, in the
centre, and tobacco and cotton in the south.

Musk oxen and polar bears are found in the far
north. The great forests are a home for the elk in
Canada and for numerous fur-bearing animals generally.
Bisons, now sadly reduced in numbers, used to range the
broad prairies in tens of thousands. The beaver is still
a common inhabitant of the forest streams. Alligators
are numerous in southern waters and the rattlesnake
is common. American birds include the humming bird
and the turkey. Fish are well represented; they include
several species of salmon, astonishingly plentiful in the
western rivers, and cod and herring upon the Newfoundland shallows or banks. The great Bank of Newfoundland
is thought to have been made by sediments from melting
icebergs.

The continent is rich in minerals, and these are
found, as usual, in the mountainous districts. Gold,
silver, iron, copper, lead, tin, mercury, coal, salt, petroleum, and building stone are found in large quantities.

The People and their Distribution.

In America we have an example of a continent where
vigorous Aryan peoples have driven the original inhabitants to the less favoured parts. The Red 'Indians'—
whose misnomer on account of Columbus' mistake in
his longitude still clings to them—are fast disappearing
in this racial struggle, and another racial antagonism

JANUARY
RAINFALL
& WINDS

■ Over 8 inches
▦ 4 - 8 "
▥ 1 - 4 "
░ Under 1 inch
← Direction of
winds

has arisen between the whites and the negro race introduced by them in the early days of settlement upon the continent.

America thus contains peoples of three of the great races of mankind: the white, black, and copper-coloured. The negroes in America are most numerous in the southern states, for they were introduced here because they could withstand the climatic conditions better than white men.   Spanish, French, and English took part in the settlement of the country.   The English element has prevailed, although each of the three has left its mark upon the inhabitants and place-names of the continent.

The distribution of the population is dependent upon the nature of the soil and the presence of minerals, particularly of coal and iron : thus the meridian of 100° W. long. divides the more thickly populated district of the east from the sparsely populated desert and pastoral lands of the west. The cold northern lands are practically destitute of inhabitants, as also are the Rockies and the Great Basin.   Any population map of North America will require modification within a few years, for the more easterly of the pastoral lands and the southern fringe of the forest belt are being rapidly devoted to wheat-culture.

The most thickly populated part of the country is in the east ; this is due partly to the presence of coal and iron and the industries connected with them, and partly to geographical position, which led to the first settlements of the whites being along the eastern border, and which now causes the bulk of the trade to be done from this side of the continent.   The well-favoured agricultural region of the Californian and Columbian seaboard has also a fair number of inhabitants, but not so many as the Atlantic coast.

JULY
RAINFALL
& WINDS

█ Over 8 inches
▦ 4 - 8 "
▤ 1 - 4 "
░ Under 1 inch
← Direction of
  winds

Canada and Newfoundland.

Position and Size.

Canada and Newfoundland together form British North America—a territory nearly as large as Europe, and embracing all the northern half of the North American continent except Alaska in the extreme north-west, from which it is separated by the 141st meridian. Whilst its western shore is washed by the Pacific, it stretches into the Atlantic on the east as far as the 52nd meridian. Its southern frontier, abutting on the United States, has a length of more than 3000 miles, and although following the 49th parallel from the Pacific Ocean to the Lake of the Woods, its course east of that lake is much less regular ; passing south-west to Lake Superior, and then following the median line of the Great Lakes and the river St Lawrence almost as far as Ottawa. It next curves round the New England States and reaches the Atlantic at the Bay of Fundy.

Surface and General Features.

Around Hudson Bay and embracing Keewatin, North-East Territory, and much of Quebec and Ontario is the low Laurentian plateau of ancient rocks with bare-topped hills and lowlands with a clayey soil, often containing lakes. Glaciers once extended over wide areas in this district, and where, as in the south-east, the sediment left by the glaciers is mixed with that deposited by great lakes which have now disappeared, there is a soil of singular fertility. The lands around Hudson Bay are of little use, either being low and swampy, or stony plains with no trees and with but little pasturage, and that of poor quality. The rivers which flow through Quebec from the plateau have numerous rapids and falls. Their power is largely utilised for the saw-mills in the timber trade of the province.

The plains or prairies stretch from the south-west of the plateau to the slopes of the Rocky Mountains. Round the lakes of Manitoba, especially to the east of the province, there are lake soils of great fertility.

The waters of these plains form an intricate network of river and lake ; the rivers go by different names in various parts of their courses, and in some cases there is water communication between the different river systems. The Mackenzie river is navigable in summer for 4000 miles, and the Saskatchewan-Nelson system is increasing in importance owing to the agricultural development of the naturally fertile soil.

The western part of the country is most mountainous. The two great ranges are the Rocky Mountains and the Cascade range, the former being mainly composed of limestone, the latter of granitic rocks. Snow-clad peaks tower above to a height of 10,000 feet and glaciers feed the rushing torrents, which leap over high falls down the forested mountain sides. The Rocky Mountains decrease in height and width as they approach higher latitudes. Although we speak of them as a mountain range it is truer to regard them as a series of parallel ranges. We shall refer to some of these ranges—the Selkirk and Gold Mountains—in connection with the minerals of the Dominion. The most westerly range of this great Cordilleran system is now partially submerged by the ocean, and appears as the long line of islands upon the Pacific coast. The rivers of this short western slope are noted for their rapidity and their wealth of fish.

The St Lawrence, which is navigable by ocean-going steamers as far as Montreal, is by far the most important river flowing into the Atlantic Ocean. It is the natural highway for the trade and population of the country. Its basin is four times the size of the British Isles, but fully one-third of this area is covered by the great chain of lakes, Superior, Michigan, Huron, Erie, and Ontario. These lakes lie about 550 feet above sea level and have a depth of 300 to 900 ft.

Niagara Falls

Many rapids and falls obstruct the passage of the Canadian rivers: the Saskatchewan is impeded by rapids at its entrance into Lake Winnipeg, and the Montmorency falls near Quebec have a height of more than 200 feet, whilst the celebrated Falls of Niagara between lakes Erie and Ontario are nearly 170 feet high. Reference has already been made to the utilisation of water power for Canadian saw mills; the Niagara Falls provide power for the electric lighting and industries of the neighbouring towns.

One highland region has not yet been mentioned : that forming the south-eastern boundary both of the province of Quebec and the basin of the St Lawrence. This is the northern extremity of the Appalachian system. Its narrower coastal slope is towards the St Lawrence.

The Canadian Coast.

The most prominent physical feature of the low, monotonous Arctic shore which is icebound most of the year, is the broad expanse of Hudson Bay. Although this inlet is more than 1000 miles long, it is only 60 fathoms deep in the middle. This remarkable fact is due to its being merely a local depression of the plateau which almost surrounds it. As a result of its shallow character it has no harbours suitable for large ocean-going vessels.

The Gulf of the St Lawrence has bold, rocky shores. Its northern entrance is by the Strait of Belle Isle. Newfoundland has good harbours among the many bays of its rocky north-eastern and southern coasts. Sable Island, to the east of the Nova Scotian peninsula, is a long sandy stretch—a menace to shipping. It has both lighthouse and lifeboat protection. The peninsula itself has low sandy shores upon its eastern side ; its western coast experiences very high tides. In the Bay of Fundy there is a rise of 60 feet due to the tide, and the St John's harbour has a reversible fall as a result of the tide—a fresh-water fall seawards at low tide, and a salt-water fall in the opposite direction at high water. The ports of Halifax and St John's have a great advantage over those of the St Lawrence in that they are ice-free throughout the year.

In the Gulf of St Lawrence, which extends for 500 miles, the chief islands are Cape Breton, Prince Edward, and Anticosti. The great lakes have in general low shores, but rugged cliffs give fine scenery to the southern shore of Lake Superior.

The finest coast scenery, however, is found on the Pacific side of the continent, where inlets of great depth but narrow width extend far into the land as winding fjords with steep mountainous sides, sometimes half as high as the Alps. Exceptionally good harbours are found at Vancouver and Fort Simpson.

Climate and Rainfall.

As a large part of a great land-mass, Canada naturally experiences an extreme or continental climate. The winters are intensely cold, but, thanks to the prevailing dryness, not unhealthy or disagreeable. With the exception of the southern part of the Pacific coast and islands, the average January temperature is below freezing point (32° F.) for the entire country. The northern regions have the coldest temperatures; all districts north of a line drawn from the south end of Lake Winnipeg to Bering Strait and East Labrador have, on the average, more than 32 degrees of frost during this month. The following *average* temperatures for January are very instructive : Montreal 12° F., Quebec 14°, Winnipeg 0°, New Westminster 37°. From these figures we see that the winter of the east and interior is much colder than that of the Pacific coast, where ocean and moist wind exert great warming influence. Newfoundland and Nova Scotia have less severe winters than other parts of the eastern district, the average temperature from January to March being about 22° F. It should be noted that the Canadian winter can only be compared with that of one other climatic area—North-Eastern Asia.

Summer isotherms over Canada curve sharply to the north along the Columbian shore region and then slope gently to the south-east across the greater part of the country. From this we see that the hottest part in July is in the south-west, *i.e.* nearest to the region of greatest heat in the continent. The 70° isotherm for July runs in its south-easterly course from the Lesser Slave Lake to the western end of Lake Superior. The Atlantic and Pacific coasts have a cooler temperature in July than the interior : St John's 58°, Quebec 60°, New Westminster 60°, Winnipeg 70°. Newfoundland is cooled in summer by the melting of icebergs which have travelled south.

In considering the extremes of temperature in Canada it is well to bear in mind that the range for the British Isles is about 20° F. Such a small range in Canada is only to be found upon the Pacific coast, where, as at Victoria upon Vancouver Island, the variation is as little as 16°. Winnipeg has a very extreme climate, the range being 70°, and even the eastern coast of Canada has a range of temperature double that of our own islands. The student should notice that the Pacific shore is warmer than the Atlantic.

As regards rainfall we may divide Canada into three regions :

(*a*) The eastern half, as far as Winnipeg, where rainfall is heavy on the coast and gradually decreases westwards.

(*b*) The very wet coastal region along the Pacific.

(*c*) The dry western half of Canada, lying between (*a*) and (*b*).

Owing to the cold Labrador current, fogs are prevalent upon the Atlantic coast.

Pear Orchard in bloom, Ontario

Agriculture.

Agriculture is practised in Canada on an extensive scale, especially in the growth of cereals. Labour-saving machinery is widely employed in this branch, and the grain is stored in huge elevators and transported in special cars and ships. The cooler, moister eastern provinces grow much oats and barley as well as a fair amount of wheat, but the hot, dry, though short summer of the 'North-West' (Manitoba and the Saskatchewan) is especially favourable to wheat culture, particularly in the eastern and therefore moister prairies. Quebec grows maize and tobacco in addition to cereals, and in the cooler parts of most provinces large quantities of potatoes and flax are produced.

The 'peninsula' of Ontario is devoted to orchards and fruit culture. Grapes are grown here in the south near the lakes, and a wine industry is being developed. Another rising fruit district is the coast of British Columbia, which possesses an admirable climate for the purpose.

Cattle-rearing and dairy-farming form important industries in the moist eastern provinces, but stock-raising is the only pursuit possible in the dry 'ranch' country lying to the east of the Rockies, and Alberta is the great cattle province.

Plants and Animals.

The summer isotherm of 50° is approximately the boundary between the zones of tundra and of coniferous forest. The forest zone spreads from one ocean to the other and has a width of 200 miles in many places. Pine, spruce, larch, birch, with poplar along the southern edge, are the principal trees found in this region, and lumbering is a great industry in almost every province. Grass plains, where there is not enough moisture for the growth of trees, stretch from Lakes Superior, Lake of the Woods and Winnipeg to the foot of the Rockies. In the easterly part of this region the rainfall is sufficient

Salmon Fishing, Canada

to repay agriculture, and this district is the most promising in the Dominion to-day.

The fur-bearing animals of Canada recall those of Siberia. The skunk, marten, mink, beaver, and bear are but a few of the many animals found here. The scanty grasses of the Keewatin district provide food for herds of reindeer. The musk ox and elk are rare, and the bison is practically extinct. Both rivers and seas are plentifully stocked with fish. The Columbian rivers are so full of salmon that it is the daily food of Indian tribes. Cod, herring, lobsters, and halibut are obtained from the Atlantic. The cod and salmon fisheries are worth £4,000,000 yearly. Lobsters, exported like salmon in the 'canned' state, produce £80,000, and the seal fishery of the northern seas is almost as productive.

Minerals.

The colony is rich in minerals : gold, coal, copper, and nickel are the most common, and iron, mica, lead, and petroleum are also found. The coal mines of Nova Scotia produce four million tons annually, and those of Vancouver Island have caused Esquimalt, near Victoria, to be the coaling station of our fleet in Pacific waters. Gold is found in Nova Scotia, Quebec, British Columbia (Selkirk Range), and Klondyke in the far north-west. The output from Klondyke amounts annually to £4,000,000. Thus the bulk of the mineral wealth is found in the east and the west, the great plains being practically devoid of minerals.

People, Race, and Religion.

The population exceeds five millions, *i.e.* a population less than that of London is spread over a country nearly as large as the continent of Europe. The native races —Eskimo and Indian—comprise not more than one-fiftieth of the people. About one-third of the Indians are found in the north-west territories, but the others are scattered all over the country. The Sioux and Iroquois tribes live in the western plains and the St

Lawrence provinces respectively. The forest-dwelling tribes are skilful trappers ; the birch tree provides them with both canoe and wigwam.

The white population, which is being increased by a quarter of a million immigrants yearly, is most dense in the valley of the St Lawrence, but the wheat-lands of Manitoba and districts further west are rapidly becoming peopled. Dawson City in Yukon is a good example of a dense population in a small area owing to the discovery of mineral wealth. The fertile Ontario peninsula has the thickest population of any area in the Dominion ; fertility of soil also accounts in part for Prince Edward Island having a greater population than any other province in proportion to area.

So many French Canadians (85 %) inhabit Quebec, that both French and English are used as the official languages of the province. The French have preserved their Roman Catholic form of religion, and Roman Catholics number 40 % in the entire Dominion.

Asiatic immigrants, both Chinese and Japanese, have settled along the Pacific coast. The Chinese perform domestic work in the western towns.

History explained by Geographical Considerations.

As we should expect from the geographical positions of Europe and Canada, the eastern coast of the latter was the first part to be colonised by white men. Again, the St Lawrence, as a far-reaching inlet, formed the natural route for colonisation, and to-day its valley forms one of the most densely-peopled areas. France and England, occupying favourable positions on the west of Europe, entered as a matter of course, upon the work of settlement to the exclusion of other European nations. Spain did not take part as she was fully and lucratively occupied in the southern parts of the continent.

Nova Scotia was the French colony of Acadie from 1605 till the Peace of Utrecht in 1713. Quebec began

as a fur station in 1601, and its capture by Wolfe in
1759 marked the close of French power in the country.
We owe Ontario to loyal colonists, who moved northwards from the States when the short-sighted policy of
the British government had caused the great rebellion
in 1776.   Not only were the settlers loyal to England,
but they succeeded in repelling the United States army
which invaded their country in 1812.

The original settlers in Manitoba were servants of
the great fur-trading companies, who founded many
stations in the north and west.   British Columbia owes
much of its importance to the great gold-rush of 1857.
Newfoundland remains outside the Dominion, and
although one would expect it to have been peopled in
the early days of the colony, its settlement was delayed
by the jealous fear of British fishing companies that
their trade would be spoilt by competition with local
inhabitants.

Industries and Communications.

The fur trade, fishing, mining, agriculture, stock-
raising, and lumbering are the great industries of
Canada.   Connected with the forest trade is the manufacture of resin, of wood pulp for paper, and, in Nova
Scotia, of ships.

The natural communications by river and lake
are impeded by frost and rapids.   Traffic via the St
Lawrence and the great lakes is stopped by ice for four
months of the year.   The Indians still surmount the
difficulties of navigation of the rapids by using light
birch-bark canoes, which draw but little water and can
'shoot' many rapids in safety ; on the return journey
they can be emptied of their contents and carried past
the dangerous parts.   Modern engineering skill, however,
has constructed canals with locks where rapids occur
upon the more important water highways.   It is thus
possible to pass by water from the Atlantic Ocean to
the head of Lake Superior.

A Canadian Log Raft

The Welland Canal avoids the Falls of Niagara, and the rapids of the St Mary River are passed by the three 'Soo' canals (one Canadian and two American) at Saulte St Marie. Boats can also pass from Ottawa to Kingston on Lake Ontario by the Rideau Canal. The proposed 'Georgian Bay' canal will connect Lake Huron and the St Lawrence via the Ottawa river and Lake Nipissing at a cost of £20,000,000.

But Canada takes greatest pride in her two long lines of railway : the *Grand Trunk* and the *Canadian Pacific*. The former taps the resources of Ontario and Quebec. One terminus is in United States territory at Portland in the state of Maine, and Detroit and Chicago are both upon the line. Quebec forms the other terminus and the railway skirts the St Lawrence and Lakes Ontario and Erie, passing through Montreal, Ottawa and Toronto.

The *Canadian Pacific Railway* crosses the entire continent—a distance of 3000 miles—from Quebec to Vancouver. It first follows the St Lawrence to Montreal, then turns westwards through Ottawa, the capital of the Dominion, and Sudbury, the nickel-mining centre, to Port Arthur upon the north-west coast of Lake Superior. Next, it traverses the rich grain-growing country both east and west of Winnipeg. Regina marks its entrance into the ranching country, which it leaves near Calgary to ascend the Rocky Mountains. Two passes are utilised, the junction being at Medicine Hat. The northern branch passes Kicking Horse Pass and the Kamloops goldfield, and joins the second, which traverses the Crow's Nest Pass and the Kootenay goldfield, before coming to an end at the twin towns of Vancouver and New Westminster.

Commerce and Ports.

The annual value of Canadian commerce is about £100,000,000. The imports include metal goods and the textile manufactures necessary for a civilised white race not largely engaged in manufactures. Natural productions (wheat, timber, cheese, silver, cattle, bacon,

Rocky Mountains: Crow's Nest Pass

and wheat-flour) constitute the exports of the country. Internal commerce is large ; the 'Soo' canals have a greater annual tonnage passing through them than has the Suez Canal.

The United States and Britain share most of the foreign trade, but the high American tariffs hinder trade with that country. *Vancouver* is the great port on the west coast. It has regular sailings of steamers to Japan, Australia, and New Zealand.

Montreal, the head of the St Lawrence navigation for ocean vessels, is the summer port for the Liverpool trade, steamers from which town usually pass round the north of Ireland, calling at Moville. Winter commerce is done with *Halifax* in Nova Scotia, and *St John* in New Brunswick, and the route chosen is that passing to the south of Ireland, steamers calling at Queenstown.

Administration, Divisions, and Towns.

The Dominion of Canada consists of nine provinces (Nova Scotia, Prince Edward Island, New Brunswick, Quebec, Ontario, Manitoba, British Columbia, Alberta, Saskatchewan) and several territories. The central government is at Ottawa, there being a British Governor-General, who holds office for five years, and two houses of parliament. Each province has also a Governor and a house of parliament, except Quebec and Nova Scotia, which possess two 'houses.'

Halifax, in Nova Scotia, is a fortified port and coaling station. *Montreal*, in Quebec, is the largest Canadian port. *Quebec* is the oldest town, and possesses wood-pulp factories. *Ottawa*, on the Ottawa river, is the capital of the Dominion. *Toronto* is a manufacturing and banking centre. *Kingston* has important colleges. *Winnipeg* and *Brandon* are centres of the grain district. *Victoria*, on Vancouver Island, has a fishing fleet. *Fort Churchill*, on Hudson Bay, has a harbour which is ice-free for five months in the year. *Dawson* is the gold-mining town in Yukon. *St John's*, in Newfoundland, has a good harbour and large cod-fishing industry.

The United States of America.

Position and Size.

The country of the United States is worthy of the name of a continent, for its area is nearly three million sq. miles and almost equals that of Europe. From the Atlantic in the east to the Pacific in the far west it measures a distance of 2,500 miles. Canada bounds it upon the north, whilst its southern boundary is formed by the Mexican Republic and Gulf of Mexico. If we exclude the northern part of Alaska the country lies entirely within the North Temperate Zone.

Surface and General Features.

The outstanding features of the surface are the eastern and western highlands, and the broad plain stretching between them. The Atlantic coast plain is found to the east of these, and the short Pacific slope to the west.

The eastern highlands are known as the Alleghany or Appalachian system. They run almost parallel to the coast from the extreme north of the country as far south as latitude 34°, and are separated from the sea by the Atlantic shore plain. In the north they are quite near the sea, but they diverge from it further south, where the coast plain attains a breadth of 200 miles. Much of this coast plain is of a sandy type and is only useful for forest growth. The part lying nearer the mountains however is more fertile, having a marl soil.

The Appalachians have their oldest rocks along their eastern side, whilst along the west flank, adjoining their more recent rocks (which themselves are *primary* in point of geological age) is the Alleghany plateau. The mountains are known by various names (Green Mountains, Cumberland Mountains, Catskills, etc.) in different states. It should be particularly noticed that they are of lowest elevation in their central region, *i.e.* between the towns of New York and Washington. This fact will be found of great importance in dealing with the history of the country.

The Yellowstone Cañon

The great central plain occupies about half the country. It ends on the west at the Rocky Mountains, in one part of which is America's National Park. This, the *Yellowstone Park* as it is called from one of the many colours of its rocks, is a magnificent district about half the size of Wales and situated at an elevation of 8000 ft. above sea level. It is a land of fantastically terraced mountains, seething clay pools, mud volcanoes and geysers. One of the latter sends at intervals a jet of water some 150 ft. into the air—a natural fountain. The Yellowstone river has fine waterfall and cañon scenery within this area of nature's marvels. The student should compare the natural phenomena of the Yellowstone region with those of North Island, New Zealand.

West of the Rockies lies the Great Basin, which in many parts is almost a rainless land. It is traversed by mountain ranges, and owes its low rainfall to the Sierra Nevada and Cascade Mountains, which lying quite close to the Pacific, rob the ocean winds of their moisture. Another of America's 'playing grounds' is situated in the former of these ranges. This is the famous *Yosemite Valley*, situated about 150 miles from San Francisco. The waterfalls of this region are its finest feature.

Rivers and Lakes.

The Hudson is the most important of the Atlantic rivers. Its valley, with that of the Mohawk, one of its tributaries, has been one of the main highways for immigration. Communication with the Great Lakes is afforded by means of the Erie Canal. Like the other rivers of the Atlantic states, the Hudson, although navigable to Troy, 150 miles from its mouth, has rapids and waterfalls in its course. These falls are important in that they provide electric and water 'power' for manufacturing processes.

The *Mississippi* has a low-lying source, much lower in fact than that of its tributaries the Missouri and Ohio rivers, which rise in the Rocky Mountains and the Alleghanies respectively. St Paul marks the head of its navigation, for here the Falls of St Anthony bar further passage. The river is very liable to floods, and embankments called *levées* are necessary for their prevention. At its mouth it has built up a large delta. This can be seen very well by a glance at the shape of the southern coast. Where the river enters the Gulf of Mexico there is a spit of land projecting into the sea. This represents the earth brought down by the river as suspended matter. The value of the river as a highway of internal communication is increased by the fact that, whilst the main stream flows from the north, its two great tributaries flow from east and west.

Coast Line.

The Western coast has few good harbours, those of San Francisco and Puget Sound being the best. This is a marked contrast to the north-eastern portion of the Atlantic coast, where, owing to land subsidence, the eastern valleys of the Appalachian system have been submerged, and now appear as roadsteads possessing deep water and safe anchorage. The eastern coast is much lower and sandier south of Chesapeake Bay, and is marked by sand reefs, swamps, and lagoons. The American 'beaches' or pleasure resorts are found here Atlanta City being one of the best known.

The sand reefs are known locally as 'banks.' They are portions of the continental shelf, which extends 100 miles from the shore, and their formation is largely due to conflicting ocean currents. The coast of Florida has coral reefs. This is a sign of the warmth and purity of the sea water. The southern shore of the continent is low and swampy.

Climate and Rainfall.

In general the United States has extremes of climate : *i.e.* hot summers and cold winters, but this statement requires a little modification ; for the coastal districts have not such extremes as the interior, and the southern and western coasts are more equable in climate than the eastern coast. St Paul, situated on the upper Mississippi, is a fair example of the continental interior ; with a

January temperature of 20° F. and a July temperature of 75° F. it has a range of 55°. New York, on the other hand, has a range of about 40°, whereas New Orleans, near the Gulf of Mexico, has only 30° range. Further, the Pacific coast has temperature corresponding in range to that of our own islands, *i.e.* about 20°.

The student should guard against the serious error of considering these ranges of temperature as actual temperatures. They do not represent the actual temperatures experienced, but are a guide to the average difference of temperature experienced in January and July. Their great value lies in the fact that they show us at a glance whether a climate is equable or extreme. The distinction will be made clearer by reference to the temperatures of St Paul and New Orleans: the latter town having average temperatures of 55° and 85° in January and July. From these we see that range of temperature is no guide to the actual temperature of winter or summer.

The hottest part of the country is the Colorado plateau (or the Great Basin) where the summers are as hot as those of the Sahara desert. Sudden changes of temperature are characteristic of the country, for *cyclones* frequently traverse the Great Plain. Owing to the anti-clockwise direction of the cyclonic winds as previously explained, places lying to the front of the cyclone have heat waves or *sirocco weather* due to hot winds blowing northwards. On the other hand, such places have cool weather when the cyclone has almost passed them, for then north-westerly winds blow from the cooler north. The Mississippi valley is also subject to *tornadoes*, or funnel-shaped whirlwinds of terrible destructiveness. They are due to the meeting of hot upper and cool lower currents of the atmosphere. Again, the presence or absence of ocean currents has much to do in determining the average temperature of the coasts. The western, southern, and south-eastern coasts have warm currents directed towards them (Pacific and Gulf Stream currents), whereas the North

Atlantic States have their shores washed by a cool current from the north, the Gulf Stream having veered from the east coast in a north-easterly direction.

Rainfall is greatest on the Gulf of Mexico and the north-west Pacific coast. The Atlantic coast has a sufficient supply of rain, as has also the Mississippi valley, although a less amount. Rainfall decreases from south to north, and from the east coast to the practically rainless Great Basin, which includes Nevada, Utah, Arizona, and South California.

Agriculture and Stock Raising.

The United States is one of the foremost agricultural countries of the world. The 100° meridian approximately divides the agricultural from the pastoral area, or rather, to be more correct, it divides the agricultural and pastoral from the purely pastoral, for in the eastern half of the country the two industries are closely mingled. Thus in the great maize-growing area round the Ohio river, millions of hogs are fed upon maize or 'corn' as it is called by the Americans.

The wheat-growing district stretches from the Great Lakes on the north to the confluences of the Missouri and Ohio with the Mississippi on the south, and from the 100° meridian to the Alleghanies on the east. The hot dry summers of the country round St Paul make it a centre for the wheat-growing industry. Washington in the north-west is also coming to the front as a wheat-producing state. Cotton, sugar, tobacco and rice are the chief vegetable products of the lower Mississippi and southern Atlantic plains. Fruit—including peaches, grapes, and oranges—is extensively produced in the fertile valley of the Sacramento in California. Florida has a similar industry, both districts being well supplied with moisture and warmth. Salt Lake City deserves mention, for round it the land is carefully irrigated, and climatic disadvantages are thus overcome.

Cotton-picking

The cattle-raising district lies largely along the Missouri and its tributaries. The plains stretch to the foot of the Rockies, and the shortness of their hot summer renders them suitable only for grass.

Plants and Animals.

The country is well wooded, with the exception of the treeless prairies, where fineness of soil, moderate or scanty rain, and Indian fires have prevented forest growth. California is the land of giant conifers such as Sequoia. In the sub-tropical south are found mangroves, cacti, and palms. Thorny, drought-resisting plants and pale grey sage scrub grow in the dry districts of the west.

The American wild animals—bear, elk, deer, mountain sheep, and goats—are fast disappearing, except in the specially reserved areas.

Fisheries.

Valuable oyster-beds have been laid in Chesapeake Bay on the Atlantic coast. Seals abound off the Alaskan shore, whilst the canning of salmon, caught in the Columbia river, is one of the most profitable industries in the states of Washington and Oregon.

Minerals.

Coal, iron, and copper are determining the position of the United States as a great manufacturing country. The presence of these, as well as of petroleum and natural gas, in the north-east has already made the district lying between the Great Lakes and the northern Atlantic coast the principal manufacturing area of America. Copper is plentiful in the Rocky Mountains as well as in the state of Michigan. The western highlands provide silver and gold, the latter also being found in Alaska. The fine public buildings in the eastern cities are partly accounted for by the presence of various building stones in the northern part of the Appalachian system. Florida, in the south-east, will gain an increased importance in the future by exporting her rich beds of phosphates for use as manure.

The People and their Distribution.

The United States offers a close parallel to Canada in its racial elements and in the distribution of its inhabitants, although, of course, differences occur; for instance, the nine million negroes living in the United States have no counterpart in Canada. As in Canada, there are remnants of Indians to be found, even in the east of the country, for instance, in the state of Maine. The eastern portion of the country is also the most thickly peopled, and the New England states may be considered as corresponding in this respect to Nova Scotia and Prince Edward Island. In both countries density of population decreases from east to west, a river (the St Lawrence and the Upper Mississippi) has a thickly peopled valley, and Chinese immigrants are found on the Pacific coast.

When we consider that the United States possessed less than six million inhabitants a century ago, about 14 millions 70 years ago, and now has 77 millions, giving an average of 25 to the square mile, we can understand that she must have drawn many of these from foreign countries. About half the foreign-born people in the States have come from the British Isles and Germany, but most European countries have also furnished immigrants. These immigrants, though poor, are as a rule hardworking, law-abiding people and rapidly become Americanised.

History as determined by Geographical Considerations.

Colonisation by European races was shared by the British, Dutch, French, and Spaniards, and the earliest settlements were naturally round the good harbours of the eastern coast. Commercial and religious reasons decided the settlement. The Pilgrim Fathers started from Plymouth in 1620 to obtain religious freedom;

similar considerations caused William Penn and his
Quaker friends to found Pennsylvania in 1681. Virginia
and Carolina had come into existence in 1584 and 1663,
and in 1667 the Dutch relinquished their station of New
Amsterdam (afterwards New York) to the British as a
result of European politics.

Colonisation steadily proceeded westwards, although
greatly hindered by the Alleghany barrier, until the
thirteen states which threw off the English yoke in 1776
had a territory bounded roughly by the Atlantic Ocean
and the Mississippi. The first half of the 19th century
witnessed great expansion to the south and west : the
purchase of Louisiana from the French in 1803 added
an immense territory stretching from the Mississippi
to the Rockies, whilst the purchase of Florida from
Spain, the annexation of Texas, and the occupation
of the Pacific region were completed by 1846. About
20 years later Russia ceded her American territory—
Alaska—to the United States government for a monetary
consideration.

The main stream of immigration westwards has been
through the low, narrow part of the Alleghanies near
New York. The development of this city as a port has
also been largely due to the navigability of the Hudson
and the easy passage its valley and that of the Mohawk
afford to the Great Lakes. If we add that New York
is the nearest port for Europe and that it possesses
a very good harbour, we can understand why it is so
important a city.

Industries and Manufactures.

Lumbering in the region south of the lakes, milling
round St Paul, and meat-packing round Chicago and
Cincinnati may be cited as typical American industries.
The New England states soon developed the cotton-
spinning industry, since they possessed abundant water-
power, a sufficiently humid atmosphere, and were within
easy reach of raw material from the South Atlantic
states. But the greatest manufacturing activity has

followed the development of the mining industry in the
north-east, where coal and iron are found together.
Machinery, railway stock, clocks, agricultural implements, paper, leather, sugar, and textiles are only a few
of the many manufactures in this district.

Communications.

The traffic by river, canal, and lake is not as great as
formerly, owing to the rapid growth of railways which
now cover the country with an intricate network.   It is
impossible to distinguish here between the numerous
lines of the north-eastern manufacturing district, but we
can note the longest lines :

(i)   The *Pennsylvania Railroad*, linking New
      York with Chicago and St Louis.

(ii) The *Northern Pacific* from Chicago and
      Duluth to Portland on the Pacific.

(iii) The *Union Pacific*, which runs due west from
      Chicago to San Francisco.

(iv) The *Central Pacific* from Pittsburg through
      St Louis to Salt Lake.

(v)   The *East Coast* through Philadelphia and
      New Orleans.

(vi) The *Southern Pacific* through New Orleans
      and Los Angeles to San Francisco.

Commerce and Ports.

The United States is the second commercial country
in the world.   Her annual foreign trade reaches the
almost incredible total of £670,000,000.   Great Britain
is her best customer, receiving about one-third of her
goods and sending her one-sixth of the goods she
requires.   New York is her premier port ; about half
the total trade of the whole country is done through
that city.   Baltimore, Boston, Philadelphia, New Orleans,
and San Francisco do almost all the remainder.   We
receive chiefly bacon, petroleum, cattle, tobacco, copper,
wood, leather, beef, and lard, from the United States,
and send in return textiles, metal goods, chemicals,
china, and glassware.

Administration.

The original 13 states have increased to 45. Each has a Parliament and Governor of its own, but also sends representatives to the Federal Parliament (the Senate and House of Representatives) which meets at Washington. The form of government is Republican, the President being at its head, and holding office for four years.

Towns.

New York, on Manhattan Island, now includes *Brooklyn* on Long Island. It has a population of four millions, and innumerable industries. A suspension bridge connects the two towns. *Boston*, the second port, has great historical interest. Leather, clothing, printing, and metal-working are some of its industries. At *Cambridge*, near by, is Harvard University. *New Orleans*, near the mouth of the Mississippi, exports cotton, oil, rice, and sugar. *San Francisco* connects the trans-continental railways with China, Japan, and Australia by means of regular steamship lines. It exports wheat, fruit, timber, meat, and wine. *Philadelphia* has more than a million inhabitants. Many of these are engaged in metal, textile, and pottery industries.

Baltimore on Chesapeake Bay is a centre for oysters, tobacco, and metal goods. *Chicago*, at the southern end of Lake Michigan, is a city of two million inhabitants. It is a great railway, cattle, and grain centre. Its packing-yards are among the most extensive in the world. *Pittsburg* manufactures iron and glass goods and refines petroleum. *Minneapolis* and *St Paul* are milling centres. *Cincinnati* has received from its packing-yards the name of 'Porkopolis.' *St Louis* has a similar industry. *Cleveland* smelts the iron brought to it from Lake Superior. *Washington* is the federal capital. *Salt Lake City* is the headquarters of the Mormons or Latter-Day Saints.

Central America.

Position and Size.

In Central America we include Mexico, the group of small states lying to the south of it as far as the Panama Isthmus, and the encircling band of West Indian Islands which form, as it were, a natural breakwater against the Caribbean Sea and the Gulf of Mexico. The Rio Grande forms the northern boundary of Mexico—a country six times as large as the British Isles, and situated half within, half outside the Torrid Zone. The Bahamas are similarly placed, whereas the remainder of the district we are now considering lies wholly south of the Tropic and stretches to within 8° of the equator. Although the islands appear small on the map, some of them are really of considerable size: Cuba is as large as England.

Surface and General Features.

The bulk of Mexico is covered by a plateau, from which rise many snow-capped volcanic peaks, prominent among which are Orizaba and Popocatepetl, which respectively reach a height of more than 18,205 and 17,784 feet. The plateau has been largely formed by the valleys between the great mountains being filled up with volcanic dust and other ejected material, so that from the level of the plateau the peaks appear much lower than they really are. The rivers are alternately dried-up water-courses and raging torrents, and are useless for purposes of communication. The majority of them are short, owing to the nearness of the rims of the plateau to the coast.

Mexico has the long narrow Gulf of California upon the west separating Lower California from the mainland. The mountainous nature of the Californian peninsula is a distinct contrast to that of Yucatan, which projects northwards into the Gulf of Mexico from the south-east of the country. The narrow isthmus of Central America is a land of mountains, volcanoes, and earthquakes. The Panama isthmus is but little more than 40 miles wide. The work of canalisation, by means of which a saving of 5000 miles will be effected in the sea route from London to San Francisco, is now being undertaken by the United States government.

Popocatepetl

The islands include the Bahamas, the Great Antilles (Cuba, Jamaica, Haiti, and Porto Rico) and the Lesser Antilles (the Windward and Leeward Isles). The majority of them have had a volcanic origin and are exceedingly fertile. The Bahamas are more barren; they are a long series of coral islands lying roughly parallel to Cuba.

Climate and Rainfall.

The Mexican interior has a more extreme climate than any of the islands or the narrower portion of the isthmus. In summer its plateau forms part of the very hot district of North America, whereas the remaining parts of the region have exceedingly equable, but tropical, climates—about 5° F. being the usual average range. They owe this to the nearness of the sea, to their low latitude and consequent little variation in the length of day, and to the prevalent North East Trades. Usually more rain falls in summer than in winter, and in general the rainfall on the north-eastern side is greater than that on the west. The mountains of Guatemala for instance receive a rainfall of 195 inches annually on their northern slope, but their summits and southern slopes receive only 100 inches and 27 inches respectively.

Natural Productions.

Altitude is one of the greatest factors in deciding which plants can grow in a country, and we may say that there are three climatic zones of vegetation as a result. The lowlands and slopes to the height of about 3000 feet have a luxuriant tropical vegetation, including mahogany, logwood, rosewood, rubber, coconut, banana, and cacao. From 3000 to 7000 feet elevation coffee, sugar, maize, and oranges are cultivated, and above this elevation are forests of oak and pine with clear spaces devoted to wheat, potato, and cattle rearing. Wild animals are numerous on the mainland but not on the islands. They include many monkeys, the puma, jaguar, tapir, ant-eater, alligator and turtle.

Agriculture is carried on by primitive methods, but the great moisture and high temperature ensure large crops. Cacao, tobacco, and sugar are the chief products of the islands.

Mexico possesses a variety of minerals, including iron, copper, and mercury as well as the precious metals,

platinum, gold, and silver.   The last two metals yield
£13,000,000 annually, silver being by far the more
important.   Gold and silver are also mined in Honduras
and Nicaragua, and the island of Trinidad has vast
supplies of asphalt which is obtained from its pitch
lake.

The People and their History.

The Mexicans of to-day are a mixed Indian and
Spanish race, although more than half the people have
not intermingled.   The majority of the inhabitants of
Mexico and the Isthmus are poorly educated, since they
suffered from Spanish oppression for the three centuries
which ended in 1823.   Mexico, after trying an imperial
form of government, has now become a republic, closely
modelled on that of the United States.   The isthmian
lands are now five separate republics.   Their peoples
are a mixture of natives, blacks and whites, and as-
similate but little.   These states are subject to sudden
and frequent insurrections, conspiracies, and changes of
presidents.

On the islands the coloured races are increasing at
the expense of the whites.   We should expect this from
climatic conditions.

The distribution of population on the isthmian
lands is interesting : on the torrid plains of the lowlands there is less than one person per square mile, for
human beings suffer much from the unhealthiness
of the climate.   In higher parts of the country,
where more healthy conditions prevail, the population
has a density of 280 per square mile.   The habitable
zone on the mountains extends to a height of 10,000 ft.

Industries, Commerce, and Towns.

The mainland has local manufactures of blankets,
felt and straw hats, pottery, leather, tobacco and filigree
work, but these are of no importance from the commercial point of view.   The manufacture and export of
cigars from Havana (in Cuba) is, however, noteworthy

Roads are bad, almost impassable in fact in many parts. Traffic is largely done by porterage, pack-mules, and clumsy ox-carts. Railways are increasing in Mexico, there being at the present time about 10,000 miles of line. The nearness of the United States is partly responsible for this. The railway from Puerto Mexico to Salina Cruz crosses the isthmus of Tehuantepec and is of the greatest importance. It will prove a serious rival to the Panama Canal as it shortens the Japanese and Chinese voyages so much, and it is estimated that no less than 1200 miles will be saved by this route from New York to San Francisco over that via Panama.

Natural productions (silver, coffee, sugar, indigo, spices, woods, and fruits) are the chief exports. *Havana* and *Santiago* in Cuba, and *Tampico* and *Acapulco* in Mexico, have the finest harbours. The trade of *Vera Cruz* is decreasing owing to its harbour being exposed to hurricanes. *Mexico*, the capital of the state of Mexico, is a half Spanish town situated 7000 feet above sea level at the foot of Popocatepetl.

CHAPTER IX

SOUTH AMERICA

Position and Size.

South America is a huge continental peninsula, almost twice as large as Europe, stretching from 12° North to 55° South latitude, and attached on the north to its twin peninsular continent by the Isthmus of Panama. It is bounded on the north and east by the Atlantic, and on the west by the Pacific Ocean. The greater part of it lies within the Tropics.

Surface and General Features.

It may be compared in build with North America, for it possesses eastern and western mountain systems running approximately north and south, and a broad plain lying between them.

The immense mountain system of the Andes extends throughout the continent from north to south for a distance of 5000 miles. Many of its peaks exceed 20,000 feet in height and are snow-clad throughout the year. In the south, many peaks have extensive glaciers, and in common with other recently elevated mountain-chains the Andes possess many volcanoes, one of which—Cotopaxi—was last in eruption in 1879. Like the Rocky Mountains, its counterpart in North America, the system consists of threefold, double, and single ranges in different parts. It is the great continental watershed, sending numerous short rivers to the west and others of very great length to the east. In width it varies from 30 to 500 miles and internal drainage systems occur in its widest central portion.

The mountains of Guiana lie in the north, and the ancient table-land of Brazil occupies much of the eastern

Pampas Grass

part of the continent.   This table-land is crossed by a network of ranges and has its steepest slope towards the Atlantic.   Its average height is 3000 feet.

South America has an exceptional number of wide plains. These occupy the basins of the Orinoco, Amazon and Parana-Paraguay, as well as much of the coast region on the north. They go by different names : the *Llanos* of the Orinoco—flooded grass plains or desert tracts according to the season, the densely forested *Selvas* of the Amazon, and the *Pampas* of the Argentine and Patagonia, which are grassy in the north but rocky and sterile in the south.

Rivers.

Each of the three great rivers of South America is navigable for more than 1000 miles. They vary in width from one to two miles, and carry an almost incredible amount of water seawards. Owing to the low elevation in the interior of the continent, they are connected by their tributaries, especially in the rainy season.

The *Orinoco* flows east from its source in the Andes, receiving numerous tributaries on both sides. It enters the Atlantic Ocean near the island of Trinidad, at which spot it has more than fifty branches traversing its great delta.

The *Amazon* drains a country 23 times as large as our own islands. Its plain is so level that the stream is only 400 feet above the sea when 2000 miles distant. So great a volume of water is sent to the ocean that the water is comparatively fresh 200 miles from shore. Its chief tributaries are the Negro and Madeira rivers. The tide ascends its great estuary for a distance of 400 miles ; the usual entrance for ships, however, is up the Rio Para mouth. The name ' Para ' at once suggests rubber, the commercial product of the tangled forests of the Amazonian selvas.

The *Parana* and *Paraguay* drain the southern Brazilian highlands and the Argentine plain. They unite near the town of Corrientes, and after traversing a frequently-flooded lowland district, empty their waters into the estuary of the River Plate, along with those of the Uruguay river.

Coast.

The coast-line is but slightly indented, and good harbours are scarce. Capes San Roque, Pariña and Horn are respectively the most easterly, westerly and southerly points of the continent. The east coast is on the whole much lower than the west. On the north stretch a thousand miles of mangrove-covered swamps. Fine cliff scenery is found along the south-west, where numerous islets and fjords are found on the coast. The continental mainland is separated by Magellan Strait (named after the Portuguese Magellan, who sailed its waters in 1520) from the island of Tierra del Fuego. The Falkland Isles, peopled mainly by British whalers, lie a little to the north-east of this inhospitable island.

Climate.

If we leave altitude out of the question (for zones of tropical, temperate, and cold temperatures are found as the elevation increases) we may say that South America does not experience great ranges of temperature, for the average January temperatures range from 50° in the south to 85° in the Argentine, whilst those for July range from 35° in the south to about 85° in the north. The climate is therefore equable, the range varying from 5° to 10° in the north and south to about 30° in the Argentine.

The continent is warmer in January than it is in July because it lies mostly to the south of the Equator, and in south latitudes summer occurs during our winter months. From this it follows that the hottest part of the continent in July lies in the north (*i.e.* within the North Torrid Zone); whilst the Brazilian highlands and the Parana basin, which lie south of the Equator, are very hot in January. The western coast is cooler than the eastern, as a result of the cool ocean current flowing northwards along that coast from the southern ocean.

Rainfall.

The distribution of rainfall is very interesting when considered as a result of the latitude and altitude of the continent and the directions of the prevailing winds. The drier half of the continent lies to the south of a line drawn from Quito to Monte Video, the only exception being the wet south-western coast. In the moister region of the north, the Amazon plain and the coasts of the Panama Gulf, Guiana, and Brazil near Pernambuco and south of Rio Janeiro, are the parts receiving most rain. An annual fall of more than 200″ occurs on the Guiana coast, Rio receives about 60″, whereas less than 10″ is experienced on the eastern slope of the Andes from Bolivia to Patagonia, and on the western coastal strip from Valparaiso to Cape Pariña.

To explain these facts we note that excessive evaporation and condensation are usual in tropical countries and consequently South America has most rain in its northern half. Again, this tropical region lies within the influence of the Trade Winds.

Effect of the Trade Winds.

The North-East Trades strike the northern coast, and, owing to the build of the country, are able to travel far into the interior, distributing their moisture as they go south-westwards. They penetrate further inland during the southern summer (*i.e.* about January), because they tend to circulate in an *anti-clockwise* direction round the low-pressure area which exists over the heated land-mass of central Brazil; and consequently the Amazon basin has its heaviest torrential rains during the summer months.

The South-East Trades bring rain to the east coast about as far south as Buenos Aires. On the west coast they blow *away* from the land, thus accounting for the low rainfall of the Peruvian and North Chilian coasts.

The 'Brave Westerlies' blow constantly upon the west coast south of latitudes 30° to 40° according to

season, retreating to the higher latitude when the sun
comes south of the Equator. They cause the excessive
rainfall on the south-west coast—a rainfall which decreases rapidly eastwards owing to the nearness of the
Andes range to the sea. Thus the Pampas of South
Argentina and Patagonia have very little rainfall, for
in addition the south-easterly trades, which might have
brought moisture, are deflected southwards along the
east coast and caused by the Brave Westerlies to form
part of their system. The rainy coastal areas round
Pernambuco and south of Rio Janeiro are explained by
the nearness of the Brazilian mountains to the shore at
these points.

Agriculture and Stock Raising.

Owing to the build and climate of the country,
agriculture is mainly practised along the coast. The
warmth and moderate moisture of the eastern Argentine,
Uruguay, and Chile are making these cereal-producing
countries ; maize and wheat are the principal crops.
Maize, which is a native plant of South America, is
also grown in low latitudes, in fact almost to the Equator.
The sugar, tobacco, and cotton production of the eastern
'elbow' of Brazil, recalls that of the south-eastern United
States. On the other hand, the north-western part of
the continent is a part of the Central American climatic
region, growing large supplies of cacao and coffee.

The plains of the Orinoco and Parana-Paraguay
basins and the eastern Argentine are the great cattle-
raising districts of South America. Sheep replace
cattle in the drier west of Argentina and along the
Andes range, where the pastures are poorer and more
scanty.

Plants.

Extensive forests and wide grassy plains cover the
greater part of the continent. The great heat and rains
of the Amazon region promote the rapid growth of trees
and undergrowth in the tropical *selvas*—a forest-covered

district almost as large as Europe. Much of this has never been explored, for it can only be penetrated by cutting a way with axes through the luxuriant, tangled vegetation. Ornamental and dye woods, rubber and coffee trees, palms, bamboos, and fig trees are matted together by an endless variety of creeping plants, whilst numerous other kinds of plants live perched high up upon the branches of the trees and send down rope-like roots to the steaming soil below.

In drier parts are characteristic drought-resisting plants, such as the cactus and agave. On the open plains, especially where only a moderate rainfall is found, there are wide stretches of grass-land eminently suitable for stock-raising.

Animals.

South America, as we should expect from its climate and vegetation, has numerous wild animals, some of which are peculiar to the continent. The puma, jaguar, tapir, and llama are the counterparts of the lion, tiger, elephant, and camel of the Old World. The sloth, ant-eater, humming-bird, condor, boa constrictor, turtle, and alligator are also extremely common.

Minerals.

The great mineral wealth of the continent is associated with the Andes, where gold, silver, platinum, iron, tin, and other metals are found. The student should compare this mountain range with the Urals and the Rocky Mountains from this standpoint. Brazil is very rich in precious stones, and Chile has a vast store of useful nitrates.

People.

The people are estimated to number thirty-six millions, *i.e.* about five to each square mile. From this we see how sparsely the continent is peopled, the main reason perhaps being the dense vegetation of the tropical interior. Barren rocky soil and dryness of climate also combine to make Patagonia practically uninhabitable.

The native 'Indian' races are in all stages of civilisation according to the extent of their connection with Europeans. Some are in the lowest stage of development, knowing nothing of agriculture, possessing no religion, and gaining food and livelihood from forest fruits and juices. Yet Peru possessed a fair degree of civilisation even before the Spanish occupation, and to-day many of the South American natives, by reason of their intermarriage with Spaniards and Portuguese, are highly civilised. These usually profess the Roman Catholic religion. British, Dutch, and French occupy Guiana in the north, and Brazil has many German immigrants. In addition, Britons are fairly numerous in Chile and the Argentine, whilst Spaniards and Portuguese are found along the coasts.

Communication, except by the navigable rivers, is poorly developed, although railways are rapidly increasing. The Argentine Republic possesses most railways at present. These ramify in the Uruguay-Parana district as far north as Asuncion, and a transcontinental line is almost completed from Buenos Aires to Valparaiso, where it will join the Chilian coast-line running south to Valdivia. The llama (or South American camel) is largely used as a beast of burden for traffic across the mountains.

Colombia.

Position and Surface.

The Republic of Colombia occupies the north-western portion of the continent. Its area is five times that of the British Isles. It is much flatter in the east, where numerous tributaries of the Amazon flow over the plains from the Andes slope. The latter range covers the western half of the country, and down its longitudinal valleys flow the chief river, the Magdalena, and its tributary the Cauca. The country possesses both

Atlantic and Pacific coasts, but the Isthmus of Panama now forms a separate state. The chief inlets are the two large gulfs of Panama and Darien.

Climate and Productions.

The climate of the west varies according to altitude, the Andes slopes being cultivated to the height of 10,000 ft.   The higher altitudes produce temperate grains and fruits, and lower down the mountain sides are maize fields and coffee plantations, followed by purely tropical growths (sugar, cacao, etc.) upon the lowest slopes and coastal plains.   The eastern plains are either savanas (*i.e.* grass lands) or selvas (forest lands) according to their supply of rain.   The former provide hides for export, the latter produce dye woods, ornamental woods, rubber, and drugs.   Minerals are plentiful in the Andes, and both gold and silver are exported.

Communications and Towns.

There are no manufactures of importance, nor are there good means of communication in the country. The Isthmian railway from Panama to Colon has now passed out of the possession of Colombia, and the navigable Magdalena is practically the only highway.   The people, who number about four millions, have a republican form of government, which meets at *Bogota*— a healthy town situated upon a plateau high above sea level.   Forest, agricultural, and mining produce is exported, whilst food and clothing comprise much of the import trade.

Venezuela.

Surface and Productions.

The Republic of Venezuela occupies much of the Orinoco basin, the vast plains (llanos) of which are devoted to cattle and horse-rearing. These llanos are almost deserts during the dry season. The northern extremity of the Andes occupies the west of the country, and in the south-east are the forested Sierra Parima, a prolongation of the Guiana highlands. Venezuela shares the Caribbean sea-coast with Colombia, and the swampy Orinoco delta lies on its eastern seaboard.

Agriculture is mainly practised in the western half of the country, where the fertile valleys of the Andes produce cacao, sugar, coffee, and bananas. Precious metals, as well as tin, iron, and copper, are found in the mountains, and much copper is exported.

The People.

The government of the country is far from stable and there have been frequent revolutions and changes of government. Although Venezuela is five times as large as the British Isles, there are only two and a half millions of people. This scantiness of population is to be attributed to the wide extent and dryness of the llanos, and to the unsatisfactory state of the government.

Communications and Towns.

The Orinoco and its tributaries afford the chief means of communication. A railway has been built from *La Guaira*, the chief port, through the capital, *Caracas*, and thence westwards towards *Valencia*, which is the centre of the coffee-growing district. Caracas has suffered from earthquakes, but is now a well-built modern town. The country round it has large cacao plantations. *Maracaibo* on the Gulf of Venezuela exports the agricultural produce of the west. The United States does much trade with Venezuela, supplying cottons, metal goods, and food, and receiving in exchange coffee, which (with cacao and rubber) is largely exported.

Ecuador.

Surface, Climate, and Productions.

Although Ecuador looks small on the map, it is as large as the British Isles. It consists of three well-marked districts : (*a*) coast, (*b*) Andes, (*c*) plains of the interior. The coastal district is characterised by an unhealthy climate due to excessive heat and moisture. The equatorial heat is relieved in the Andes by their elevation, and in this central zone of the country are many magnificent mountain peaks, notable amongst which is *Cotopaxi*, the highest active volcano in the world. The mountains are very rich in metals, including gold, silver, copper, iron, and lead. Precious stones are also mined in this district.

The eastern flatter portion of Ecuador is composed of the rainy selvas, where rubber and drugs such as cinchona (from which quinine is made) are obtained in large quantities. Mining is more important than agriculture.

People, Communications, and Towns.

Like other South American republics Ecuador is but poorly peopled. There are only one and a quarter million people in the country, and Europeans number less than half this total. Before the Spanish occupation, the land formed part of the empire of the Incas, a native race which possessed a fairly high civilisation, but stagnation resulted from later Spanish oppression.

Railways are practically absent : a short line connects *Quito*, the capital—situated 9000 ft. above sea level—with its port, *Guayaquil*. The llama is used as a beast of burden over the mountain passes. Lack of good roads, as a result of the mountainous nature of the country, is a great drawback to trade. The exports from Guayaquil include cacao, cinchona, rubber, copper, and other metals, and ' panama ' hats.

Peru.

Surface.

The Peruvian republic is divided into the same
three types of country as Ecuador, but its area is
about four times as great.   The coastal plain is narrow
throughout its length, and the much broader eastern
plain lying beyond the Andes is drained by the Amazon
and its tributaries.   Tropical forests cover the eastern
plains and they are only penetrable along the courses
of the rivers.   Native collection of rubber and drugs is
the only industry in these selvas.

Industries.

Pasco in the Andes is the great mining centre, both
gold and silver being obtained.   The upper mountain
slopes are devoted to grazing, and large flocks of vicunas
and alpacas provide hides and wool for export.   Maize
is the chief cereal grown, and other vegetable products
are cacao, coffee, and tobacco.   Agriculture is increasing
in importance, as the result of more extensive irrigation.

People and Towns.

The majority of the people, who number four millions,
are of Indian and mixed 'Indo'-European race.   Before
the conquest by Pizarro, Peru, like the neighbouring republics, formed part of the empire of the Incas.   Under the
new system of self-government, the country is increasing
its railways and other means of communication.   *Lima,*
Pasco, and *Cuzco* are all connected with the coast by rail.
Lima, the capital, was founded by Pizarro in 1535.   Its
houses are built of sun-dried bricks.   *Callao,* its port
on the Pacific coast, exports manures (guano and nitrates), wool, bark, cacao, and sugar.   Much of the trade
is in the hands of American and Chinese merchants.
Cuzco, on the plateau not far from Lake Titicaca, was
the old capital of the Incas.

Bolivia.

Surface and Productions.

The Bolivian republic, which took its name from General Bolivar, who aided in the successful revolt against Spain, is an inland country four times the size of our islands. It possesses no coast-line at the present time, having lost its Pacific coast as the result of a war with Chile. Fully half the country is occupied by the Bolivian plateau, the widest portion of the Andes system. Rich mines of gold and silver are found here, the annual output amounting to £3,000,000. The silver mines of Potosi have been renowned for centuries but they do not produce as much metal as in former years. The broad north-eastern plain is thickly forested and produces cinchona and rubber. It is drained by the Madeira river, one of the largest tributaries of the Amazon. The trade in cinchona is decreasing, owing to successful plantations of the tree in India and south-eastern Asia.

Industries, Trade, and Towns.

Agriculture is not of great importance in Bolivia. The people, who are chiefly descendants of the native Inca race, are principally engaged in mining or pastoral pursuits. Alpaca and vicuna wool are obtained from the mountain flocks. The llama is the chief beast of burden; in fact it is the only animal which can be used for mountain traffic. The chief railway line curves from Lake Titicaca and the plateau, through *Potosi* and the Andes to the Chilean port of *Antofagasta*, which exports coffee, cocoa, ores, silver, rubber, and Peruvian bark. *Sucre* is the seat of government, but *La Paz* is the capital. This town is situated about 10,000 ft. above sea level, quite close to the towering peaks of the Andes, and in the centre of the cinchona district.

Chile.

Surface, Climate, and Productions.

The republic of Chile is a long, narrow coastal strip lying to the west of the Andes through more than 30° of latitude. Its coast is regular in the north, but in the south it possesses many fjords and islands. The character of the prevalent winds produces different climatic zones. In the north, where the south-east trades blow away from the coast, there is the torrid Atacama desert, which is useless for agriculture and pasture. The central zone is the most fertile, for it receives rain from the westerly winds and produces much wheat, barley, wine, and fruit. Many cattle are kept here and careful attention is being given to dairy-farming. Sheep-rearing is important in the south of the country, and here also are wide forests upon the mountain slopes.

Chile is well supplied with metals and manures, and although both gold and silver occur, copper is the metal of greatest value in trade. The manures include guano and sodium nitrate. Indeed, we may call Chile the land of nitrates.

People, Trade, and Towns.

Most of the inhabitants are of European stock, but of course there are native Indian races as well. These vary from the Chango labourers in the north to the Fuegians of Tierra del Fuego in the south. Most of the towns upon the plain are connected by rail, and *Valparaiso* will soon be in communication with *Buenos Aires* by a line crossing the Andes through the Uspallata pass and tunnel. The country is in a very settled state, and is prosperous and progressive. It possesses a good army and navy, and is now one of the most important republics of South America. *Santiago*, the capital, is a handsome modern town. Its houses are low so as to avoid as far as possible the effects of earthquake shock. *Valparaiso*, its port, exports wheat, flour, copper, silver, and guano. *Iquique*, the northern port, ships nitrates. The chief imports are food, machinery, and clothing.

Argentina.

Surface, Climate, and Productions.

The Argentine Republic is the second largest state in South America. It is fifteen times the size of the British Isles, and occupies much of the southern half of the continent. It is flanked on the west by the Andes range, and its northern area consists of the Parana basin, the southern of the wide pampas. Minerals, though plentiful, are neglected for agricultural and pastoral industries. The great range of latitude and elevation produces great differences of climate and consequently a great variety of crops—maize, tobacco, sugar, grapes, flax, and wheat. Argentina has a great future as a wheat-growing country, and sends us quite one-half of the wheat it produces. The chief wheat-growing district is the province of Buenos Aires.

The southern pampas feed millions of cattle and sheep. These are kept upon ranches of wide extent, and provide wool, hides, tallow, and preserved meat for export.

People and Towns.

Argentina is the most progressive South American republic. There is a constant stream of immigrants from Europe, and it has more Europeans in it than any of its neighbours. Railways are rapidly increasing. Monte Video in Uruguay and Buenos Aires are the termini of lines connecting the towns of the Uruguay and Parana valleys. The cross-country line to Valparaiso and Santiago has already been mentioned. This line will save 2000 miles in the journey to Valparaiso. *Buenos Aires* has a splendid harbour and is regularly visited by many lines of steamers. Its population is over a million, and it has nearly three-fourths of the trade of the country.

Buenos Aires : Sheep Farm

Uruguay and Paraguay.

Uruguay consists of grassy plains enclosed on three sides by the Atlantic, the Plate estuary, and the river Uruguay. It is a well-watered country about half the size of the British Isles, and is widely devoted to cattle and sheep-rearing. *Monte Video*, the capital, and *Paysandu* have large meat-packing yards. Ox tongues, beef, and extract of meat are the chief articles exported.

Paraguay is entirely an inland country, being bounded by Brazil, Bolivia, and Argentina. Forests occupy the northern part, whilst the country round Asuncion is low and swampy. Cotton, tobacco, sugar, and indigo are the main agricultural crops ; rubber is obtained from the forests, and cattle-rearing is rapidly increasing. Two vegetable products deserve special mention : the *manioc* root which is the staple starchy food of the people, and *maté* or Paraguay tea. The latter is made from the powdered leaves of a kind of holly, and is largely drunk in South America. The two chief exports are *maté* and hides ; and, like all other South American states, Paraguay imports clothing and metal goods. *Asuncion* is the capital.

Brazil.

Surface and Productions.

Brazil is the largest country in South America, in fact it occupies one-half of the continent and is as large as the United States. It has 4000 miles of coast-line, whilst its land frontiers touch ten other states. It comprises the basins of the Amazon and upper Parana, and a vast highland region in the east. From its great extent it has a very diversified climate. The Amazon selvas yield rubber, mahogany, satin and rose woods, dyes and drugs. These impenetrable forests partly explain why quite half of Brazil is uninhabitable. Coffee, cacao, sugar, cotton, tobacco, flax, and rice are amongst the varied agricultural products. São Paulo is the great coffee-producing state, and more than half the coffee is exported from *Rio Janeiro*, the principal seaport. Cattle-rearing is done mostly upon the southern plains, where the country is more open. The mountains are rich in minerals, including gold and precious stones, but the main exports from the country are of vegetable and animal products.

People, Trade, and Towns.

This is the only country in South America where Portuguese is the official language. An emperor of Portuguese extraction ruled Brazil as recently as 1889, from which time the government has been republican. The Amazon is the natural highway for commerce, and the few railways at present in existence are short lines running a little distance inland from the ports. There are altogether about 6000 miles of railway in the country, but this is very little compared with its vast size. Brazil has cable communication with Lisbon in Portugal.

British trade with Brazil amounts to £14,000,000 annually. The United States is the best customer for coffee and sends foodstuffs in return. The chief ports are *Rio Janeiro, Pernambuco, Bahia, Para,* and *Santos.* Hides, tobacco, rubber, coffee, cotton, and sugar are the chief articles exported.

The Guianas.

The Guianas lie north of Brazil and east of Venezuela.   They consist of low swampy plains rising on the south to the Guiana highlands.   Sugar, rum, molasses, coffee, cacao, and cotton are produced.   The temperature is high and the rainfall heavy.   The climate is thus very unhealthy for Europeans, and coolies are employed on the sugar plantations. *Georgetown, Paramaribo,* and *Cayenne* are the chief towns of British, Dutch, and French Guiana.   The French use their province as a convict station.

QUESTIONS AND EXERCISES

Chapter I. Mathematical Geography.

1. Of what value is the study of Geography ?

2. Describe the shape and size of the earth.

3. Explain why we have alternating day and night.

4. How is it possible for there to be a 'midnight sun'?

5. Why has the earth been marked out into zones? Give the names and boundaries of the zones.

6. Define Latitude and state the reason for the slight variation in the length of a degree of latitude.

7. Why does the length of a degree of longitude differ so much in various parts of the world ?

8. Why is it colder in winter than in summer ?

9. Find from a map of the world the latitude and longitude of Paris, New York, Sydney, Tokyo, and Cape Town.

10. If it were noon at Greenwich, what would be the local (or sun) time at the above places ?

11. Draw a diagram showing the positions of earth and sun when it is winter in the northern hemisphere.

12. Find a place on the globe where it is midwinter day when it is midsummer night with us. State the reasons for your choice.

13. Why are plane maps inaccurate? Compare the accuracy of a plane map of North America with that of one of the Thames basin.

CHAPTER II. LAND AND WATER.

1. On an outline map of the world insert the names of the continents and their chief peninsulas, the oceans and the directions of their main currents.

2. What is meant by the Continental Shelf? Say what you can of the relative depths of the oceans, and the variations in depth in any single ocean.

3. Account for the fact that, speaking generally, the oceans are never frozen.

4. Compare the temperatures of land and water at different times of the year.

5. Distinguish between waves, tides, drifts, and currents.

6. Account for the facts that the Indian is the warmest ocean, and that the west coast of Canada has a warmer climate than the east coast.

7. Where and why do 'Polar' waters flow towards the Equator?

8. Why do Atlantic and Pacific Ocean currents take a clockwise course in the Northern Hemisphere, and an anti-clockwise in the Southern?

9. Give instances where ocean currents are (i) deflected, (ii) subdivided by coming into contact with land-masses.

CHAPTER III. CLIMATE AND THE DISTRIBUTION OF LIFE.

1. What are isotherms? How do the world's isotherms differ in January and July? Account for the difference.

2. What is the cause of wind? Define isobar, trade wind, monsoon, doldrums, sea breeze, cyclone.

3. Account for the west coast of Britain having a heavier rainfall than the east.

4. What effect has a mountain range upon rainfall? Which would have the greater effect: a range running (i) parallel, or (ii) at right angles, to a prevalent ocean wind?

5. Name three very wet and three very dry regions upon the globe. Give reasons in each case.

6. 'In passing from a tropical valley to a mountain summit we traverse diverse belts of vegetation.' Explain this statement.

7. Choosing any district you please, indicate how far man has altered (*a*) its flora, (*b*) its fauna.

8. Name six arctic, temperate, and tropical animals and plants. Show, if you can, how they are fitted for life in the conditions under which they are found.

CHAPTER IV. EUROPE.

1. Compare and contrast the Mediterranean and the Baltic Seas.

2. Indicate on a blank map of Europe the general relief of the continent and the action of its chief watersheds in determining the direction of the rivers.

3. How does the seasonal distribution of rainfall vary in different parts of Europe?

4. What do you mean by (i) an insular, (ii) a continental climate? Quote examples from your own continent.

5. What effect has the amount of rainfall upon the range of temperature? Give instances.

6. Summarise the distribution of European trees, and in particular explain the reason for the peculiar type of tree found in the Mediterranean district.

7. 'Europe may be divided into climatic belts by the northerly limits of culture of its various cereals.' Is this statement wholly or only partially true?

8. Contrast the grass lands of east and west Europe.

9. Account for *Irish* linen, *Russian* leather, *Hollands* gin, *Bohemian* glass, *Swedish* knives, *Dutch* pottery, and *Swedish* matches.

10. Explain the main factors determining the density of population in any district you choose.

11. Distinguish between Celt and Slav, isotherm and isobar, tundra and steppe.

The British Isles.

1. Between what limits of latitude and longitude do the British Islands lie?

2. Give a short account of the relief of either Scotland or England, indicating the chief 'divides' and the rivers which flow from them.

3. Describe a journey along the western coast of Great Britain from north to south. Draw a sketch map to show the positions of the places you mention.

4. Why do the winter isotherms cross Great Britain from north to south? What difference would you expect to find in the directions of the summer isotherms, and why?

5. Compare the temperature of Britain with that of continental Europe.

6. Shade a blank map of the British Isles so as to represent the mean annual rainfall in the various districts.

7. What are the conditions which decide whether a given area shall be devoted to pastoral or agricultural pursuits? In the latter case, what factors determine the character of crop produced?

8. Give the names and positions of six towns on our coasts engaged in the fishing industry.

9. Draw a map showing the positions of our coalfields and mark one important town upon each.

10. From what districts in Great Britain do we obtain lead, copper, and tin respectively?

11. What industries arise directly from agriculture? Indicate the positions and industries of Bedford, Kettering, Yeovil, and Dundee.

12. Insert upon a blank map the positions of the chief towns engaged in the iron trade.

13. Account for the woollen industry being carried on in south Scotland, Yorkshire, and Wiltshire.

14. Name six towns in Lancashire engaged in the cotton trade, and indicate their positions relative to Manchester and Liverpool.

15.   Why is linen manufactured in Ulster and in east Scotland?

16.   Give instances of towns arising at places of strategic importance.   Account also for the greatness of Glasgow, Liverpool, and London.

17.   Why has canal traffic declined in Britain?   In what parts of our islands do we find canals, and why?

18.   Draw a sketch map of three important railways radiating from (*a*) London, (*b*) Dublin.

19.   What two classes of goods constitute the bulk of our imports?   Why is this?   Trace the more important imports to the countries which produce them, and state by which ports they enter our country.

20.   Enumerate the routes from London to Norway, Germany, the Low Countries, and France.

21.   Write a short essay upon the distribution of population in the British Isles.

France.

1.   State the boundaries of France, pointing out where the frontier needs to be specially guarded.

2.   Describe the build of the country and deduce from this the directions of the principal rivers.   How does the relief of the country affect the character of the coast in different parts?

3.   Write a short account of the climate of France, and emphasise the differences between the climate of Paris and that of Marseilles.

4.   Why is Biarritz one of the rainiest places in France?

5.   Account for the mildness of the winter on the Riviera.

6.   Name six agricultural crops of importance in France and state in which parts of the country they are principally cultivated.

7.   Coffee, cider, and wine are three typical French beverages.   Why?

8.   Give an account of the two chief French coalfields and the industries connected with them.

9. Draw a sketch map of the country and insert the chief wine-growing districts.

10. Write an account of the silk industry in France.

11. Give the positions of the following towns and add a note on each: Lille, Marseilles, Roubaix, Brest, Paris, Rouen, Bordeaux, Nancy, Calais, Cognac.

12. Draw a sketch map of France showing the railways, and indicate their continental connections. What would be the shortest route from London to Rome?

Belgium.

1. How do the geographical position and build of Belgium affect its climate?

2. Compare and contrast Belgian and British agriculture, giving special attention to

(a) the kinds of crops grown,

(b) the methods of cultivation.

3. How would you explain the fact that Belgian steel girders were used in the construction of a large railway station at Birmingham?

4. Draw a sketch map to show the relative positions of Antwerp, London, Ostend, and Dover.

5. Account for Flanders being a weaving centre in the Middle Ages. Whence did she obtain wool in those days? Contrast present day conditions.

6. Name the chief Belgian towns engaged in iron, linen, and cotton industries.

Holland.

1. Explain the following statement: 'Holland is composed of sediment conveyed from Scandinavia and Central Europe.'

2. Why would a list of Dutch exports be an untrustworthy guide to (a) the vegetable productions, (b) the manufactures of the country?

3. Compare the climate of Holland with that of France.

4. What are polders, dunes, and dykes?

5. 'The sea has been Holland's greatest enemy and also her greatest friend.' Illustrate this statement by reference to the country's history and geography.

6. Why is Holland one of the wealthiest countries of the world?

Germany.

1. Between what limits of latitude and longitude does Germany lie? Name the countries touching Germany upon the east, south, and west.

2. Insert the chief rivers upon a blank map of Germany. Is it an advantage or a disadvantage to Germany that many of her rivers rise in other countries?

3. Draw a sketch map of the Rhine. Insert two tributaries. Indicate on the map the regions which are remarkable for their beauty or their industry. Mark six towns and state their importance.

4. Contrast the climate of Friesland with that of East Prussia and of Baden. To what extent does the North Sea affect the climate of Germany?

5. On a blank map of Germany show, by shading, the wheat, vine, hop, and beet-growing districts.

6. To what extent has the presence of coal aided the industrial development of certain districts in Germany? Give details.

7. Write an essay on the German people and their position in Europe at the present day.

8. 'Germany, once one of our best customers, is now a formidable rival.' To what is this due? Indicate parallel changes which have occurred in the industrial history of the two peoples.

9. Name the chief German ports, state their exact positions, and also give the chief articles forming the trade of each.

10. Where are the following, and for what are they noted: Breslau, Nuremberg, Meissen, Düsseldorf, Chemnitz, Munich, and Frankfort?

Denmark.

1.   Contrast the build, geological structure, and climate of Jutland with that of Iceland.

2.   How would you explain the fact that Iceland and the Faroe Isles belong to Denmark ?

3.   Was Shakespere correct when in speaking of Elsinore he wrote :

'The dreadful summit of the cliff
That beetles o'er his base into the sea.' ?

4.   Account for Denmark's insignificance as a manufacturing country.

5.   Give a list of her imports and exports, and show how each article is determined by the climate and natural productions of the country.

6.   Draw a sketch map of the Sound, and mark the positions of corresponding Danish and Swedish ports.

7.   Can you account for Denmark—a weak country— retaining the command of the Baltic entrance ?

Scandinavia.

1.   Describe the position and build of the Scandinavian peninsula.

2.   Contrast the rivers and coasts of Norway and Sweden.

3.   Explain the great emigration of Norwegians to North America.

4.   Shew the relation of the climate and geographical position of Scandinavia to its natural productions.

5.   How would you explain the fact that Scandinavia is rich in minerals, whilst the neighbouring country of Denmark is singularly poor in mineral wealth ?

6.   If there be no coal in Scandinavia, how is it possible for the larger towns to have textile and iron industries ?

7.   Quote instances where portions of Scandinavia and Denmark have been made into islands by the construction of canals.   State the commercial advantages derived from these canals and draw a sketch map to show their position.

8. With what Italian city is Stockholm frequently compared? What are the chief industries of these two cities? In what direction is the line joining them, and through what European countries does it pass?

Russia.

1. What effects have (*a*) extent, (*b*) build, (*c*) nearness to Asia, upon the climate of Russia?

2. Enumerate the rivers flowing from the Valdai Hills, and state the character of the districts through which they flow.

3. Account for the building of St Petersburg. Why is its position advantageous, yet unhealthy?

4. What reasons would you give for the intemperance of the Russian peasants, and why are they drinkers of *spirits*?

5. Say what you can about (*a*) steppes, (*b*) tundras, (*c*) black lands.

6. Write a short account of the Russian system of government, comparing it with those of Great Britain and France.

7. Account for the diversity of wild animals found in Russia.

8. Give the positions and industries of Odessa, Moscow, Lodz, Nijni-Novgorod, St Petersburg, Archangel, and Slatoust.

Austria-Hungary.

1. At what points would Austria-Hungary be most open to hostile attack and what countries would be likely to attack from these points?

2. What geographical, racial, and political causes have led to the recent annexation of Bosnia and Herzegovina by Austria?

3. Why has Hungary such important wine, wheat, and pastoral industries? Compare its rainfall with that of eastern England.

4. Draw a map of the Alps and show the positions of the chief passes and tunnels.

5. Where is the 'Iron Gate' of the Danube, and why has this part of the river been canalised by the Hungarian Government?

6. Explain the following statement: 'Austria has been peopled from the north-west, Hungary from the east.'

7. Why does Fleet Street obtain much of its paper from Austria and Scandinavia?

8. Why is Budapest sometimes written Buda-Pest? Give six other Austro-Hungarian towns, their positions and industries.

The Balkan Peninsula.

1. Account for the relative dryness of the eastern half of the Balkan peninsula.

2. 'Roads and railways follow the course of rivers.' Illustrate this statement by reference to the Balkan peninsula. Draw a map to show the course of the railway from Vienna to Constantinople.

3. Indicate briefly the curtailment of the Turkish Empire in Europe. Why is 1878 an important date in the history of Turkey?

4. Make a list of the natural products of this region and show their dependence upon altitude and latitude.

5. Why is Russia said to have designs upon Constantinople?

6. What is meant by the 'problem of the Near East'? State simply the chief points in this problem.

Switzerland.

1. Draw a map of the country showing the Alps and their highest peaks, and the valleys of the Rhone, Rhine, and Inn.

2. Account for the fact that most Swiss villages are lit by electricity, in spite of the absence of coal.

3. Zurich manufactures cotton and silk goods. Whence does she obtain her supplies of raw materials?

4. What do you mean by glacier, föhn, avalanche?

5. The chamois is scarce in Switzerland, yet the country exports 'chamois leather.' What animal has been substituted for the chamois in this industry, and why ?

Italy.

1. Insert upon a blank map the chief mountains, rivers, and islands of Italy.

2. Is there any connection between the recent formation of the Italian Kingdom and the heavy taxation which is at present in force in the country ?

3. Contrast (a) the temperature, (b) the rainfall of northern and southern Italy at different times of the year. Account for these differences in climate.

4. What goods do we send to Italy and what do we receive in return ?

5. Draw a map to show the Alpine passes and railway tunnels from Italy to three neighbouring countries.

6. Why does Italy export raw silk instead of manufacturing all of it herself ?

7. Can you explain why Corsica and Sardinia belong to different countries ?

8. Explain the paradox that Genoa, a seaport, exports most of her goods *inland*.

9. Why is irrigation so necessary in Italy ?

Spain and Portugal.

1. Contrast the relative importance of Spain and Britain (a) during Elizabeth's reign, (b) at the present time. Give as far as possible the reasons for your statements.

2. Account for the dryness of the Spanish plateau.

3. What is the historical reason for Madrid's central position in the country ?

4. When, and why, did Portugal separate from Spain ?

5. What are huertas and sierras ?

6. What fruits are exported from this peninsula? Account for Portugal exporting rubber when none is produced in the country.

7. What would be the probable route of the Romans when they entered upon the conquest of Hispania? Give the reason for your answer.

8. Why should chocolate be a general beverage in Spain and Portugal?

9. Compare the climate and natural productions of Britain and the Iberian peninsula.

Chapter V. Asia.

1. Give an account of the build of the Asiatic continent.

2. What is meant by systems of internal drainage? Give examples. Why are they usually found in connection with plateaux?

3. Name the islands and seas of eastern Asia. How would you account for the fact that the Yellow Sea is the shallowest of the whole series?

4. Divide Asia into climatic areas, showing clearly where the coldest winters, the hottest summers, and the greatest and least ranges of temperature are experienced.

5. What countries experience 'monsoons'? State the cause of these winds and their effect upon fertility and density of population.

6. Write a short essay upon the vegetable products of Asia.

7. Why are the Pamirs called the 'cradle of the human race'? Illustrate your answer by a sketch map of Asia showing the distribution of Asiatic races at the present day.

8. Draw sketch maps of (a) the Siberian railway, (b) the sea route to Japan, marking the positions of the more important towns or seaports *en route.*

Russia in Asia.

1. In what respects may Siberia be expected to develop during the next century?

2. Contrast the climate and productions of Siberia with those of Transcaucasia.

3. In what part of Asiatic Russia is irrigation playing an important part? Why is it necessary in this region, and what are the chief agricultural products?

4. What various animals are used for transport purposes in different parts of the Russian Empire? Show in what ways each of these animals is fitted for its work.

5. Draw a map of the Russian railways in Central Asia and indicate how they are connected with the caravan trade of China, India, Bokhara, and Afghanistan.

6. Show by reference to climatic conditions and vegetable products that the Ural Mountains are only an imperfect barrier between Europe and Asia.

Japan.

1. Compare the geographical positions of the British and Japanese islands.

2. Indicate briefly how Japan has altered her internal conditions and external position among the nations during the last fifty years.

3. What were the main causes which led to Japan's success over Russia in 1905?

4. Along what lines is it to be expected that Japan will develop during the next fifty years? How will these developments affect the articles she now imports and exports?

5. 'The United States obtains most of its tea from the west.' Explain this statement, and draw a map showing the route traversed and the towns concerned.

6. What connection exists between the depth of the Sea of Japan and the frequency of volcanic and earthquake phenomena in the Japanese islands?

7. Explain why the following articles are found among Japanese exports : bronzes, camphor, paper fans, lacquered goods, and lucifer matches

China.

1. Why has China proper a population forty times as dense as its outlying provinces?

2. What crops are grown in (*a*) North, (*b*) South China, and how do elevation and humidity determine the character of the crops grown in southern China?

3. Compare and contrast the Japanese and Chinese nations from the following points of view: (*a*) origin, (*b*) general appearance, (*c*) adaptability, (*d*) general habits.

4. Draw a map showing the relative positions of China and Japan. Name the chief Japanese islands and insert the more important physical features of China.

5. Why is the Hoang-ho frequently called 'China's sorrow'? Can you draw any parallel between this river and the Rhine in their lower courses?

6. Describe the various routes by which Russia and India can communicate with China. Draw a sketch map to illustrate your answer.

South-east Asia.

1. Draw a sketch map of this district. Shew, by shading, to whom the various parts of it belong. Insert Singapore, Manila, Bangkok, and Batavia.

2. Account for the tropical temperature and excessive rainfall of south-eastern Asia, and show particularly the effect produced by central Asiatic regions of high and low pressure upon climate.

3. What are the chief natural products of south-east Asia? Compare them with those of Japan. Explain the presence of any additional products.

4. Explain why Turkestan (lat. 35° N.) has a hotter July temperature than Sumatra (lat. 0°).

India.

1. Describe the build of India and show how elevation determines the agricultural products.

2. What effect has the opening of the Suez Canal had upon the trade of (*a*) Bombay, (*b*) Calcutta, and why?

D.

3. What is meant by (*a*) Punjab, (*b*) Doab, (*c*) cyclone?

4. Give an account of the distribution of rain in India. Has this any connection with the fact that India is one of the most thickly populated Asiatic countries?

5. In what regions of India are wheat, rice, opium, and coffee grown? What climatic conditions determine the position of these crops?

6. Draw a sketch map of the Ganges basin and mark the position of six important towns. Indicate what industries are carried on at each.

7. Insert on a blank map the chief Indian railways. Show in particular the development of the system along the passes of the north-west.

8. Account for the Indus having no important tributaries in its lower course. Compare its value as a highway with that of the Ganges river.

Afghanistan.

1. Describe and account for the climate of the Iranian Plateau.

2. Draw a map to show the strategical importance of Afghanistan. What do you understand by a 'buffer-state'?

3. What effect has the geographical nature of their country had upon (*a*) the character, (*b*) the organisation of the Afghans?

Persia.

1. Compare the size, build, and climate of Persia and Afghanistan.

2. Why are Russia and Britain so jealously watching each other in these two countries?

3. What effect has Persia upon the trade and importance of Damascus?

4. Sketch the important events which have recently occurred in the Iranian plateau.

Chapter VI.   Africa.

1.   Give a brief account of the build of the African continent, and insert in a blank map the positions of the four largest rivers, the great lakes, the plateaux and deserts. Indicate also the positions of the equator, the two tropics, and the meridian of Greenwich.

2.   Say what you can of the rainfall of Africa, and state which parts receive rain (*a*) all the year through, (*b*) in January, (*c*) in July.   Show how the amount of rainfall affects the distribution of population.

3.   Explain park lands, Bantu, fetich, oasis, tsetse.

4.   Amplify and discuss the statement that Africa has been invaded from all sides, and briefly give the reasons for such invasion.   What is meant by the 'Partition of Africa'?

5.   Show the effects of (*a*) winds, (*b*) ocean currents upon Africa and South America.   How is the African climate influenced by the Asiatic land-mass upon the north-east?

The Barbary States and the Sahara.

1.   'Morocco owes its rain to the Atlas Mountains and cyclonic winds.'   Explain this statement, and show by a map why Morocco is a more fertile country than Tripoli.

2.   Explain why the Sahara is a sandy waste.

3.   What do you mean by a 'Mediterranean' climate? Illustrate your answer by reference to both northern and southern coasts of that sea.

4.   Explain wadi, shott, simoom, alfa.

5.   Give a list of the vegetable products of these states and compare them with those of (*a*) northern, (*b*) southern France.

6.   Say what you can of Fez, Carthage, Biserta, and Marakesh.

Senegal, Niger, and Congo Districts.

1. Compare the climate of these regions with that of the Barbary States. Does the rainfall occur in these two districts at the same times of the year? Give reasons for your answer.

2. Compare the natural products of this region with those of tropical South America. Account for any similarities and differences.

3. A map of the Guinea Coast shows most towns as being near the sea. Account for the positions of these. Also state the reasons for the positions of (a) Leopoldville, (b) Kano.

4. Draw a map to show the three routes possessed by the French to the southern Sudan. Insert any British and German territories lying near those of France.

5. Account for the density of population in Nigeria.

The Nile Basin.

1. Draw a map of the Nile, insert its chief tributaries, and show the positions of the cataracts. Mark the Egyptian portion of the Cape-to-Cairo Railway, and explain how this railway overcomes the difficulties caused by the cataracts.

2. Discuss the rainfall of the Nile basin. Explain the regularity of the rise in the river's level, and show how this is closely connected with the question of latitude.

3. Enumerate the vegetable products of this area. How does the following Scriptural quotation apply to the crops of the Nile valley and the speed of the Nile current: 'Cast thy bread upon the waters, for thou shalt find it after many days'?

4. Say what you can of (a) barrage, (b) sudd.

5. Why is the Nile delta more thickly populated than other parts of the river valley?

6. Give a brief account of the history of Egypt. What geographical considerations have caused it to have a very different history from Abyssinia?

7. Draw a map showing (a) the overland route, (b) the sea route from London to Bombay. Has the opening of the Suez Canal had little or great influence on the trade of the Barbary States? Give reasons for your answer.

The Eastern Plateau.

1.   Draw a sketch map to show European possessions in this district.   Indicate how (*a*) commerce, (*b*) physical features have decided the positions and boundaries of these possessions.

2.   Compare and contrast the natural products of this district with those of (*a*) the Congo (*b*) the Nile valleys.

3.   Account for the coastal plain producing different commodities from those of the interior highlands.

British South Africa.

1.   Account for the importance of (*a*) Cape Town, (*b*) Johannesburg.

2.   Explain spruit, kopje, veld, karroo, and kloof.

3.   Name the South African industries in order of importance and show how geographical conditions determine this order.

4.   Compare the climate and rainfall of the coast of South Africa at the following places : (*a*) near Cape Town, (*b*) near the mouth of the Orange river, (*c*) near Port Elizabeth, (*d*) near Durban.   Explain especially the reasons for variation in the seasons at which rain falls at these places.

5.   What is mohair?   Account for it being a product of South Africa.

6.   Insert on a blank map of Africa the parts of the Cape-to-Cairo Railway which have already been constructed.   Of what value will the line be when finished?   Compare it with (*a*) the Canadian Pacific, (*b*) the Siberian Railway.

7.   Give examples of systems of internal drainage in Africa.   Give reasons for their positions.

8.   Give South African place names which are indicative of (*a*) native, (*b*) Dutch, (*c*) British occupations.   Briefly sketch the history of South Africa, and show why the railway was so important in the war of 1899–1902.

CHAPTER VII.

AUSTRALIA AND NEW ZEALAND.

Australia.

1. Shade a blank map of Australia to show its vertical relief. Account for the direction and length of the rivers, and the presence of lakes and inland drainage systems.

2. Say what you can of the following : trepang, marsupial, scrub, emu, karri, wattle, jarrah, dingo.

3. Compare the rainfall of Australia with that of South Africa, and in particular show the differences caused by the former being bounded by the sea, and the latter by land on the north.

4. Account for (a) the floods, (b) the droughts of some parts of Australia.

5. Insert the January and July isotherms of Australia upon a blank map, and give your reasons for
  (a) the different temperatures shown,
  (b) the different courses taken
by these isotherms.

6. Summarise the present distribution of the Australian population, giving geographical reasons.

7. State (a) the chief wheat and fruit districts, (b) the chief horse-raising districts of Australia, and explain how the climate determines where these industries are carried on.

8. Account for certain colonies producing sheep only, and others both sheep and cattle.

9. Insert on a blank map the chief Australian seaports and the railway lines running from them. Indicate the chief articles exported from these ports.

10. Say what you can of the following : Sydney, Pine Creek, Coolgardie, Bourke, Port Darwin, Launceston, Ipswich, Mildura, Pt. Augusta, Wimmera.

11. What are the great drawbacks to the pastoral industry of Australia, and what attempts have been made to remove them ?

12. What geographical and historical conditions have decided that the white inhabitants of South Africa and Australia are great coffee and tea drinkers respectively ?

New Zealand.

1.   Compare the positions of New Zealand and the British Isles.   In what way do the latter have the advantage, and what use has been made of that advantage?

2.   Why does Australia receive rain from the east and New Zealand (in general) from the west?   During what season do the South-East Trade Winds bring rain to New Zealand and which parts of the country benefit by them?   Does South Island profit by them?   Give reasons.

3.   Give an account of the build and natural phenomena of New Zealand.   Are the latter an advantage or a disadvantage to the colonisation of the country?

4.   Mention Australian and New Zealand place-names which are evidently of native origin.   Compare the native races of the two countries.

5.   Write a short essay on the plants of these two countries, giving as far as you can the reasons for their peculiarities, and the uses to which the plants have been put by civilised races.

6.   Draw a map to show the position of New Zealand relative to Australia and America.   Insert the chief ports and trade routes.

7.   What do you understand by the word 'antipodes'?

Chapter VIII.   North America.

1.   Describe the general build of the North American continent and name the most important rivers which flow to the three oceans washing its shores.

2.   What is (a) a blizzard, (b) a cañon?   Explain clearly how these phenomena are produced and why we do not meet with them in Europe except in a modified form.

3.   Compare the conditions of barometric pressure existing over Asia and North America in summer and winter.

Does any part of North America experience 'monsoons,' and, if so, which, and why?

4. What is the effect of the Rocky Mountain axis upon the climate of North America?

Compare and contrast the distribution of rainfall in the continents of Europe and North America.

5. Why is the 100th meridian of west longitude so important in considering (a) the climate, (b) the nature of the land, (c) the rainfall, (d) the industries, (e) the density of population in North America?

6. Account for the different races of mankind dwelling in North America and their distribution over that continent.

Canada.

1. What do you understand by the term 'a glaciated region'? Give examples in Canada and North Europe. What physical characteristics would you expect such regions to show, and why?

2. Describe the Cordilleran system of mountains in Canada. Draw a sketch map to show how (a) rivers, (b) railways pass from this system to the Pacific Ocean.

3. Divide Canada into climatic areas as regards temperature and rainfall. To what extent do these areas coincide? Compare the Canadian climate with that of England. Is it fair to call Canada 'Our lady of the snows'?

4. Enumerate the successive zones of vegetation found in crossing Canada (a) from north to south, (b) from east to west. Emphasize the climatic conditions which determine these zones.

5. What qualifications should an intending emigrant to Canada have? Give reasons for your answer.

6. Briefly describe the colonisation of the country and the present distribution of the population. Why does Canada advertise so largely in Britain, especially in rural districts?

7. Draw a sketch map to show (a) the St Lawrence basin, (b) the route of the C.P.R.

8. Show on a map the trade routes between Canada and (a) Europe, (b) Japan, (c) New Zealand.

United States of America.

1. By what route did the French people the province of Louisiana ? Account for them acquiring such a large territory when British settlers were comparatively near.

2. Draw a sketch map to show the chief physical features of the United States.

3. To what extent is the climate of the United States affected by altitude, latitude, nearness to the sea, winds, and ocean currents ?

Show the 90° and 75° July isotherms upon a blank map. What can you deduce from the positions of these isotherms ?

4. Explain why at their confluence the Mississippi waters are clear and those of the Missouri yellow and turbid.

5. Account for the manufacturing and commercial importance of the New England states.

6. Draw a map of the Mississippi basin and mark on it the chief animal and vegetable productions.

7. Explain levée, tornado, cyclone, 'sirocco weather.'

8. Shade a blank map of the States to show the range of temperature experienced. What effect have the North-East Trade Winds upon the climate of South California ?

9. Iron firms of the United States advertise largely in the village cafés of Normandy. What do they advertise and why do they do so ?

Central America.

1. Draw a map of Central America and the West Indies to show how the winds influence the rainfall.

2. Summarize the vegetable productions of this region. Account for them being so varied and state approximately at what elevations they are cultivated.

3. Explain the following statement : ' The practice of European governments, who assist agriculturalists in the production of certain crops, has ruined the trade of Jamaica.'

4. Account for the decline of European power in this region.

Chapter IX. South America.

1. What effects have the trade winds upon the South American climate? Draw a map to show their course, and the countries affected by them.

2. How do you account for the fact that the independent South American states are all republics?

3. Explain selvas, savanas, llanos, pampas, and campos.

4. Give ten place-names which show that the Spaniards held possession of South America. Quote other place-names which appear to you to be of native origin.

5. Name the chief products of the South American forests. Where are the most promising agricultural regions and what crops are likely to be produced in these districts in the future?

6. Can you explain the scarcity of manufactures in this continent?

7. Write brief notes on llama, maté, Peruvian bark, vicuna, and cacao.

8. Say what you can of the following: Cotopaxi, Potosi, Quito, Rio Janeiro, Para, Lima, Valparaiso, and Bogota.

9. What reasons are there for thinking that Argentina will rival the United States?

INDEX OF PLACE NAMES

D.